# *JOB SEEKER'S CAFE*
# The Complete Series

## How To Get Employed

An Old Oak Media Partners, LLC Self-Help Series Publication

Kenneth R. Grow

# Job Seekers Café - The Complete Series
389 Total Pages

By Kenneth R. Grow
Written for Old Oak Media Partners, LLC - Personal Self-Help Series

© 2014 by Old Oak Media Partners, LLC
Downey, California, USA

 QR Code for: www.oldoakmediapartnersllc.com

All rights reserved; except as permitted under United States Copyright Act of 1976, no part of this publication may be reproduced, stored in a retrieval system, or transmitted in any form or by any means, electronic, mechanical, photocopying, recording, or otherwise, without the prior written permission of Old Oak Media Partners, LLC. Although every precaution has been taken in the preparation of this eBook, the author and publisher assume no responsibility for any errors or omissions. Nor is there any liability assumed for damages resulting from the use of information contained herein.

**Note:** This publication contains the opinions, ideas, and experiences of its author. It is intended to provide helpful and informative material on the subject matter covered. It is sold with the understanding that the author and publisher are not engaged in rendering professional services in the eBook. If the reader requires personal assistance or advice, a competent professional should be consulted.

The author and publisher specifically disclaim any responsibility for any liability, loss, or risk, personal or otherwise, which is incurred as a consequence, directly or indirectly, of the use and application of any of the contents of this eBook.

ISBN 13: 978-1-940557-12-0
ISBN 10: 1940557127

Employment, Job Hunting, Job Searching, Self-Help, Education, Jobs, Job Interview, Resume, Power Statements, Elevator Speech, Me In Thirty Seconds

*Other books by Kenneth R. Grow*

**Five Easy Steps To Achieving Your Goals Now!**

ISBN 978-0-615702-88-9 (2013)

**The Companion Workbook For**

**Five Easy Steps To Achieving Your Goals Now!**

ISBN 978-1-940557-00-7 (2013)

## Dedication

*This book is dedicated to all I have worked with in helping those in need of employment and to all those who would listen and take the required action to move forward in their lives.*

*Without my family's support this book would not have been possible.*

## Table of Contents

| | |
|---|---:|
| Introduction | 1 |
| Guide For A Job Seeker | 5 |
| Basic Breakfast Plate | 47 |
| Fresh Garden Salad | 73 |
| Mentor Plate Special | 103 |
| Application Pizza | 133 |
| Sampler Plate | 161 |
| Rock Solid Resume | 191 |
| The Power Burger | 237 |
| The Thirty Second Sandwich | 257 |
| Skill Builder Special Salad | 283 |
| Appendix | 351 |

**Job Seekers Café**

# Introduction

This project is part of a Personal Self-help Series of eBooks that began as an idea how to make job searching simpler by making the process as easy as selecting from a café menu. There were a total of nine menu items, each in an eBook, and one eBook written as an overview that was offered free to anyone who wanted to download a copy of the **Guide For A Job Seeker**.

The nine eBooks were offered online for purchase individually or in a specially priced combination package. The package offered significant savings and provided the entire Job Seekers Café menu through an instant download. Those who are new to the world of job searching need to know how to prepare to get a job. To some it will be lots of work, for others it will be a logical course of study to become prepared to obtain the results desired, getting the job they really want.

We made every effort to make this series valuable to: an individual who has recently completed their education and has no job experience, an individual who is seeking to move to another company, or for some one looking to make a change in their career direction.

Each of the nine eBooks deal with a specific topic to prepare for one's job search activities. In today's competitive job market those who take the time to prepare themselves with the contents of this book will have an advantage over the other job candidates.

Job Seekers Café - The Complete Series is a consolidation of all the eBooks into one printed book. Some changes have been made so the forms can be found in the appendix. Many of the forms are found in several of the other eBooks and by putting the forms into the appendix it reduces the number of pages and the costs of printing. None of the instructional or informative text has been left out.

You will notice that on the outer margins of this and most other pages there are Scholar Margins, where you can make notes or comments about what impressed you when reading the material. Perhaps you might have a question and you will put a question mark to remind you that you need to find clarification of the text and the concept presented. This was part of the eBook series and proved to be of benefit to most readers.

This book is printed in a larger format with larger sized fonts than most other books printed on the subject of job searching. It was designed to be easily read with plenty of white space for notes or comments. The information is presented in a more conversational tone than many other books on the same subject.

We hope you find it to be an easy read and not an ordeal to be suffered through. There is also some consolidation made regarding some parts of material that appears in multiple sections, a reference is made back to the original section where the information was first presented. The appendix will have the various forms referenced throughout this book in alphbetical order to make it easier to find. Filled in examples of any forms will be left within each of the sections to make things easier for the reader's reference.

In the beginning of each section you will find a Section Table Of Contents to help you find the information you are looking for to help you in your job search activities.

All the forms are also located on our web site and can be downloaded for free for your personal use. There are many other items on our web site that we hope you will enjoy.

We wish you the best of luck in finding the job you desire.

Old Oak Media Partners, LLC

# Chapter 1

# Guide For A Job Seeker

# Chapter 1
# Guide For A Job Seeker

## Guide For A Job Seeker

Are you having some trouble getting a job? Maybe you're new to the job market. Maybe you've lost your job and need new employment. Maybe you're looking to add or replace a job for extra income. Before you begin, you need to know that some of the 'rules' for job seeking have changed. We're presenting this guide to help you understand these 'rules' and show you all the skills required to get the job you are looking for.

Some of these skills you may already have while others may be new. Some of you may just need a little review to sharpen those skills. Whatever your current situation and skill level, we are here to help.

This guide is only meant to give you an idea of the various items and activities you will need to accomplish to be successful in finding a job. For more complete information about each concept presented in this guide, please check out the **Job Seekers Café Menu.**

We know it is tough out there and the more you know, the better your chances are for getting the job you are seeking. Job searching is a full-time job if you are not employed. If you are looking to change to another job, it will require additional effort besides your existing job.

We hope this guide will prove to be of great value to you in your job seeking efforts. Good luck!

## Section Table of Contents

| | |
|---|---|
| Introduction | 7 |
| Steps To Success | 9 |
| Reduce The Time | 11 |
| Right Goals, Right Results | 13 |
| A Mentor, A Coach, Or Both? | 15 |
| Master Job Application | 17 |
| Networking and Resources | 19 |
| Scripting | 21 |
| Resume For Results | 23 |
| State Your Case With Power | 25 |
| Me In Thirty Seconds | 27 |
| Interview Preparation | 29 |
| Own Yourself / Sell Yourself | 33 |
| Capitalize On Your Experience | 35 |
| Know What To Expect | 37 |
| Conclusion And Review | 39 |
| Grow Into Your Career | 43 |

# Section 1

# Introduction

This introduction should not be ignored. The information on these pages will help you understand how you can get the most out of this guide and the contents herein. Take your time and read this guide thoroughly. Take notes and when a form is recommended, be sure to print one out and use it as a tool to help you build the skills you need to secure the job you are seeking.

You will notice that on the outer margins of this and most of the other pages there are Scholar Margins, where you can make notes or comments about what impressed you when reading the material. Perhaps you might have a question and you will put a question mark to remind you that you need to find clarification of the text and the concept presented.

Some of the material presented may be familiar and some may be new to you. The information is being presented through time tested and proven concepts that have helped countless individuals find the job or career they have sought. Some concepts might seem 'silly' or 'old-fashioned' to you. All we can say is that they work.

We are assuming that you are new to job searching and so we are going to start at the beginning. Think of it as a job seekers' *'boot camp'* of sorts. Don't worry, if you have been through a boot camp before, you will find this one much easier and a bit more friendly.

The purpose of this guide is to give you the basic principles of how to correctly job search. Yes, there is a right way to do it. Some will think they can do it on their own, and maybe they can. But with knowledge and tools that you will learn from this guide you will begin to see why some individuals find jobs quickly while others seem unable to even get called in for an interview.

Nothing in this guide or in the **Job Seekers Café Menu** is difficult to understand or implement into an action plan. However, you must gather up your internal motivation, take action, and continue taking action until you find what you are looking for. There are many items that will be presented in this guide; the more you master the easier it will be to get hired. Don't short change yourself thinking you only need to do a few. Build a strong foundation and you will be successful.

# Section 2

# Steps To Success

In this section you will learn the steps necessary to secure employment. We know there are plenty of books out there that tell you how to look for a job. Many are very good books with lots of valuable information. Others will have you read about what others have done in the past. Here, we want you to be in the present looking at and preparing for your future.

You will learn about the 'mechanics' of preparing to look for a job. If you are currently unemployed then you will need to begin reading and put into practice the information contained in this guide immediately. If you are looking to 'up grade' or find another job, then you will still need to read and put into practice the information with some sense of urgency. You should have a time line in mind of when you would like to make the job change.

Perhaps the most difficult part of job searching is trying to deal with and survive unemployment, or the anxiety of anticipating a change of career or current employment. Trying to find employment can be very frustrating and challenging for the individual and their family. Finding a job might take longer than most individuals expect. You will need to set your sights on a realistic time frame to find a job.

Budgets might get tighter and leaner. You must create a financial budget that can carry you for several months. Live within your means by carefully evaluating all expenditures and shop only for items that you need, find on sale, or at a discount store. Taking this advice will reduce the financial stress that you might feel. (**See Appendix - Simple Budget Form**)

Sometimes, finding part-time or temporary employment can get you through a rough patch. But remember your ultimate goal and never give up on it. You might even consider selling off some items that you can live without to get some cash. Do everything in your power to avoid going deeper into debt. Find ways to reduce your expenses. Turn down the heat and air conditioning. Use a couple of extra blankets or open a window. Consolidate all your shopping to conserve fuel and transportation costs. Make gifts or give the gift of your time rather than spend money on something less personal.

Use coupons and take advantage of the close-out items that a market might have discounted. Eat more meals at home and less at restaurants. Make use of what you have. Spend more time reading a book from a library and less time at a movie theater. Use your time wisely. Spend some extra quality time with the family and less on outside costly entertainment.

Seek help from those who can help you prepare a resume, work with you on putting together a job search plan, or mentor you with their knowledge and wisdom. Keep your mind busy so you have less time to think about your current situation. Be focused on your plan.

Your time will best be utilized by keeping yourself fit by exercising your body and your mind. Get plenty of rest so you can wake early and get an early start each morning. If you are still employed, be sure to set up doctor and dental appointments before you leave your current job. Maximize any current benefits before they are lost.

There have been many studies about the results of job searching and obtaining employment. Those who have a plan and stick to the strategies and techniques greatly reduce the time it takes to secure employment. Those individuals who take the time to learn the 'how to' get a job will get a job faster than those who do not feel it worth their time to learn those skill sets.

Remember that a first impression is a lasting impression. Pay attention to the section about grooming and dress standards you will find later in this guide. Many well qualified candidates failed to get a job, not because of the lack of needed skills, talents, or abilities. They left an impression of not being professional in their grooming and dress standards with the interviewer. After all, the interviewer is also human and will be influenced by appearance concerning fitting in to the organization's culture and policies.

You will greatly improve your chances for finding the right job with the right company or organization if you will do a little research. Make sure the organization has your same values. Be sure they are a growing company and have a long-term business plan for success. There is one secret that will be explained later in this guide as to how to differentiate yourself from other candidates by doing some research about the organization.

# Section 3

# Reduce The Time

As mentioned before, there have been many studies about job search results. What is confirmed in nearly every study is that those who are successful are those who prepare to learn the skills required to secure a job. They then applied the techniques and strategies they had learned and demonstrated that they were the ideal candidate to fill the position. These studies also show that those who have prepared themselves for job search activities will find employment in about half the time, they will average an almost 20% higher salary and report higher job satisfaction with their new job.

This reduction in time comes with proper job search preparation. You must have the correct agenda and work your plan. Don't get lazy and hope that you get a job offer because you think you deserve one. Do your due diligence and use the job searching skills you will learn to your advantage.

Use various forms to plan your job search activities, record your efforts, and hold yourself accountable for the results you are obtaining. Keep a list of who you have contacted, what possibilities that contact might offer, and know if you should keep them on a future contact list. **(See Appendix - Job Search Activity Log)**

You can lie to others, and you can lie to yourself. However, you must be honest about your efforts if you really want to see successful results. Just walking through a mall and gathering up business cards is not job searching. No matter how many cards you collect it is still not job searching. Neither is just sitting at a computer and filling out online applications.

Fill out those online applications only for those organizations you are seriously considering working for and then follow up with those companies or organizations to see if they did indeed receive your application. If they did, you now have another opportunity to ask them if they would like a copy of your resume. Take it to them, in person preferably. If you mail it to them, contact them again to see if it was received. Ask them if you could schedule an interview with the hiring manager. Showing interest without being pushy can score some points, show that you are a serious candidate, and that you are truly interested in working for the organization.

You must have a detailed plan to follow if you want to have success in the shortest amount of time. A detailed plan will also help to keep you focused on what you need to be doing and when. Without a plan you will waste precious time in non-productive activities that will delay your securing a job. **(See Appendix - Job Search Checklist)**

Hold yourself accountable for the time you dedicate to finding a job. Have someone whom you trust review your efforts. Ask for their honest opinion about where you can better spend your energies to get the results you are seeking. Respect their thoughts and comments as constructive feedback that will help you. Don't take offense just because something might be said that you feel is an unjust criticism. They are trying to help you and they might be able to see things more clearly than you can. Be grateful for any assistance that is offered to you.

The next section will deal with setting goals as they relate to job searching activities. These goals will be planned the same as any goal you will seek to achieve, except here in this guide we will try to limit them to job seeking activities. Setting your job searching goals properly will help you see positive results much sooner.

# Section 4

# Right Goals, Right Results

Goals must be properly set if they are to be achieved. There are simple rules to follow when setting goals and working on them. Remember, these are your goals and you are accountable to yourself to set them and work on them. When you set goals you will need to have a sense of urgency. The goals will not work on their own. You must be pushing forward every day toward the goal you set. It is up to you to hustle to get your goal accomplished. If you never start, you will never achieve your goal.

We begin a discussion about a goal being defining as exactly what it is that you want to accomplish. In the case of seeking a job, finding the right job is your goal. Once you identify it, you then work back to the current moment and see how long it might take you to be hired. Your goal might be to have a job that requires additional skills or education that you currently lack. That does not mean that it is not a worthy goal. It means that to accomplish this goal you will have to acquire the skills or education required. So you have a longer-term goal that might take several medium-term goals to accomplish. And each goal will have several mini goals we call action steps, that must be accomplished before you will be able to achieve your ultimate goal. **(See Appendix - Goal Setting Form and the Action Step Form)**

Goals can be broken down into much simpler and easier steps in order to accomplish them. Within each step there are other smaller steps that you must be aware of. When you know exactly what it is that you want to achieve, it is time to start writing your goals. Remember, to make a goal concrete, write it down. A dream is not written down and soon becomes a fading memory.

The first step to writing a goal is to keep it simple. Don't get so caught up in the small details that you never move forward. Next, keep it real. Dreams are nice but we live in a world of reality. Your goal must be achievable. It also must be clearly defined. If you don't understand what it is you want to do, no one else will know either. And most important of all is that you must take action. Without action nothing will be achieved.

One subset you must also consider when writing your goal; you must keep balance with all facets of your life. If you aren't balanced you are making things more difficult for yourself. It is also important that you measure your progress. In order to be held accountable you have to know if you are making progress toward you goal. If you are making progress you will soon reach your goal. If you are not, you are wasting time. Another thing that you must consider when you begin working on your goals is that you will begin a paradigm shift from where you are now to where you want to go. We all have a fear of change. We enjoy our comfort zone and sometimes change feels uncomfortable. So we remain in a 'frozen' state of being unable to move forward because we have a fear of the unknown that waits ahead of us.

If you have never written a goal about job searching, here is a very basic layout of how to set a goal. First you decide what it is that you want to accomplish. For example, preparing a resume to get results. So your goal is to write a good resume. The first action step will be to gather all the information you will need in order to write the resume. The next action step is to organize the information so there will be a logical flow of information (chronology). Then you will have an action step to begin to write your resume using the information you have gathered and organized so you can make a clean, neat, and organized looking resume. An action step will be to review it several times to see where it might need improvement. Once done to your satisfaction, have someone else read it. Get their opinion and polish it once more.

Send the resume on a test flight. Ask several individuals to read it and give you their opinion if it looks and reads right. If the information is not understood, it will be rejected. Make sure it is understandable. Once it has been written, revised, re-written, revised, and re-written again it might be ready to be printed and submitted to prospective employers. At this point you might be able to say you have accomplished your goal of writing a good resume.

If after several interviews and sending out many copies of your resume you still have not found employment, you should review your resume to see if you might have left out some important detail or did not have the clarity you expected. Just keep polishing it until you do get a job.

In the next section you will be introduced to the importance of having a mentor and a job coach.

# Section 5

# A Mentor, A Coach, or Both?

Many tend to confuse the roles associated with a mentor and a coach. A mentor is one who will work with behaviors, concepts, customs, and will help one 'learn the ropes' of an organization. A coach will work with performance skills to achieve a desired result. So the question becomes: "Do I need both a mentor and a coach to help me prepare to work on my job search?" The answer is yes, no, and maybe. A job coach will be able to help you by making sure you are making contact with as many potential employers as possible. They will review your efforts and suggest ways in which you might improve your results by making adjustments to your job search approach.

The mentor, on the other hand, can help you write your goals because they will have a better idea of what you can do and counsel with you about what it is you are trying to accomplish. Both have their place and both can be of great value to you. Mentoring is a longer process helping one evolve to a position while coaching is done to achieve specific performance results.

Can the same individual be both the mentor and the coach? Yes, if they have the necessary skills to do both. Many individuals do have both skill sets and will be willing to help you. At times they will be acting as a mentor and at other times they will be acting as the coach. If you can recognize the difference and apply the message then you will be fine. Mentoring can be more passive in training than coaching. Coaching tends to be more "at-the-moment" training.

Mentoring can be either structured or unstructured. With structured mentoring there is accountability. And it can be formal or informal. With coaching it tends to be more 'one on one' practicing repeatedly until the desired outcome is obtained.

Both a mentor and a job coach can be extremely valuable in finding a job. This is your team so you should listen and follow their advice and wisdom.

You will be surprised how much faster you will be able to find employment using a mentor and a job coach.

Next section, the Master Job Application Form and why it is important.

# Section 6

# Master Job Application

Having a Master Job Application is one of the best tools you can use in looking for a job. This is a detailed and informative master information sheet about you. It is the foundation you will use in writing your resume, power statements, Me In Thirty Seconds, and when you are filling out a job application at a prospective employer's business or online.

This is not an application that you will drop off like you would a resume. It will be a 'ready reference' form that you will refer to often while seeking a job. You will carry it with you like your personal identification and other papers required by employers, only you will use it to help speed up the time it takes to fill out applications in person or online.

The information contained within the Master Job Application can be the foundation and an outline for a powerful resume that will be read. Your accomplishments will be turned into the power statements that will help differentiate you from all the other candidates. Your Me In Thirty Seconds will describe you in an impressive, self-confident, and professional manner.

The Master Job Application we offer is a two page form that will have all the information about you that you will need when filled out completely. We recommend you go to our website and download a copy. **(See Appendix - Master Job Application Form)** On our website there are many other forms that you might find useful in helping you with your job seeking activities.

Remember, the Master Job Application form must be filled out completely to have maximum value. It is a history of your past jobs, education, skills, and accomplishments. If you find a significant gap in your time line, be sure to fill it in. If you did not work you will need to address the gap, which might be due to taking care of aging parents, caring for children, going to school, or volunteering to help a worthy cause. Whatever reason you give, be prepared to support it with some documentation if possible.

Now that you have a firm foundation to work on, the next section will help you build your personal network and resource list.

# Section 7

# Networking And Resources

To some individuals trying to build a network of contacts is as painful as having their gums scraped. It is the nature of some to avoid asking others for help even when the need for help is great. Most people are willing to help someone in need. Even if they don't have an answer, they may know someone who might be able to give the assistance requested.

Building a network is not that hard and is easily accomplished when you ask someone for help. Once you get their answer, ask another question. Ask for two other names of people they know that also might be able to help. Write down all the contact information and add to your network or resource list. After a few contacts you will have a long list of individuals on your network list to whom you can go for help. **(See Appendix - Network and Resource Forms)**

Resources are those individuals you know or who will be able to help you in some manner. Make a list of all those you know who will be willing to help you and then classify them. Identify those who can be a direct help resource, those who can be of indirect assistance, and those who will know of others whom you might contact. Other resources can be websites with information about job searching methods and suggestions. All information is good and the more you have, the better decisions you can make.

Your network and resources are very valuable and you must make sure you express sincere gratitude for any leads or help they provide you. You may have to call on them often and you don't want them to think you are taking advantage of them. Both your network and resource list will have lots to offer so use them responsibly.

Remember, networking is not asking for a job—only to help you find leads that can help you find a job.

In the next section we will discuss scripting and how it works to help you build your network and resource list. When worked properly you will see your network and resources multiply quickly.

# Section 8

# Scripting

We have all answered the telephone and heard, "Hello, my name is, I can save you money on your . . ." What you have been subjected to is a sales script that is being read to you. Immediately you sense that it is without passion and sincerity. It sounds artificial and stilted. Yet the premise behind scripting should not be condemned due to those who do not understand the purpose of the script and how it should be used.

While building your personal network you will have to make calls to many individuals to obtain help in your quest to secure a job. Writing down what you want to cover in these conversations is a perfectly sound strategy. It must be done, however, carefully and succinctly to be effective.

Begin by listing what questions you want to ask and what items you need help with to move forward. Then write it all down in a logical progression so you will appear to be organized. At first your script will sound crude. By reading it several times out loud you will begin to notice what parts need to be worked on to make it have a better flow.

After several revisions and rewrites, present it to a few friends you are comfortable with and ask them for their comments. They should be able to make a few suggestions that should help you understand how you can make it sound natural and not like a memorized script.

There are some basic formats for writing an effective script. Begin with a warm greeting. Give your name and ask for the name of the individual you will need to contact. You should offer a 'relief' valve for the other individual just in case it is not a good time to talk right now. "Is this is a good time to talk to you?" "Would you mind if I could take a couple of minutes of your time?" This way you are acknowledging that they might be busy and you want to show respect for how valuable their time might be. If they are too busy to talk to right then, ask when would be a good time for you to call them back. Remember to be professional and thank them for their time talking to you no matter how short it might be.

Once you begin to go into your script, explain your reason for calling. Use positive statements like, "I am in the job market," not "I need a job," or "I just got fired and I am looking for any job available."

This is also a good time to use your Me In Thirty Seconds or a couple of power statements. After your initial greeting, your statement of who and what you are, and an explanation of why you are calling, ask the standard networking questions:

1. Do you know of any job openings in your company that might fit my qualifications?

2. Can you recommend anyone who hires or manages people who do what I do?

3. Do you know two people who work in my field of experience who might be able to assist me?

Remember that while networking you are not asking for a job, but for guidance and information. Don't push for a job while networking. That is not the purpose or the intent of networking or how your script should be focused. **(See Appendix - Scripting Form)**

You should have several scripts prepared for various situations in which you might find the need to address things or question more specifically. You should have a script written for your telephone calls, another to use during a face to face interview, and one for casual encounters with friends or people who are introduced to you as potential resources.

The most important thing to remember is the script you use must sound like your natural self. In all cases this is not a 'stump' speech where you get on your soap box and pound on your audience until you get what you want. If you do it right, you will have a list of networking contacts who will be willing to help you in the future if you find a need for their services. Leave a friendly impression with all your contacts.

The following section will be about producing the right resume for your purpose. Your resume should be a powerful representation of all your qualifications for the position you are seeking.

# Section 9

# Resume For Results

Your resume is one of the most powerful tools for your job search efforts. It can open doors, or close them. It depends on how it is written. There are many styles and types of resumes being submitted everyday. Some get noticed, get read, and make a positive impression. Your resume should set you apart from all the other applicants for the position you are applying for. The wrong style or type of resume can eliminate you from consideration just by its appearance. There are certain acceptable styles and formats for various types of job seekers. If you are just entering the workforce with no experience the resume can be very simple. If you are well seasoned with plenty of experience and education you will need to have one that will showcase your work history, education, and accomplishments. **(See Appendix - Resume Worksheets)**

Resumes that are neat, clean, and easy to read are the best. Don't think you need a hundred bullet points to list your personal characteristics. These are not easily read and after an interviewer reads a couple of them they tend to become numb to the content since they all start to look so much alike. Interviewers are busy and don't have time to read each bullet point. They are only interested in facts which are best presented in sentences that reflect the characteristics they are looking for in an employee.

You want your resume to get results. If you are not getting the results you expect, then look at your resume and try a different style or do a new resume type. One interviewer might prefer one style and another interviewer another. However, all interviewers like a well-crafted resume that is easy to read so they will be able to locate the information they want to know about the job candidate.

If you have someone else write your resume for you, be sure to read it and know what it contains. Many job candidates were asked a question about their resume and they did not know the answer. Read it, know it, be it. Nothing is so frustrating to an interviewer than to read a well-written resume about an individual that states how they are self confident and an outgoing individual only to see them walk into the interview displaying self doubt and lack of self esteem. It brings into question the validity of the rest of the information on the resume.

The next section will help you state your case with power.

# Section 10

# State Your Case With Power

The words you use, spoken or written, have power. 'Word-smithing' is an art and making the use of the right word or words can make or break your chances for being hired. There are many power words, but some are over used. Be mindful of the words you are using and try to avoid trendy words or phrases. There are many words you can still use that can make the impression you want to achieve with an interviewer.

Power statements are a couple of sentences that will state a situation, what you did, and the results of your efforts. Just the basic facts. They can also be used to answer an interviewer's question. **(See Appendix - Power Statement Form)**

You might write a paragraph or two to make a statement that can be easily edited down to a couple of lines by using the more powerful words that will target only the important point you are trying to make. Don't feel that you can just talk on and on. Keep it short and let the interviewer move on to the next question.

Some schools of thought say you should have about five power statements. Others will recommend at least thirty or more. Once you become familiar with the power statement concept, you can easily mold and modify them to apply to a variety of questions or situations. A power statement should be less than fifteen seconds and closer to ten to be effective. Once you go on too long the power is gone and the message lost.

Some of the best examples of real power statements are the short quotes you read that in just a few words will deliver a whole message of inspiration. When writing your power statements use the least amount of words you can to say what it is you want to say. Keep the statements short so their power will be greater. Too long and they become too diluted to have the effect you desire.

In the next section, Me In Thirty Seconds, you will learn how to expand your power statements to make a short confident story about who you are.

# Section 11

# Me In Thirty Seconds

Me In Thirty Seconds is also known as the 'Elevator Speech' because it can be spoken in about the time it takes to travel a few floors in an elevator. This tool is used to make an impressive statement about who you are, what you have done, and what you can do. When crafted just right it can answer many questions rather quickly so the interviewer can move forward in the interview process.

There are two basic Me In Thirty Seconds. One will be about your job qualifications and the other about you as an individual. You do not have to limit yourself to only the two kinds. You should have several that you can use to better address a question that might be asked of you. A question might be asked about what you enjoy doing when not at work, which might be different than a question as to what you do while not at work. A subtle difference that the interviewer is looking to learn more about you. You would not want to use the same Me In Thirty Seconds to respond to the two questions. You might enjoy going to the beach when not at work. Yet, you mow the lawn, work in the garden, or go shopping while not at work. So be prepared to handle various questions that might seem to be the same, yet require slightly different answers. **(See Appendix - Me In Thirty Seconds Form)**

A Me In Thirty Seconds or Elevator Speech is an expansion on the power statement. It just goes on a bit longer but still uses power words to state facts about your qualifications or your personal interests. Prepare several and practice them until they become a natural extension of your confidence. Even the best crafted Me In Thirty Seconds, if not delivered with confidence, will not have the impact you expected.

The Me In Thirty Seconds is generally prepared to answer the question, "Tell me a little bit about yourself." If the general discussion preceding the question was job related, use your job related Elevator Speech. If the conversation was about you as an individual then go with the more personal one.

The next section will give you information on how best to prepare for a job interview.

# Section 12

# Interview Preparation

Preparing for a job interview involves several things. One is to 'dress for success' and look professional. On the job you might wear very casual clothing, however for a job interview take the time to dress appropriately to show respect to the interviewer so they know how serious you really are about the position they are trying to fill. If you are a man and show up for an interview in a business appropriate suit and tie, you will have the advantage going in over those who show up in just slacks and a collared button shirt. If you are a woman and show up dressed nicely you will have an advantage over those who choose to show up in designer pants and a trendy top.

Job interview questions are generally based on some sort of psychological evaluation principles. You may be asked over the course of the interview three questions that are very similar, asked slightly differently. The interviewer is not trying to trip you up, they are trying to see if you are answering the questions correctly and with some consistency.

There are many resources available about what is currently being asked in job interviews. It is good to know in advance what you might expect some of the questions to be so you will know how to answer them correctly. If you do not understand a question that is being asked, feel free to ask them to repeat it or to rephrase it. You might even ask them to explain the question to you since you do not want to give a wrong or false answer.

Generally speaking, there are four areas in which an interviewer will draw questions from. The first area is about your work history and how it relates to the position you are applying for. The next area will be about you as an individual on a more personal level. The third area is about the position being offered and the organization. Finally, about where you see yourself in the future.

At the conclusion of the interview, the interviewer might ask you if you have any questions about the job or the company. Here is a chance to really show how serious you are by asking some good questions. Some might relate to items you thought might be asked and were not, and so you would like to know the answer. Another question you could ask is about educational opportunities that the company might offer some assistance in.

We are including a list of things to consider about preparing for a job interview. This list is not all-inclusive, however it does address the basic and best practices about how the job seeker should be groomed and dressed. Your opinion of these conventions is not important. Your adherence to these conventions is what is important. Remember, you are trying to make a favorable impression with the interviewer and all with whom you may come into contact during this time. A comment by a receptionist or another employee could have some bearing on your chances of being hired.

You are a guest who has been invited into the company or organization to be evaluated to see if you are the right candidate for the position. Be a bit humble yet confident in your demeanor and certainly don't try to take charge of the interview process. No matter the outcome of the interview, be sincere in thanking all involved for the opportunity to meet with them, for the interview, and the time they spent with you.

Surveys of hiring managers and interviewers have shown that candidates with lower personal standards of dress ranks high as to why an individual will not be considered for hire.

1. First impressions are important. Be on time. If the appointment is at 9:00 am, you should be there ready for the interview no later than 8:50 am. Arriving there at 9:00 am is considered late. Your personal appearance will also have an impact on the first impression you make. Being dressed appropriately is a sign of respect regarding the importance the interview has to you and to the interviewer.

Dress Standard for Women:

- A suit preferably with a skirt, conservative in color

- Minimal jewelry, conceal tattoos, minimize piercings

- Avoid perfume or strong-smelling hair treatments

- Hair should be neat, clean, and combed or brushed if long, it may be pulled back so you will not be brushing hair away from your face throughout the interview

Dress Standard for Men:

- A suit, collared shirt, and tie, all in conservative colors

- Avoid jewelry except for a conservative wrist watch

- Clean shaved face; any beard or mustache must be neatly trimmed and in a conservative style

- Very light aftershave or none at all

- Conceal any tattoos, and minimize piercings

- Hair neatly trimmed, clean, and combed

2. Know something about the organization by doing some research. Don't confuse them with one of their competitors. Find out some history, the current place in the market they serve, and be prepared to ask questions that will demonstrate that you have an interest in working for them.

3. Set the tone at the opening. Know the name of the interviewer. Ask someone to tell you how to pronounce the name correctly if it is an unfamiliar sounding name. It is important to get the name correct. Enter the interview room with confidence, have a warm and friendly smile, keep direct eye contact, and give a firm handshake and pronounce the name of the interviewer correctly as you introduce yourself. If this is not the one whom you had the appointment with they will let you know and generally take you to the one who will be doing the interview.

It is possible that you will be escorted to the interviewer's location in another part of the building. If someone referred you to the interviewer or helped you secure the interview appointment, acknowledge the fact that you appreciate the relationship and the trust they have in offering you this opportunity.

4. Every organization and each interviewer will have a set of interview questions they like to use. Many questions are similar with some slight variations. Interviewers do this daily and they know what they like to ask and what answers they as individuals like to hear. To give a set number of standard interview questions that are used would be hard. Some interviewers

like to ask more about vocational skills and experience, while others might after reading your job application and resume spend more time getting to know more about you as a person. There are many resources online and at your local library about job interview questions. You might consider reading the **Job Seekers Café Menu** item **Skill Builder Special Salad,** where you will find over one hundred sample interview questions, suggested answers, and explanations of what the interviewer is looking for.

Most interviewers will ask you to tell a little about yourself. This is not an open-ended license to give your life story. Here is where you would deliver your Me In Thirty Seconds speech. If you have been discussing vocational skills, then use the one about your job experiences. If you have been discussing you personally, then use the speech about your non-working interests.

5. If you are prepared for the interview you will do just fine. Prepare so you will know how to answer the questions being asked. Do not try to wing it or try to impress the interviewer with clever answers. That is not what they want to hear. Answer with confidence by using a power statement where appropriate. Take a breath to pause before you answer so your mind can be clear about the question asked.

After each interview or meeting you should conduct an evaluation on how you think you did. We have a form to help you with this evaluation and it can be a record that will help you improve your interview skills. We recommend that you go to our website and download a copy to use in your job search activities. **(See Appendix - Interview Evaluation Form)**

Next we will talk about Owning Yourself and Selling Yourself. If you take ownership and can sell yourself with confidence you will have a better chance of acquiring the position you are seeking.

# Section 13

# Own Yourself / Sell Yourself

Whether you like it or not, when looking for a job you are a salesperson selling yourself. Before a salesperson goes out to sell their products, they have to be convinced that their products are suited to meet the customer's need. You need to have a positive attitude about who you are, and take full ownership of yourself.

This is a simple but highly effective way of exhibiting self-confidence, because no one can know you or know what you can do better than you. When responding to questions use the introduction as follows:

"**I am** ..." (qualified, willing, a team player, etc.)

"**I have** ..." (experience, education, demonstrated, etc.)

"**I can** ..." (follow instructions, learn quickly, do the job, etc.)

Whatever words you choose to add behind the introduction words now demonstrate that you have taken ownership of the statement you are making. These ownership words help you sell yourself because you have now identified who you are, what you have done, and what you can do. These become power statements that leave a positive impression with any interviewer. Very few job candidates will use these ownership words, so when you do you have a better chance of securing the position.

You should practice using these ownership words with a variety of interview questions. See which ones work best for you. Remember, by practicing and listening to how you sound, you will develop your natural voice which creates a sense of self-confidence.

Capitalizing on your experience will be presented in the next section.

# Section 14

# Capitalize On Your Experience

Our lives are a summary of all of our experiences. You might feel some experiences are very important and others not so important. When you list or detail many of your experiences the prospective employer can gain a better understanding of who you are and how you can help the organization.

If you served in the military, volunteered your time giving service to those in your community, or attended seminars to help you grow personally you should consider using those experiences. This may be what puts you ahead of all the other applicants for the position being offered. Most employers know that a well-rounded individual makes for a better employee. And the objective of all organizations is to staff all positions with the best possible employees.

Many job candidates have listed or presented experiences from their life that were of similar interest to that of the interviewer. With a 'connection' of a similar interest the interview may be detoured with a conversation about that shared interest, thus making the interview more personal.

When all of the qualifications have been weighed, experience is the point of differentiation. If a degree is required for the position, only those candidates with a degree will be invited in for an interview. If all applicants have the same degree, there are only a few things left that will separate them. Experience will normally make the separation process easier for the employer to make the right decision to meet the needs of the organization.

Make sure that you have something to bring to the table that will make you stand out against all other applicants. Differentiate yourself by capitalizing on your experiences.

Knowing what to expect after the interview will be discussed in the next section.

# Section 15

# Know What To Expect

Before leaving an interview, ask some questions to clarify what you should expect in the near future. Will they call you, or should you follow up with them in a few days? When will they be making their final decision as to who will be hired? Are there other positions within the organization you are qualified for besides the position you interviewed for?

Asking these questions you will know what to expect and it will make you look a little more professional. You don't want to keep calling to see if you got the job and end up losing it because you bugged them about it. Sometimes, you might be high in the running for one position but someone else got it who had more experience. If you don't ask about other positions available within the organization where you have the qualifications you might not ever get the chance to be considered.

You should send a letter of appreciation to the interviewer thanking them for the opportunity to be considered for the position. In this note let them know you look forward to hearing from them soon. Many times an offer is made to a candidate and the others excused. The candidate selected might refuse the offer because the wages are not acceptable, or because they got a better offer from another company. Rather than go through the whole process again, the hiring manager will look at all those interviewed and make another choice. If you showed gratitude for the opportunity for being considered you might improve your chances of getting an offer.

In the next section we will conclude and review what information has been presented. Following that is a bonus section about how to Grow Into Your Career.

# Section 16

# Conclusion And Review

There has been lots of information presented in this guide. This is by no means a complete resource on the subject of job seeking. It is however a guide to help you, the job seeker, understand that there are lots of parts in putting together a job search action plan.

It all begins with your commitment to devote whatever resources and time you have available to be actively engaged in seeking employment. At this time there are many pressures that build up that will cause frustration. If you are unemployed there are additional distractions that might keep you from putting forth your best efforts. Understanding and dealing with unemployment is critical. If you still have a job, and are seeking a new one, there will also be a unique set of survival challenges.

Budgets get tighter, stress levels rise, and normal small irritations become major crises. If you are unemployed and it is taking longer than you planned, you might have to seek some temporary work to help out with your living expenses. You won't get wealthy working part time, but it can make your overall life a bit more 'stress-free' during this time.

Employed or unemployed you should ask for some help. There are many who will be happy to help you find suitable employment. Write out a plan of action and follow it. Contact as many people as you can who will help you. Dress for success and be sure to follow the suggestions about grooming presented in this guide. Having done research about an organization that you would like to work for can be an advantage over the candidates for the position you are applying for.

Be prepared to do your job search activities. Use the forms suggested and hold yourself accountable for your time and efforts. Follow up with those whom you have provided job applications, resumes, or had an interview with.

Without a written plan you will not be able to hold yourself accountable and you will waste too much time and too many resources that should have been used to make contacts to secure employment.

You will have to set some goals (daily, weekly, etc.) You have to go out and find the job—it will not come to you while you are sitting on the couch next to the telephone. Make your goals simple, realistic, achievable, and defined, and take the necessary actions to achieve them. Keep your life in balance. Don't be afraid of the changes that might come your way. Review every detail of what transpired with every contact. What could you have done better? How can you improve your presentation? List what you must do to improve so you can quickly find the employment you are seeking.

Find a mentor and a job coach. They can and will be a great asset in helping you prepare for and find employment. They usually have many contacts that will also be willing to help.

You will need to begin with a Master Job Application. This one tool will be of great help in reducing the time to think through every application you will fill out. It is also a great outline for your resume, Me In Thirty Seconds, and in building your power statements.

Build your own network and resource list. You will be amazed at how many names and items you already know. Use them to help build your list even more. Be sure to thank those you use because you may have to contact them again.

When writing your scripts, be aware that you first need to put down the message you want to convey, then polish it by reading it aloud and working it into your natural voice. Don't let it sound like a standard 'sales' pitch. Keep your scripts positive and to the point. Remember to always ask the three standard networking questions found on page twelve of this guide.

Your resume is one of the most powerful tools you will create. Make sure it is one that is properly written. If it is hard to read, then chances are it won't be read. Make it clean, neat, and give a complete detailed history about yourself. Good resumes get read. Great resumes get results.

When talking on the phone, or in person, you will want to state your case with power. Using power statements can demonstrate that you are confident and can back up your words. Make sure to write many power statements to be able to address any question that might be asked of you.

Your Me In Thirty Seconds (Elevator Speech), when properly presented, will impress the interviewer. Remember that you will need one to use regarding your job qualifications and another one that will be used to describe you as an individual.

Prepare for the interview like you are truly interested in being hired. Many an applicant will just show up and not understand why they were not hired. This is about presenting yourself and showing respect to the interviewer and their organization and that you are grateful for this opportunity. The interview is very important and you should be completely prepared for it.

Own yourself by making statements that show you take full responsibility for who you are. Be positive about what you have done and can do. Let the interviewer know that you are qualified and meet the requirements for the position.

Experience is what you are selling to a prospective employer. It might be the skills you have learned on the job or when you were getting your education. Be prepared to capitalize on your experiences to demonstrate that you are the best candidate for the position.

Knowing what to expect and how to follow up with those with whom you had an interview are both important. You want to be respectful and not 'pester' them. You want to be professional about it. Offer to contact them in a few days and secure their permission to do so. Then make sure you follow up and make the contact.

*Thank you for allowing us to serve you this guide.*

*We wish you every success*

*in your job seeking activities. Good luck!*

*Please visit our*

**Job Seekers Café Menu**

*and order up some information on how to make the most of your job search efforts.*

# Section 17

# Grow Into Your Career

Once you secure employment your journey has just begun. To really succeed you will have to continually grow and develop your skills and abilities. Most organizations want to grow and expand. The best way to achieve this growth is to have those who work for them also develop individually. Take advantage of any training that is offered. The more you show an interest in improving your skills and knowledge, the more the organization will be willing to help you achieve your goals concerning advancement or moving to another position.

There are seminars, classes, trade shows, and opportunities out there and if you are proactive in expressing your desire to attend them, chances are you will be able to participate in them. Never pass on an opportunity to improve yourself or learn more about the business you are engaged in. If you are willing to move forward, the organization will be more willing to help you.

Many companies offer tuition assistance for employees to continue their formal education. If you lack a bachelor's degree or a master's degree you might be able to complete them with financial assistance from your employer. Some might pay a percentage of the total cost while others may offer a complete scholarship. You might have to ask them since this might not be something that is pushed by management. There are many organizations who also offer assistance to those who are in need of a high school diploma or a G.E.D. Most managers know that an educated workforce is a productive and efficient work force.

Your organization might be involved in trade associations or groups to which you might be able to offer your talents. Don't ever be afraid to gather information and share your knowledge with management on how things might be improved or how the organization might be able to save some money.

You are still responsible for you. Don't let others deny you of this. Take responsibility for your future by setting your goals and then achieving them. If you have time to complain about how unfair something might seem, you have the time to improve yourself and your circumstances.

**Be the best you can be in what endeavor you so desire.**

# Chapter 2

# Basic Breakfast Plate

# Chapter 2
# Basic Breakfast Plate

Start off your job search activities with a complete agenda for being successful in finding a job. Topped off with a personal log of contacts, follow-ups, and referrals. Comes with forms to help you stay organized and focused on getting a job quickly.

## Section Table of Contents

| | |
|---|---|
| Introduction | 49 |
| Where Am I Now? | 51 |
| My Personal Plan | 55 |
| Scripting | 57 |
| Reducing The Time | 61 |
| Taking Ownership | 63 |
| The Total Package | 65 |
| Conclusion And Review | 69 |

# Section 1

# Introduction

Welcome to the **Job Seekers Café**. This menu item is entitled **Basic Breakfast Plate.** You will find that this menu item will satisfy your hunger in preparing you to find new employment quickly. A complete basic breakfast that will start you off right. This menu item will give you the resources you will need in order to find and obtain employment. You might even say it is more than you can handle. Yet, the more you can handle will make all the difference in you finding the job you really want much sooner.

Some of the items you will find on this basic breakfast plate will be tools that will help you get organized and stay on track. There will be a selection of fresh answers to old concerns about job seeking. Yes, the 'game' has changed somewhat from times past. There are more individuals applying for fewer jobs and the competition is getting brutal. One of the main purposes for this series of eBooks is to help 'differentiate' you from all the other candidates.

You will notice that on the outer margins of this and most other pages there are Scholar Margins where you can make notes or comments about what impressed you when reading the material. Perhaps you might have a question and you will put a question mark to remind you that you need to find clarification of the text and the concept presented.

Surviving unemployment can be difficult. So we are offering some suggestions that should help you endure this period of time. There will be more pressures placed upon you by others and yourself. Keep a positive attitude and always look for the good things. Even if you didn't get hired by an organization, evaluate each step you took and how you interviewed and learn from the experience. Improve your presentation and take ownership of your statements by speaking with confidence and understanding the process. Knowing where you are now will help you know where you need to start.

Every company and organization will have their own employment practices and policies. Some of the employment rules are governed by national, state, and local laws. They must be followed and additional ones will be handed down from the human resources department of major corporations that will set the standards for job position qualifications. Small businesses will be a little more flexible in their hiring criteria, however they still are looking for someone to do the job they are trying to fill.

You may have to find some part-time work to help supplement your cash flow requirements. Don't let this get in the way of your main objective of securing the job you want. If you are always worrying about your finances you will have a hard time focusing on your job searching activities. Find the time to exercise both your body and mind. Don't let them go to waste while waiting to find a job.

Reference will be made throughout this eBook about concepts that can be found in some of the other **Job Seekers Café** menu items. While each eBook is a standalone publication about a given subject, the entire collection of menu items has been prepared to help a job seeker be totally prepared to reduce the time it takes to get a job.

# Section 2

# Where Am I Now?

Where you are now is where you need to start. This can be, and usually is, a different place than someone else. You may be looking for your very first job, to change employers, or you have recently become unemployed for any one of a variety of reasons. It is important to remember that the same basic principles apply to everyone who is looking for employment. As you sit waiting for a job interview you will be surrounded by those who are looking for their first job, a change of employers, and those who have become unemployed recently.

Who will be hired is the big question. Experience and educational requirements will have an impact on which candidates will be considered for an interview. Those selected for the interview will not only be asked plenty of questions, they will also be observed on how they present and conduct themselves. So it should not come as a surprise that the most common reason a candidate fails to get a job is that they did not come to the interview wearing appropriate clothing, or had issues with their personal grooming.

Where are you now? This is the question that must be answered first. You will have to get some paper and start making some lists. Begin by listing your strengths. What is it that you do so well that someone would want to hire you? Now list your education, skills, and talents. Finally, list the experiences that you have had throughout your working life to date. You might think that something was not that important or was a minor point of your working career. List it anyway. It might just be what you need to pass over another candidate who lacked that particular experience.

Now make some more lists. The first one is: What is your dream? The second one is: What jobs have you had in other fields where you have experience? Finally, the third one is: What jobs are you willing to settle for if you can't find one from the other two lists?

Take these last three lists you have created and write down what are the educational requirements and the amount of experience you need to have in order to be considered for such a position. Remember, years ago all you needed was a high school diploma to get a decent job. Today those jobs are going to college graduates or those with specialized technical training.

If you happen to find that you meet the requirements for your dream job, then great! If not, do you know what you need to do to get the education or experience required for the position? How long will that take? How much will it cost? There might be a position similar to the one of your dreams that might offer the experience you need. It might even allow you the opportunity to continue your education to meet the position's requirements.

Differentiation is what will move an applicant toward being a candidate for further consideration. Then it is what additional value that the candidate can bring to the position. The company or organization is looking out for what is in their best interest. They are not concerned about what interests you. Most organizations want the best qualified employees they can find, hire, and retain.

Perhaps the most important part of surviving unemployment is keeping yourself occupied by looking for a job. If you are still employed and looking for a change in employers you will experience a little more stress and anxiety than normal. Seeking a new job and not finding one can be frustrating for both the job seeker and their family. Most individuals think they will find a job within a very short period of time. Times have changed, securing a good job takes a lot more time than most people realize. Be realistic about your time frame so you won't be too upset by any delay you might encounter.

If you are unemployed or new to looking for a job you should have worked out a financial budget that will carry you through until you get a job. Here is the time you will need to be careful how you spend your money. Take advantage of sales, coupons, and clearance items. The more you save the longer your money will last. At the back of this eBook you will find a copy of our Simple Budget Form for your use. You can also download a copy free from our website. **(See Appendix - Simple Budget Form)**

There are many facets to job searching, and to help you stay organized and focused you will find a Job Search Checklist form at the back of this eBook. This checklist contains many items that you must master in order to increase your chances of getting the job you are seeking. Each item is important and can easily be accomplished with just a little time and patience. Several of these items will discussed in this eBook, while others will be more fully explained in other eBooks within this series. You can also download a free copy of the checklist from our website. **(See Appendix - Job Search Checklist)**

There are several steps that must be taken in order to be successful in finding a good job. If you took the time to write the lists in the paragraphs above you have taken a couple of those steps already. One of the most important tools you will have will be your Master Job Application Form. This form is one you will carry with you when you go on location to fill out a job application, or have on hand when filling out an application online. By having all this information readily available you will cut down the amount of time it takes to complete any job application. **(See Appendix - Master Job Application Form)**

In the next section we will discuss your personal plan for finding a job.

# Section 3

# My Personal Plan

Your personal plan will be your guide. What you plan to do will be up to you. We will give you some suggestions that have a proven track record for getting the results job seekers are looking for. You should find a mentor or a job coach who will be able to help you work on your plan. They will be able to give you the support and encouragement you will need by seeing that you are working your plan properly. Both a mentor and a job coach will have experience that they will be able to share with you so you can avoid making some of the more common mistakes made by job seekers.

Your plan must contain your ultimate choice of a job. This could be your dream job if you are so qualified, or a better job than the one you currently have. Remember, when unemployed you are now 'self-employed' and you are expected to work forty or more hours each week on searching for a job. If you are committed to really looking for a job, then forty hours would be a short work-week. The more time you put into looking for a job the sooner you will find one. You could just sit and wait for a job to come find you, however you could have found one much sooner by looking for the job yourself.

Part of your plan will be to work on the items contained on the checklist. In the boxes under the drafts you could put a starting date and a to-be-completed-by date. All the items on the checklist can be completed within sixteen to twenty hours. This time frame comes from years of experience of helping individuals master each item. The more time you put into preparing for job searching the more you will get out of it. After dress and grooming standards the reason someone is cut out of the running is lack of preparation to find a job. The more confident you present yourself and the more you can state your qualifications the more prepared you will be to answer the interviewer's questions.

We know that most individuals do not like to sell things. Yet you have now become a salesperson, selling yourself to a prospective employer. Are you confident in your 'product'? Are you able to back up any claim you are making with regards to the 'fitness' of the product to fill the needs of the employer? The greatest strength a salesperson has is the knowledge of their product. Who knows you better than you? Now you can see the reason for making those first few lists.

You now have lists of what you have to offer to fill an employer's needs. Now would be the time to add another list to your first set of lists. What are you doing right now for self-improvement? Are you taking any classes or doing any research at the library or online to improve your skills, talents, or knowledge about your chosen career? Have you considered keeping up with the trade journals in your field so you are not 'out-of-touch' with what is going on in the industry?

It might even be getting in better shape physically. Start going to the gym or doing some exercise to get your body in shape (or maintain it). How is your diet? Should this be part of improving the quality of your life? When we refer to exercise we include both the body and the mind. We are not proposing that you play video games all day long. We are thinking of crossword puzzles and mind games that will keep you mentally sharp. We do talk about keeping things in balance and the body and mind are two important things about you that work best when you have them balanced.

In the following section we will discuss scripting and how to do it properly.

# Section 4

# Scripting

Have you ever answered the phone and immediately you can tell that the one who is calling you is reading from a script? "Hello. My name is ... and I am calling to tell you how you can save some money. Would you like to save some money? Great, let me tell you how ..." Many times these calls are made without passion or sincerity. They will sound artificial which makes you begin to question why they are calling you. Many of these callers are working in a 'boiler room' and there is a great deal of pressure to get you to use the service or buy the product they are selling.

Your script will not be selling anything. The script you will use will be one for those you have on your networking and resource list. You are trying to gather information from those on your list about any jobs or opportunities they might know of that could be of help to you. You will find that most people like to help others. This will not cost them more than just a few minutes of their time and they will feel good that they were able to be of some measure of help to you.

There are three basic scripts that you will need. One will be used with someone you know. This will be the easiest one to create and use. The second one will be for those who were referred to you by someone else. Being a referral, these will also be easy to use. Finally, the third one will be to someone that you do not know. This is not as hard as you might think. Once you have contacted those you know and several of the referrals, calling those who you don't know will be a little easier. The more people you call the easier it will become to call on almost anyone on your network and resource list.

Every script you write should have six basic components:

1. A greeting

2. A quick question regarding if this is a good time to talk

3. Explanation of why you are calling

4. Use of your Me In Thirty Seconds or a couple of power statements

5. Asking the three networking questions

6. Closing by thanking them for their time

Each script will use the basic script model with only a few differences in what questions will be asked. No matter what script you are using there are a few things that you must do exactly the same. These include asking the three standard networking questions.

The three networking questions are:

1. Do you know of any job openings in your company that might fit my qualifications?

2. Can you recommend anyone who hires or manages people who do what I do?

3. Do you know two people who work in my field of experience who might be able to assist me?

Creating a script is not hard and at the end of this eBook there will be a scripting form that can help you write your scripts. The scripting form is also available on our website. **(See Appendix - Scripting Form)**

The purpose of writing a script is to keep you focused on the purpose of your call. The purpose of your call is to network, not to ask for a job. By having a written script you will be able to get your questions asked and answered quickly so you won't take too much of the other person's time.

Although we are talking about having a script it is important that you practice it over and over until your natural voice takes over. This way you will sound more confident and will have removed some of the roughness of the script.

The script will sound more natural when you use the proper greeting. When the individual answers the phone say, "Hello, _____ (name of contact), this is _____ (your name). Is this a good time for you to talk to me for a minute or two?" This lets you identify with the contact and lets them know your name. Asking them if this is a good time to talk with you is showing respect for the contact's time. They might be in a meeting or just leaving to visit a customer. You are giving them an opportunity to talk with you now or at a later time when it is more convenient. This will let them know how important you consider their time. If it is not a good time you should ask them when would be a good time and make arrangements to contact them later at that time.

If this is a good time to talk to them, continue with your explanation of why you are calling them. This should take less than ten seconds. Then give one of your Me In Thirty Seconds or a couple of power statements. This will give them information about you that they will need to be better prepared to point you in the right direction. Now you will ask the three networking questions and take note of the answers they give you.

You will close the call with a sincere 'thank you' for the time and any names or referrals they gave to you. Remember, you might have to contact this individual again later and you want them to have a positive feeling toward you. Their time is valuable to them and if you express your appreciation they will be open in the future if you should ever need to call them again.

If you were referred to someone your greeting will be slightly different. You would say, "Hello, _____ (contact name), my name is _____ and _____ (name of who gave you the referral) suggested that I call you. Is this a good time to talk to me for a minute or two?" Then continue as you would for a call to someone you know.

The main difference here is that if they answer 'yes' to first of the three networking questions and you are talking to the manager or interviewer, you can ask to set up an interview. Ask them when it would be convenient for them to have you come in for an interview. If the answer is 'no' then continue to ask the second and third networking questions. Again, thank them for the time they spent with you and if you were able to set up an interview you can repeat back the time and date and state that you are looking forward to meeting with them. Then keep the appointment.

If you are calling someone you do not know or were not referred to then you would ask the person who answered the phone for the name of the manager or hiring manager. Then you would say, "Thank you. May I speak to _____ (name of manager) please?" When connected to the manager you say, "Hello, _____ (name of manager), my name is _____. Is this a good time to talk to me for a minute or two?" Then continue as you would for a referred contact.

Remember, the purpose of scripting is to keep you focused on what you need to be asking to build your network and resource list. It is not to be asking for a job. If you do happen to get a 'yes' to one of the three networking questions, that's great. However, you should ask for two referrals that you can add to your network and resource list in case you can't secure an interview at this time with this contact.

Scripting is a part of the overall job-seeking package. If you don't get all the other parts it will be much harder for you to find a job. Take the time to prepare for your job search activities. Practice your scripts until you are feeling confident that they are in your natural voice and not as if you are reading a 'canned' script. The more natural you sound the better.

In the next section we will discuss how to reduce the time it takes to get a job.

# Section 5

# Reducing The Time

There have been many studies done about job searching results. These studies conclude that those who are prepared with the skills and 'tools' to find a job will find one much sooner than those who don't prepare to search for a job. What are some of these skills and 'tools' needed to be prepared to search for a job?

The best skill you can demonstrate is one of confidence, in both your speech and in the manner you present yourself. Some have this characteristic naturally, while the rest of us have to practice demonstrating and speaking with confidence. It won't take very long with some practice to become comfortable with improving your confidence level.

In this eBook we have mentioned several worksheets and forms that can help you get organized and stay on track. Create some job searching goals with some realistic dates for completion. Hold yourself accountable for working on your goals and to put in the hours of preparation it takes to be fully prepared for your job search activities. Use the lists you have written down. Be sure to fill out completely the Master Job Application Form, have a well crafted resume, a polished Me In Thirty Seconds, and several power statements that have been reviewed, perfected, and are ready to go.

Review interview questions and practice answering them with someone who wants to see you succeed. The better you can answer the questions correctly, the better chance you have of getting a job offer. If you have filled out applications online, be sure to contact the organizations to make sure that they received them. Then ask if they want a copy of your resume and how they would like you to get it to them.

After every contact or interview take the time to evaluate how you did. This will help you improve your presentation so the next person you contact will get something better than the last one. Don't worry, you will not get so perfect that nobody will hire you. With constant improvement you increase your chances of being hired that much sooner.

The next section will deal with taking ownership.

# Section 6

# Taking Ownership

Taking ownership is taking responsibility for yourself. This includes what you say and what you do. You have the ultimate control of what you do and when you do it. Don't get into the habit of only job searching when the weather suits you. If you will brave a storm to get to an interview chances are you will have better odds of getting the job than those who stayed at home, even if they may be more qualified for the position than you.

Even if a question is asked that might be a bit embarrassing or painful, take ownership of your answer and tell the truth. "Yes, I did make that mistake on a previous job many years ago. I was embarrassed then and still am to a certain extent. I learned from that mistake to be more cautious about safety. Because of it, I am always thinking about safety first on the job and keeping those I work with safe at all times." Take a negative and turn it into something positive.

When speaking about your experience be sure to use the ownership words to begin your statement. "I am …" "I have …" "I can …" These words show that you own the statement that follows. The words have more power than words like: "I think …" "I could …" "I will …" Be positive and use ownership words to begin your responses to questions asked about you and your experiences.

Remember that you are selling something that you own, yourself. You are you because of your education, experiences, and your environment. Know your strengths and capitalize on them. Turn your weaknesses into strengths by telling how you overcame them.

You will have to do the majority of this work of job searching by yourself, so you have to take time to prepare properly and take ownership for the results you receive. Improvement is also your responsibility. Take pride in what you have done. It is a good indicator of what you will do in the future.

The next section will be about putting it all together in the total package.

# Section 7

# The Total Package

While many of the items in the 'total package' have all ready been discussed in previous sections, we will present a brief description of each part. Don't feel that you can't master them all. You can because over the years we have seen many who 'feared' to even try to acquire these skills master them all within a couple of days.

**Master Job Application Form. (See Appendix - Master Job Application Form)** This is the foundation for many of the other parts of the 'total package'. Listed here is your education, experience, and many other things that will get a hiring manager's attention to your qualifications for the position they are trying to fill.

**Resume. (See Appendix - Resume Worksheet)** Your resume is more of a description in words of what is contained on your Master Job Application Form. Most of the information contained within your resume will have come from your Master Job Application Form.

**Me In Thirty Seconds. (See Appendix - Me In Thirty Seconds Worksheet)** This is a concise statement of your qualifications for the position being offered. Most of the information used will also be from your Master Job Application Form. You should have several of these that will best suit the questions that will be asked about you. Some will be about your work experience and others about you.

**Power Statements. (See Appendix - Power Statement Worksheet)** These are statements that are used as responses to questions asked during an interview or when you are networking. Normally these are based on information contained on the Master Job Application Form. They are usually about three sentences that demonstrate your qualifications, or used when making an 'ownership' statement regarding your experience. Make sure you have plenty of them to respond to any question that will be asked of you.

**Career Goals. (See Appendix - Goal Setting Form)** These are goals that relate to your vocational goals. They are slightly different than your personal goals. The goals you have should be realistic and attainable. If you have the education and experience for the job you should have a realistic expectation of getting it. If you lack the education for your 'dream' job you will have to get it first.

**Network and Resource List. (See Appendix - Network and Resource List)** You will need to build a network and resource list of individuals and other resources where you can find help in finding jobs opportunities. This list is very valuable because you will have at your disposal a list of those who can help you match your qualifications with jobs they know you can do. More jobs today are found through networking than all the other methods combined.

**Introductions and Greetings.** Since you only have one chance of making a good first impression you will need to know how to introduce yourself and how to properly greet others. This also would include how to properly close an interview, which will be the last impression you will make with the interviewer. Be sure to do them properly.

**Interview Questions. (See Chapter 10 - Skill Builder Special Salad)** It is important that you understand the interview process and respect it. It is not an interrogation, it is an opportunity for the interviewer to ask you some questions to see if you will fit into the culture of the organization. From your application and resume they will have an idea of your qualifications for the position. Now they want to know how you will fit into their work environment. Practice the questions and understand how to properly answer the questions. It is important that you display confidence in how you sit and present yourself. The interview is also about observation of your appearance and demeanor.

**Mock Interview.** The mock interview will help you get comfortable with the interview process. It will give you the opportunity to practice and perfect your answers. It will also allow your 'mock' interviewer to give you some feedback on how you are doing so you can make adjustments where needed.

**Video Interview and Review.** After a couple of mock interviews you should be more comfortable about being interviewed. If possible, have a video made of an additional mock interview in which you can see yourself and how you sit, react, and answer the questions. It will open your eyes to many small things that you were not aware of doing, yet that can be distracting to an interviewer without you knowing it. Review the video with several individuals who are willing to help you perfect your performance.

**Dress and Grooming.** This is one of the most important parts of job search preparation. In doing your research on the company or organization you should have noticed how the employees dressed and groomed themselves. When you go to a company to fill out an application or speak to someone about the company and the position being offered, you should be dressed and groomed in a professional manner. Wearing a suit or business attire is always acceptable. Be sure to cover all exposed tattoos and remove all piercings. Make sure your clothing is clean, pressed, or ironed. Do not wear excessive perfume or aftershave and be conservative with your jewelry.

**Budgeting Your Time. (See Appendix - Simple Budget Form)** This is important if you want to find a job in the least amount of time. You will have to make your own schedule and stick to it. A good rule of thumb is to have at least two face to face interviews per day. You should be making ten or more phone contacts per day with your network and resource list. With each contact you should be gathering two more referrals to add to your list. Yes, you will be very busy. But what else do you have to do?

**Job Search Activities Log. (See Appendix - Job Search Activity Log)** After several contacts it will be hard to remember who you have met, where you have filled out applications, and where you have sent your resumes. This is the log you will keep to record who you have contacted and what transpired. You should be making a minimum of ten contacts per day if you want to see your efforts rewarded quickly. Review these forms often and you should be able to see where you might be able to improve your job searching efforts. This log can also help remind you of what follow up items still need to be addressed. Being organized and following up with those you have contacted will help you get a job.

There are more things that you could add to this list, however these are the ones you should focus on. Keep busy and the time will pass quickly. You will find employment before you know it. It is all in your hands.

The concluding and review section will be next, followed by many of the forms referenced in this eBook.

# Section 8

# Conclusion And Review

This eBook began with where you need to start. This is where you are now. You can't skip ahead and there are no shortcuts. From this starting point you will have to start gathering the information you will need in order to find a job. You were to make several lists that will help you identify your talents, skills, education, experience, and many other important items to help you through the process of seeking a job.

Be realistic about the job you are hoping to get. If you lack the education or the experience the organization has set as a condition of employment you should have a 'plan B' ready. It is not wise to set your sights on only one job if you have no expectation of even getting it. Use your time and resources to your best advantage. Don't waste time chasing unrealistic dreams where those same energies and time could have produced viable employment opportunities.

If you are currently unemployed you will need to have a plan on how you will survive. You will also have to adjust your spending habits so what funds you do have will last until you obtain a job. Create a budget and stick to it. Watch how and where you are spending your money. Money is not the only thing you will have to budget. You should budget your time to be productive in your job search activities. Schedule a time to be calling those on your network and resource list and to set appointments for interviews.

There are many things that you will have to do to prepare yourself for looking for a job. These tasks may not be fun, but they are necessary to complete if you really want to get a job in the shortest amount of time. Write out a plan. This plan should include all the items you need to have ready before you begin your job search activities. There are several forms mentioned in this eBook that are available free. Use them to you advantage. They will help you stay focused and on track.

In order to build a great network and resource list you will have to write some scripts that you will use to get help in finding out where the jobs are. We suggest that you write it, read it out loud, and make changes until it sounds like your natural voice. Practice it until the script becomes a natural extension of you. There is plenty of information about scripting in this eBook and there is a copy of a Scripting Form at the end of this eBook. Copy it and use it.

Time is of the essence and you will need to reduce the amount of time it takes to get a job. This means you can't afford to waste your time. If you are unemployed, your new full-time job is job searching. Some of this time will be used to prepare yourself by building lists, practicing interview questions, and making phone calls. If you need to look up something online, you can do it in the evening when you won't be scheduling any interviews.

We talked about the 'total package' and how important it is. The more you prepare and do to get ready to go out and job search, the faster you will find a job. The most basic items you should have when you begin are your Master Job Application Form, a great resume, a polished Me In Thirty Seconds, and some power statements. Next, you should have a network and resource list that will keep you busy. To help you stay on track and help you move forward you could seek assistance from a mentor or job coach to work with you, helping you through the maze to get the job you want.

One of the most important forms is the Job Search Activity Log. This will document your time and record who you have contacted along with information about any follow-up items you need to do. The forms we have made available are tools to help you stay organized, see what you have to do, and record what you did.

We hope that you enjoyed the **Basic Breakfast Plate** and will take the time to look at our other menu items at the **Job Seekers Café**.

*Thank you and come back soon!*

# Chapter 3

# Fresh Garden Salad

# Chapter 3
# Fresh Garden Salad

Pick your own goals and achieve them. Learn how to set goals for job seekers using time tested methods. Keep organized and on track to find employment quickly. Served with forms to get you organized and headed for success.

## Section Table of Contents

| | |
|---|---|
| Introduction ........................................... | 75 |
| What Is A Goal? .................................... | 77 |
| Keeping It Simple ................................. | 79 |
| Keep It Real .......................................... | 81 |
| Making It Achievable ........................... | 83 |
| Define Your Plan .................................. | 85 |
| Take Action ........................................... | 87 |
| Conclusion And Review ...................... | 99 |

# Section 1

# Introduction

Welcome to the **Job Seekers Café**. This menu item is entitled **Fresh Garden Salad.** You will find this basic garden salad is made of fresh ideas and concepts that will help you set your job searching goals. It is a refreshing 'back-to-basics' simple salad that has all the ingredients to satisfy your job searching hunger, with a light dressing of 'how' to get the most out of your job searching efforts. This is real 'comfort food' that will help you see what you need to do and what you have done. Enjoy the great taste of knowing where you are going.

While other salads will be loaded up with many other items to give you a variety of tastes and textures, this Fresh Garden Salad contains just the season's freshest from the garden harvest. Enjoy the simplicity of setting goals that can and will be achieved.

You will notice that on the outer margins of this and most other pages there are Scholar Margins where you can make notes or comments about what impressed you when reading the material. Perhaps you might have a question and you will put a question mark to remind you that you need to find clarification of the text and the concept presented.

This eBook will take you through the proper way to set up your goals. A goal is more than just a dream or a desire. It is a written plan on how you will achieve your objective, no matter what it is. If it is not written down, then it cannot be called a goal.

There are many parts to setting a goal. One of the things you must consider is to make the goal simple. This doesn't mean it will be easy, it will just be simpler to understand and to track your progress. Each goal will need to be realistic and not some wild impractical 'thought-it-might-be-fun' experiment. A goal should be completely defined. If you are not sure, ask for some help so you do not waste time trying to figure out where you went off track. Your goal should also be achievable. You have limitations and you must admit that there are some things that you will not be able to do. This could be a physical limitation or you might currently lack the experience or education required for the position you are seeking.

The most important part of any goal is that you must take action. This includes doing what you must do to stay on track and on your time schedule. If you continually put off working on your goals, your time line will keep extending. Then one day you will wake up and wonder what ever happened to your goals. You are in charge of you and you have to be willing to hold yourself accountable for your actions or lack of actions.

We have tried to give you all the tools you will need to write your own goals. There are forms that you will be able to use that will be your 'map' to where you want to go. They will also show you where you have been. Goals need to be measured as to the progress you are making toward their achievement.

There will be some suggestions on setting up some beginning goals to get you off to a great start. Once you get used to setting goals and seeing how rapidly you progress, you will incorporate goal setting in all the other facets of your life.

Reference will be made throughout this eBook about concepts that can be found in some of the other **Job Seekers Café** menu items. While each eBook is a standalone publication about a given subject, the entire collection of menu items has been prepared to help a job seeker be totally prepared to reduce the time it takes to get a job.

# Section 2

# What Is A Goal?

You have dreams, wishes, desires, and aspirations to become more successful in your life both vocationally and in your home. You can look around you and see that there are those who seem to be 'living' the dream. Why are they living it and you aren't? Chances are they took that dream and made it a goal, taking the time to see what it would take to achieve that dream and then writing out a plan. Then they took the action required to achieve their dream. You will notice that many of these successful individuals are very average individuals who have achieved a measure of success that others envy.

There have been many studies of successful individuals and there is always one common trait in each of them. They all had written goals and a plan to get to where they wanted to be. These are those who did not want to let life tell them who or what they would be. They charted their own course, set sail, and kept to their plan.

Just like gardening, setting goals is a process. You want to enjoy the results of your efforts. With gardening you have to prepare the soil, plant the seeds, and while waiting for the plants to ripen you will be watering, weeding, and fighting off the bugs that threaten your efforts. With goals it is much the same. You have to prepare yourself, write your goals, and put in lots of work trying to overcome all the obstacles that life will put in your way.

This eBook has been written so that the novice goal setter can easily get started. Yet it will provide the more seasoned goal setters some new and fresh ideas on how they can accomplish their goals in a timely manner. Some (both novice and seasoned) will try to accomplish more than they can handle. When they fall into this trap they tend to get discouraged and stop working on their goals. This is why it is so important that you keep your goals simple.

The first few sections will deal with the basics of how to set goals. Other sections that follow will show you how to use these basics to set your own goals and achieve them. The right goals will get the right results, so we will help you write the right goals so you can get the results that you expect.

Throughout this eBook various forms will be suggested that you can fill out. The forms can be found on our website and can be downloaded for free. Several of the forms can be found in the back of this eBook and copied for your personal use. Please use the forms suggested. They are designed to help you stay focused and on track to get where you want to go as soon as possible.

Change your dreams into goals. Change your goals into achievements. Change your achievements into a successful life. Working on goals is a journey of change. That change should be embraced and celebrated. As you become more successful you will have more that you will be able to share with others. The more you share, the more you will receive.

In the next section we will begin our discussion on goal setting basics, starting with keeping it simple.

# Section 3

# Keeping It Simple

We tend to write grand goals and post them on the refrigerator so we can see them. Trouble is, we don't usually do much more than that. This might explain why most individuals don't achieve their goals. The secret to achieving your goals is just to work on them.

Your goal should be written in a simple format so it is easy to see what you are wanting to achieve. Don't complicate your goals. Use simple terminology so they won't get lost in the confusion of your life. By making your goals simple it is easier to break them down into manageable bite-sized pieces. These bite-sized pieces, or 'mini goals', are referred to as action steps. These action steps are generally to be completed in less than two weeks. Each action step you complete should be moving you toward achieving your goal.

Where will you begin? You begin by identifying where you are now and where it is you would like to be in the future. Since you will have more than one goal you will need to prioritize them in order of importance. Don't try to do too much at a time. If you are prioritizing and working diligently on your action steps then things will move quickly for you.

When your goals are well-written you will see that the action steps are just stepping stones that lead to your goal. Do your action steps and goals in order. By skipping around you might miss or overlook an important foundational piece that you will have to go back and complete in order to be moving toward your goal. Worse yet is that you could be well off course before you have to stop and go back to the beginning. Don't waste time and resources thinking you are actually saving time. Stay the course and keep on track.

How many goals can you work on at one time? The answer depends on how organized you are. Each goal will have a target date to be achieved by. These target dates will vary for each goal. Each goal will have several action steps that must be accomplished before you can complete your goal. Some action steps might be as simple as making a phone call for information about a class you need to attend. Others will take a little longer since they might involve taking a class that will last several weeks or months. These action steps will be to attend the classes, study the material, read the books, take the tests, and pass the tests. Once you have accomplished these action steps each week and passed the final exam, you will have accomplished your goal.

When you complete an action step or goal, you need to write a new one. After a short period of time you will begin to see results from these efforts and you will see that you are getting closer to your ultimate goal. You will also notice that each action step and goal is much easier to accomplish than you thought.

We define simple as uncomplicated, yet not necessarily easy. Write out your goals and break them into manageable bite-sized pieces that we call action steps. Just as the name implies, you must take action if you want to make any progress toward your goal.

In the next section we will present how to keep your goals real.

# Section 4

# Keep It Real

Imagination is the spring of innovation and invention. It is also the basis for daydreaming and fantasizing. While innovation and invention contribute to the benefit of mankind, daydreaming and fantasizing only consume the time of the individual engaged in these activities. If one puts in too much time daydreaming and fantasizing it will begin to have an effect on productivity, profitability, and one's home life.

As you write your goals you will have to keep them real. Unrealistic action steps or goals are a waste of time in pursuing. Just because you have written a goal will not make it real. A real goal or action step means you can achieve them since they are stepping stones that will take you to the next level. If they are real you will also be able to measure your progress and personal growth.

If you are setting goals for a position that requires a degree and you don't have one, this would be considered as being unrealistic. We are not saying setting a goal to get the required degree or technical training is unrealistic. In fact it is a very realistic and desirable goal to be achieved. It just won't be achieved in time for the current position being offered.

There are a couple of quick and easy tests you can perform to see if your goal or action step might be real. Do you know of others who have been in a similar situation as you currently find yourself that were able to change their lives in the direction you want to go? Are you aware of the resources they used to achieve their goals and do you have access to those same resources? Do you have both the financial means and the time available to achieve your goal?

There are just some things that you won't be able to achieve because of your own limitations. These could be financial, physical, mental, educational, or due to a lack of resources available to you at this time. You might also lack the skills, talents, and abilities required for a particular position. Some limitations can be overcome, while others might be considered a permanent limitation you must live with.

Part of setting any goal is to know the time frame in which it should be completed. This time frame must also be realistic. Don't put the date so far out that you begin to think that there will always be plenty of time to work on the goal. Write your goals with the understanding that time is of the essence. The sooner you complete your action steps the sooner you will achieve your goal. This means you will be able to start working on the next one and you will be able to accomplish more in less time than you have planned.

Goals are usually stated in their time frame category. Goals that will take over ten years to accomplish are considered to be in the 'life goal' category. Those goals that will be completed in less than ten years are in the 'long-term goal' category. If the goal can be completed in less than two years they fall into the 'medium-term goal' category. The 'short-term goal' category includes those goals that can be completed in less than six months. The action steps you will write to reach your goals are to be completed within one to two weeks.

In a later section of this eBook you will be shown examples of how to set goals to prepare properly to begin job searching, along with appropriate action steps. The goals presented are short-term goals that can be completed in less than six months. (The goals used as examples can be completed in less than a week.) You can always finish a goal well before the target date. Because a goal to find a job is less than six months, we do not mean to imply that it will take you six months to find a job. You should be able to find one much sooner if you are diligently working on your action steps and goals. The example is only to give you a 'visual' of how a real goal can be written and achieved.

In the next section we will discuss how to make your goal achievable.

# Section 5

# Making It Achievable

A goal can be real and achievable. A goal can be real and not achievable. The difference is that a real goal can be done, yet you might not be able to achieve it. This can be due to lack of education, experience, or financial resources. It can also be due to very real obstacles or obstructions that you will not be able to overcome. We've all had goals that were not achievable due to circumstances beyond our control. This could be a temporary or a permanent situation that we must accept. Goals must be both real and achievable, not one or the other.

There is also the question of this being the best time to achieve the goal or whether you should work on more important goals right now, delaying those that can wait until a later time. You might have a goal that is simple, real, and achievable that might not be in your best interest since it might have a negative impact on your family. Working on any goal that is not in your best interest at this time means you are wasting both time and resources that could have been put to more productive use.

Some questions you might ask yourself to see if your goals are achievable are just common sense questions. Will this goal or action step move me toward my ultimate goal? Do I have the resources and time available to achieve my goal now? Do I really have the passion and commitment to do all that is required to achieve my goal?

Many goals are abandoned because the individual becomes tired of not seeing the results expected. Goals take time to achieve and figuring the proper time frame is very important. To see how you are doing you will have to measure the results you are getting. This means that you must be organized and keep accurate records of how you are doing.

Watch out for congested spots and take the time to study the situation carefully. Make adjustments early and as often as needed. It is much easier to fix things as you go than to get near completion and have to go back and make drastic changes that will cost you more time and resources you could have used on other goals. Goal setting is about the journey. Goal achievements are the mile markers you place on your path of life.

The next section will be about defining your goals properly.

# Section 6

# Define Your Plan

You will need to define your plan in complete detail so you will know exactly what you will need to do to accomplish your goal. To define your goal takes a little bit of work, but the time you spend to list everything you need to do will actually save you plenty of time later. Some items you will be able to move to a higher priority and others to a lower priority. Work on the most important action step or goal that will move you toward the life you want to live.

As you look at where you are now and where you would like to be, you should begin to formulate in your mind just what action steps you will need to accomplish in order to achieve your goal. Arrange your action steps so their flow moves you toward your goal. Keep your action steps moving you in as straight a line as possible to your goal. Each one should be supportive of the next action step you will work on.

By having your goals written down and defined you can make quick reviews to see that you are on track. If you see that you have gotten off course, make the changes to get back as soon as possible.

Throughout this eBook we continue to bring up the need to keep organized and to prioritize your goals and action steps. This will help you measure what you have accomplished and to clearly see what you still have to do in order to accomplish your goals.

A very important concept when it comes to writing your goals is to keep your life in balance. While we shift our priorities throughout each stage of our life it is keeping an overall balance that helps us move forward. There are seven facets in our life; health, family, spirituality, self-improvement (education), community, career, and finances. In this eBook series we will focus on the self-improvement and career facets. The other five are just as important, but not for our purposes of helping you secure employment.

As you begin this adventure you will realize that you will have to make some sacrifices. What we mean is that you will have to give up something now in order to achieve your goals later. Change is good, for it means movement toward your goals. We tend to fear change because we do not like leaving our comfort zone. To grow and change toward a goal we must step out of our comfort zone and embrace the changes we are making. You might have to sacrifice a few hours of television to write your goals and then to work on them. Most of the sacrifices you will be making will be to write and work on your goals. It is just that simple. You will have to determine what and how much you are willing to sacrifice to achieve your goals.

Doing your due diligence is an important part of defining your goals. Know what it is that you want, what will be required, and what will be expected to achieve your goals. Know the time frame and the financial costs if any. The more you know, the better you can define what it will take to accomplish your goals.

The next section will be about taking action to complete your action steps and achieve your goals.

# Section 7

# Take Action

The easiest part of goal setting is doing the planning and research, then writing the goals on a piece of paper. The hardest part is to overcome your fear of change and take action on those goals. The preceding sections have given you the information on how to properly write a goal. This section will help you put into action the plans you have made to reach your goals.

There are several forms you will need to have in order to begin writing and working on your goals and action steps. There are other forms that you will need to work on to accomplish the example goals you will be presented with in this section. These forms can be found in the back of this eBook and can be downloaded for free from our website. The first forms you will be working with are the **Goal Setting Form (See Appendix - Goal Setting Form)** and the **Action Step Form (See Appendix - Action Step Form)**. These are the forms where you will write your goals and the action steps you will take to achieve them.

The other forms are the ones you will need to complete as foundational items to have a proper job searching plan designed for successful results. You will need the **Job Search Checklist (See Appendix - Job Search Checklist)**, **Master Job Application Form (See Appendix - Master Job Application Form)**, and the **Network And Resource List (See Appendix - Network and Resource List)**.

On the next several pages you will see examples of a Goal Setting Form, some Action Step Forms, a Master Job Application Form, and the Network and Resource List. These forms make job searching much easier by compiling all the information you need in an organized program. The forms are simple to fill out and will keep you on schedule to complete your goals and action steps in a timely manner. The last form presented in this section will be the Job Search Checklist. This checklist is your guide to make sure that you are doing all you can to be totally prepared to enter the job search 'jungle' with all the tools you will need to 'survive' and succeed.

| | |
|---|---|
| **My Goal** | Prepare my foundational items for job searching. |
| Facet | Self-help and career facets |
| Start Date 3-1-14 | Target Date No later than 3-21-14 |
| My Objective | To fill out my Master Job Application Form and to start building my Network and Resource List. |
| My Plan | To write action steps that will help me reach this goal. |
| | Copy or download the Action Step forms, 3 of them. |
| | Copy or download the Master Job Application Form. |
| | Copy or download the Network and Resource List form. |
| My Resources | For my Master Job Application Form I will use my work history and school records. For my Network & Resource List I will use my phone contact list, friends, relatives, and use the internet to find help. |
| My Results | |

**This is an example of how the Goal Setting Form should be filled out.**

Chapter 3 - Fresh Garden Salad

| | |
|---|---|
| **Action Step No.** _1_ For My Goal: | Prepare my foundational items. |

Master Job Application Form

Facet: Self-help and career facets

Start Date: 3-1-14 | Target Date: 3-3-14

My Objective: Fill out the Master Job Application Form completely with all dates, positions held, contact names, addresses, and phone numbers. Verify all the information for accuracy!

My Plan: Copy or download the Master Job Application Form and begin filling it out today.

My Resources: Find my old employment records in the file cabinet. Missing items to be sought out by contacting previous places I have worked. Gather my school transcripts to verify dates.

My Results:

**This is an example of how the Action Step Form should be filled out.**

# MASTER JOB APPLICATION FORM

This generic Master Job Application Form complies with federal and state laws against discrimination; however, the user must exercise caution by checking local laws that might have additional restrictions. This form when filled out will contain personal information that you might wish to keep confidential.

## GENERAL INFORMATION

| Name (Last) | (First) | (Middle Initial) | Home Telephone |
|---|---|---|---|
| Smith | Jessica | A | 818 555 1212 |

| Address (Mailing Address) | (City) | (State) | (Zip Code) | Other Telephone |
|---|---|---|---|---|
| 1332 E. Main St. | Homeville | CA | 90026 | (818) 555 - 3579 |

| E-Mail Address | Are you legally entitled to work in the U.S.? |
|---|---|
| jasmith123@mynet.com | ☒ Yes  ☐ No |

## Position

| Position or Type of Employment Desired: Assistant Clerical Supervisor | Will Accept: ☒ Part-Time ☒ Full-Time ☐ Temporary | Shift: ☒ Day ☐ Swing ☐ Graveyard ☐ Rotating |
|---|---|---|

Are you able to perform the essential functions of the job you are applying for, with or without reasonable accommodation? ☒ Yes  ☐ No

| Salary Desired | Date Available |
|---|---|
| Open | 3-31-14 |

## Education and Training

High School Graduate or General Education (GED) Test Passed? ☒ Yes  ☐ No
If no, list the highest grade completed:

### College, Business School, Military (Most recent first)

| Name and Location | Dates Attended Month/Year | Credits Earned Quarterly or Semester Hours | Credits Earned Other (Specify) | Graduate? | Degree And Year | Major or Subject |
|---|---|---|---|---|---|---|
| Homeville College, Homeville, CA | From 09/08 To 06/12 | 134 | | ☒ Yes ☐ No | BA 2010 | Business Admin. |
| | From To | | | ☐ Yes ☐ No | | |
| | From To | | | | | |

| Occupational License, Certificate or Registration | Number | Where Issued | Expiration Date |
|---|---|---|---|
| | | | |
| | | | |
| | | | |

| Languages Read, Written or Spoken Fluently Other Than English |
|---|
| Spanish |

## VETERAN INFORMATION (Most recent)

| Branch of Service | Date of Entry | Date of Discharge |
|---|---|---|
| | | |

## SPECIAL SKILLS (List all pertinent skills and equipment that you can operate)

MSWord, Excel, PowerPoint, Access, Outlook, Adobe InDesign, Adobe Illustrator, Photoshop, Windows

*Sample Master Job Application Form*

Chapter 3 - Fresh Garden Salad

## WORK EXPERIENCE (Most Recent First)   (Include voluntary work and military experience)

| | |
|---|---|
| **Employer** Homeville Hardware | **Telephone Number** ( 818 ) 555 - 1776 |
| **Address** 145 N. State Street, Homeville, CA 90026 | |
| **Job Title** Office Supervisor | **Number Employees Supervised** 3 |
| **From (Month/Year)** 7/2010 | **To (Month/Year)** 3/2014 |
| **Hours Per Week** 40 | **Last Salary** $14.75 hour |
| **Supervisor** Jack Johnson | |

**Specific Duties**
Handled purchase orders, invoices, accounts payable and receivable, assisted with payroll, and helped with customer service when needed in the store.

**Reason For Leaving** Owners were retiring and closed business.   **May We Contact This Employer?** ☒ Yes ☐ No

---

| | |
|---|---|
| **Employer** Ron's Cafe & Diner | **Telephone Number** ( 818 ) 555 - 9120 |
| **Address** 1483 Hwy 29, Homeville, CA 90026 | |
| **Job Title** Shift Supervisor & Waitress | **Number Employees Supervised** 6 |
| **From (Month/Year)** 6/2007 | **To (Month/Year)** 7/2010 |
| **Hours Per Week** 30 | **Last Salary** $11.35 hour |
| **Supervisor** Ron Ortega | |

**Specific Duties**
Made shift schedules for peak customer demands and helped with the inventory, receiving, and ordering of food and supplies as needed.

**Reason For Leaving** Finished my degree, wanted an office job.   **May We Contact This Employer?** ☒ Yes ☐ No

---

*(Sample Master Job Application Form — remaining employer sections blank)*

## Check List

- ☒ Correct contact information & phone number
- ☒ All addresses are correct
- ☒ All dates have been verified
- ☒ All education is correctly listed
- ☒ Resume complete
- ☐ Me In Thirty Seconds complete
- ☐ Power Statements complete
- ☐ Job Search Activity Log entries made as contacted

**Action Step No.** _2_  **For My Goal:** Prepare my foundational items.

Network and Resource List

**Facet** Self-help and career facets

| Start Date 3-1-14 | Target Date 3-5-14 |

**My Objective** Fill in a minimum of 15 contacts each day so by the end of the week I will have 75 contacts with their names, phone numbers, and addresses with a priority contact rating.

**My Plan** Copy or download the Network and Resource List form and begin filling it out today.

**My Resources** Use my cell phone contact list, neighbors, friends, and members of my church. List also those organizations that can possibly help me with referrals.

**My Results**

> This is an example of how the Action Step Form should be filled out.

Chapter 3 - Fresh Garden Salad

## Network And Resource List

| No. | Name Of Resource | Contact Information (phone number, address, e-mail) | Priority |
|---|---|---|---|
| 1. | Bill Jones | 555-2786    1232 N. First St., Homeville  bill.jones@mynet.com | A |
| 2. | Tom Stanton | 555-8951    1275 N. First St., Homeville  stantont@mynet.com | A |
| 3. | George Larsen | 555-6585    326 E. Poplar Ave., Homeville  georgelarsen23@mynet.com | A |
| 4. | Cindy Allen | 555-3467    254 W. Elm Dr., Homeville  cinal75@mynet.com | B |
| 5. | Joyce Brighten | 555-5584   367 Snow Springs Dr., Homeville  joycenjohnbrighten@mynet.com | B |
| 6. | Rex Knox | 555-3698    155 N. Third St., Homeville  rex.knox@mynet.com | A |
| 7. | Jill Howell | 555-6984    268 N. Third St., Homeville  howelljill@mynet.com | A |
| 8. | Sam Paterson | 555-1456    674 N. Pine St., Homeville  sampaterson@mynet.com | B |
| 9. | Neal Campbell | 555-4587   389 Snow Springs Dr., Homeville  nealcampbell@mynet.com | A |
| 10. | Willie Boxton | 555-7845    154 W. Desert Dr., Homeville  willieboxton@mynet.com | B |
| 11. | Earl Krandal | 555-1679    548 E. Jefferson St., Homeville  earlkrandal@mynet.com | A |
| 12. | John Rayburn | 555-3574    637 W. Adams St., Homeville  rayburn.jk@mynet.com | A |
| 13. | Temp One Jobs | 555-4376    238 N. State St., Homeville  info@temponejobs.com | C |
| 14. | Homeville College | 555-2813    Campus Placement Office | C |
| 15. | Pastor O'Grady | 555-9173    Pine St. at Desert Dr., Homeville  pastor.tomogrady@church.net | A |
| 16. | | | |
| 17. | | | |
| 18. | | | |
| 19. | | | |
| 20. | | | |

**Sample Network And Resource List**

| | |
|---|---|
| **My Goal** | Track my job search preparedness |

| | |
|---|---|
| Facet | Self-help and career facets |

| | | | |
|---|---|---|---|
| Start Date | 3-1-14 | Target Date | No later than 3-25-14 |

| | |
|---|---|
| My Objective | To complete my job search preparedness by using the Job Search Checklist. |

| | |
|---|---|
| My Plan | To write action steps that will help me reach this goal. Copy or download the Job Search Checklist form. Schedule a time to complete the Job Search Checklist before the end of the month. |

| | |
|---|---|
| My Resources | Completed Goal and Action Step Forms |

| | |
|---|---|
| My Results | |

**This is an example of how the Goal Setting Form should be filled out.**

Chapter 3 - Fresh Garden Salad

---

**Action Step No.** __1__ **For My Goal:** Track My Job Search Preparedness

Job Search Checklist

| Facet | Self-help and career facets |

| Start Date 3-1-14 | Target Date 3-10-14 |

**My Objective** Begin to track status on Job Search Checklist items as they are worked on. Want to complete the following at least 4 items by the target date of 3-10-14.

**My Plan** Copy or download the Job Search Checklist form today and begin filling out the progress being made on each item that is being worked on.

**My Resources** Various eBooks from the Job Seekers Café menu that will provide the information on how to do the various items I am not familiar with or need to better understand.

**My Results**

> **This is an example of how the Action Step Form should be filled out.**

Page 95

## Job Search Checklist

| Complete | Item | 1st Draft | 2nd Draft | 3rd Draft | 4th Draft |
|---|---|---|---|---|---|
| 3-3-14 | Master Job Application Form | 3-1-14 | 3-3-14 | | |
| 3-18-14 | Resume | 3-6-14 | 3-9-14 | 3-14-14 | 3-18-14 |
| 3-5-14 | Me In Thirty Seconds (1) | 3-3-14 | 3-5-14 | | |
| | Me In Thirty Seconds (2) | 3-3-14 | | | |
| | Me In Thirty Seconds (3) | | | | |
| | Me In Thirty Seconds (4) | | | | |
| | Me In Thirty Seconds (5) | | | | |
| 3-5-14 | Power Statement (1) | 3-3-14 | 3-4-14 | 3-5-14 | |
| | Power Statement (2) | 3-3-14 | | | |
| | Power Statement (3) | | | | |
| | Power Statement (4) | | | | |
| | Power Statement (5) | | | | |
| | Career Goals | 3-1-14 | | | |
| | Network & Resource List | 3-1-14 | 3-2-14 | 3-3-14 | |
| | Introductions & Greetings | | | | |
| | Interview Questions & Answers | | | | |
| | Mock Interview | | | | |
| | Video Interview & Review | | | | |
| | Dress & Grooming Standards | | | | |

**Sample Job Search Checklist In Process**

As you can see, there is nothing complicated here. Things are kept simple yet well defined as to what it is you want to accomplish. Knowing what it is and how you will get there will make it easier to measure your progress. Also, you will see the items that you still have to complete in order to be totally prepared for your job search activities.

The next section will be the conclusion and review of what has been presented in this eBook. After the conclusion and review section you will find copies of the forms mentioned and used throughout this eBook.

# Section 8

# Conclusion And Review

We hope that you found this eBook on setting goals very helpful. When written properly, goals can be achieved much faster. Successful individuals write goals that are simple, real, achievable, and defined, then they take action toward accomplishing them. As a general rule, you will spend more time on your goals than you will money. Both your money and time must be budgeted in order to get the most from your efforts and resources.

Goal setting is a process that will require your energies to achieve. When your goals are simple this means you can easily see what it is you are trying to accomplish. Simple also implies that you are breaking your goal down into manageable bite-sized pieces called action steps. Keeping your goals real means you won't be wasting time on a wild dream that you cannot reach. Every goal you write down should be achievable. This means that there is a greater chance that you will succeed and do the things necessary to make the changes in your life that will take you to where you want to be. Defining your goal will make sure that you have done your due diligence to understand all that you must do to get where you want to go.

The most important part of goal setting is taking the action required to move yourself forward. Without action nothing will ever be achieved. Action is sometimes the most difficult part because we all seem to have a fear of the unknown. This fear holds us back from experiencing growth and reaching our potential. In order to grow and develop, or move from where we are now to where we want to be, we have to take the risk of changing our behaviors. We must increase our knowledge, skills, abilities, and talents in ways that will open up opportunities that we currently deny ourselves.

There are several forms that have been made available for your use. You are free to use them for your own personal use. Forms are merely a record of what you want to do and a record of what you have done. This is important so you can measure your progress toward your goal.

We hope that you enjoyed the **Fresh Garden Salad** and will take the time to look at our other menu items at the **Job Seekers Café**.

*Thank you and come back soon!*

# Chapter 4

# Mentor Plate Special

# Chapter 4
# Mentor Plate Special

This special plate is the secret that can really satisfy your craving for being totally prepared to get the job you really want. You will learn who can be your best mentor and how they can get you prepared to get a job that you can make into a career.

## Section Table of Contents

Introduction .......................................... 105

The Origins Of Mentoring .................. 107

What To Look For In A Mentor .......... 111

Styles Of Mentoring ............................ 115

Duties Of The Mentor ......................... 117

Duties Of The Mentored .................... 119

Objectives ............................................. 121

Accountability ..................................... 125

Why Mentors Mentor ......................... 127

Conclusion And Review ..................... 129

# Section 1

# Introduction

Welcome to the **Job Seekers Café**. This menu item is entitled **Mentor Plate Special.** This plate will satisfy your hunger by understanding how a mentor can make a difference in your vocational life. Both the mentor and the mentored benefit greatly by this passing of knowledge and experience. The mentored gets the benefit of learning from one who has been there and the mentor has the satisfaction of seeing someone grow and develop much faster to a higher level.

This eBook is written to help you understand who is a good mentor. It will also help you see how the relationship between the mentor and the mentored works. Some individuals will confuse a mentor with a coach. They actually have different roles and purposes although they seem to travel down similar tracks. In this section we will discuss coaching and in another section of this eBook we will discuss mentoring.

You will notice that on the outer margins of this and most other pages there are Scholar Margins where you can make notes or comments about what impressed you when reading the material. Perhaps you might have a question and you will put a question mark to remind you that you need to find clarification of the text and the concept presented.

The term coaching first appeared in English vocabulary about 1849 in Thackeray's novel *Pendennis*, roughly related to academic tutoring, the art of perfecting a performance, or the teaching of a certain set of skills. Common to the word mentoring, coaching has been around longer than the word or its definition. Coaching has been more related to job tasks, sports, and academia due to the 'performance' relationship to achieve a particular outcome. This relationship has also been brought into the workplace by managers coaching the techniques and processes to be completed by employees relative to the functions of the job task requirement. At times this may have to be repeated often to achieve and maintain the consistency of the desired results. Coaching is an activity often aimed at a group. Yet, when an individual is coached, they are often dealing with a single performance issue or set of particular performance tasks or procedures.

Mentoring, on the other hand, is directed more at an individual and involves sharing expertise and experience in several areas related to personal or career development through discussions and assignments. The assignments are measured for accountability to see if the concepts discussed were fully understood. The process can proceed at a pace which the mentor and the mentored feel comfortable. While some mentoring concepts might require days, weeks, or months to complete, the lessons are reinforced with each mentoring session until both the mentor and mentored are satisfied with the desired results.

Mentoring and coaching are two distinctly different concepts that are often used in the wrong context. Mentoring is about personal and career development (concerning customs, habits, and behaviors). Coaching is about performance expectations to be achieved, repeated, and then improved (concerning task, technique, and productivity).

You might be mentored in career development (learning the expectations of business relationships). This is best achieved by a mentor who is not in your direct line of reporting or supervision, although you might be coached in how to perform various tasks, functions, and procedures related to your position at the same time. This coaching should be the responsibility of your direct line manager or supervisor since they are in the best position to coach you in the tasks to be learned and accomplished. Normally both the mentor and job coach work well together since both have the goal of helping the individual reach their potential much faster than waiting for the individual to discover these things on their own.

The term mentored will be used throughout this eBook in reference to the one who is being mentored by the mentor. The term 'mentee' can also be used to refer to the one being mentored. In some articles or books on the subject of the mentoring process you might see the term 'mentee' used.

Reference will be made throughout this eBook about concepts that can be found in some of the other **Job Seekers Café** menu items. While each eBook is a standalone publication about a given subject, the entire collection of menu items has been prepared to help a job seeker be totally prepared to reduce the time it takes to get a job.

## Section 2

# The Orgins Of Mentoring

The practice of mentoring is as old as mankind. The word mentor comes to us because of Homer's poem *The Odyssey*. According to the poem and Greek mythology, Odysseus was the King of Ithaca, which was a small city-state on an island in the Ionian Sea located off the west coast of Ancient Greece. Odysseus was preparing to join with the Greek Alliance whose forces were about to set out to sea and wage war against the Trojans to return Helen, who was kidnapped by the Trojans, back to her husband, Menelaus the King of Sparta.

The city of Troy was a well-fortified establishment on the north western coast of Ancient Turkey. The Aegean Sea would have to be crossed and it would be a long sea voyage and campaign to rescue and return Helen to her husband Menelaus. Odysseus would be leaving his wife, Penelope, and their son, Telemachus, there in Ithaca for an extended period of time.

Odysseus was concerned about his household while he would be gone and he asked his trusted and older friend, Mentor, to watch over his household and family. Odysseus knew his friend well, for they had been companions during several earlier campaigns, and he had learned much from this older sage. Odysseus trusted Mentor and asked him to share his wisdom, knowledge, and experience in teaching Telemachus the skills, expectations, and requirements to prepare for the future. Odysseus knew that someday Telemachus would become the King of Ithaca after his death.

Mentor was considered to be a teacher, a trusted advisor, and a protecting role model. He took this responsibility seriously and did not want to let down his friend Odysseus. While the story does continue on with others who appear to Telemachus in the form of Mentor at various times, they all continued to guide and encourage Telemachus to develop into the man Odysseus wanted his son to become.

Nearly every article or book written about mentoring will refer to *The Odyssey* as where the term was first defined. Yet, even before Homer wrote his poem, individuals have been taught, trained, and educated by others. Knowledgeable individuals would take others under their 'wings' and teach them how to study, learn, and gain experience in what they would need to prosper in their lives.

So it goes also for much of the time since Homer wrote his poem that many have benefited from being mentored. Many individuals have been tutored, educated, and given the knowledge and insights by others who were older, wiser, and were willing to share what they knew. Those mentored could then take advantage of opportunities to move forward faster in their lives.

Fénelon (1651-1715) was a French Roman Catholic archbishop and writer who was asked in 1689 by Louis XIV the King of France to be the tutor to the seven-year-old Duke of Burgundy who stood second in line to become king. When Fénelon was first introduced to the Duke of Burgundy the child was very unruly and spoiled. It was not until about 1693 that Fénelon first published his book *Les Aventures de Télémaque* (*The Adventures of Telemachus*) with Mentor being one of the leading characters. Fénelon used the book to tutor (mentor) the Duke of Burgundy in learning how to become a more responsible individual who would one day be the King of France. By the time Fénelon finished with him, the Duke of Burgundy exhibited self-control, and had a greater understanding and appreciation for the responsibilities of being a king.

It wasn't until about 1750, when *Les Aventures de Télémaque* was translated into English, that the word mentor was introduced to the English language along with the definition as 'one who is wise, a tutor, advisor, teacher, role model, and an inspiration who will correct and challenge someone to reach greater heights in their life.' *Les Aventures de Télémaque* was one of the first books to introduce the concept of a mentor and what role they had in influencing an individual's course through life.

In 1759 Louis Antonine de Caraccioli (1723-1803) published *Vertable le Mentor ou l'edycation de la noblesse.* In 1760 this was translated and published in English as *The true mentor, or, an essay on the education of young people in fashion.* This essay and many others that followed were based on the writings of Fénelon.

The 1979 book titled *The Seasons Of A Man's Life,* by Daniel J. Levinson, introduced a more updated concept of the mentoring process in the United

States. In general, Levinson presents his thoughts on the term 'mentor' to apply to one who is roughly about a half a generation older, who is willing and able to help another in their development at an accelerated pace. Over the next several years mentoring enjoyed rapid growth in many career fields.

There has been considerable study regarding the value of mentoring. In the United States it might seem that mentoring has been more career oriented (focused). However, it is now slowly including the European developmental (well-rounded) mentoring approach. Mentoring is about enhancing one's ability to gain knowledge and experiences that will accelerate their growth in any facet of life. This might be physical, emotional, spiritual, educational, relational, or career related.

Many top executives are asked to mentor junior managers to 'groom' them to be the future leaders in industry. Doctors and nurses have always been assigned to those just entering the field of medicine as mentors to help the 'newbies' get up to speed. Most successful organizations will conduct in-house mentoring and there are many other organizations that will seek to find mentors for a specific area where help is needed from a professional mentor. Mentors have proven their worth by sharing their knowledge and experience to help others reach heights they would otherwise not reach on their own.

In the next section we will discuss what to look for in a mentor.

## Section 3

# What To Look For In A Mentor

You might have the mindset that only a select few are fortunate enough to have a mentor help them in their career development. While it is correct that there are few in numbers who have mentors, it is not because of a lack of qualified mentors. Most individuals tend to think that they don't require any help in their career development and so they neglect to seek out a mentor to help them.

This eBook will try to keep its focus on a mentor who will be of greater value to you in the career and self-help facets of your life. The qualifications of being any type of mentor are roughly the same and they can be found just as easily if you take the time to look for them.

Many large organizations and corporations have a mentoring program in place to some degree. Some have very formal assignments and match-ups that are designed to achieve specific outcomes. Some organizations can tap into a trade association or mentoring service to find the appropriate mentors for their needs. You should ask your company or organization if they have or offer a mentoring program.

There are two types of mentors. The personal mentor is the one we will be discussing since it has the element of a living person who you will be able to interact with at various times. The curriculum mentor can be a real life individual or a fictional character that we classify as a hero or role model that we have read or heard about, or an educational recorded audio or DVD. These will lack that personal and immediate contact that has the greater value that will be career specific in real time. We all have our heroes and role models we respect and look up to because of what they might have overcome in their life.

As mentioned in a previous section, mentors are usually about a half a generation older that the mentored. This is certainly not a 'cast-in-concrete' rule. Take care to select a mentor who has the skills, knowledge, and experience to share with you that which will help you achieve your goals. It is also best if your mentor is not a direct line supervisor over you. It is best to have a mentor from another department or from another location. There can be some issues if the mentor and mentored have a direct line connection. Some discussions can't be held in an open and frank manner because questions might not be asked or answered for fear of offending or possible retaliation. There needs to be a trust between the mentor and the mentored that the discussions will be confidential and will deal with the desired customs, habits, and behaviors required to move forward in one's career.

When the mentor is not in a direct line of supervision they can be more objective in their discussions how certain situations can be handled. The mentored should never feel that they will be punished or will have something held against them. Sometimes it allows information on how the relationships of various parts of the organization interact that are unique to its business model. It should never be an opportunity to 'bash' a supervisor or manager. It should be about gaining a better understanding of the processes and procedures to know the expectations that are inherent within the business culture.

You might ask your manager who they would recommend as a suitable mentor for you. They might even suggest that you take some college courses dealing with business management or organizational behavior so you will have a solid foundation before being assigned or recommended to a mentor. Much of the decision will be based on what your career goals are and the direction you want to go. Some organizations will use the European model of being well-rounded so you may be assigned various mentors in different departments to gain the experiences required for future promotions.

Career mentoring is best done face to face on a regular schedule. This way progress can be measured and assignments can be timely. Two hours per month would be adequate for the face-to-face meetings. This could be a two-hour block, or two one-hour blocks, whatever is the most convenient for the mentor and the mentored. With today's technology it is possible to have remote mentoring meetings via video conferencing. This has its own set of challenges, but can be managed and deliver successful results. The most important thing to remember is that it is the time spent regularly between the mentor and the mentored that will produce the most results.

The best mentor is one who you can respect and admire for what they have accomplished in their life so far, who will also have the experience and knowledge that you need to move forward. This is a relationship built on trust and both must make sure not to compromise that trust.

This is your life and assembling the best 'team' to help you move forward is your responsibility. You must hold yourself accountable to make sure you are progressing in the direction you want to go. If you find that you have gotten off track, get back as soon as you can so you can keep going in the right direction.

In the next section we will cover the different types and styles that relate to mentoring.

# Section 4

# Styles Of Mentoring

The type of mentoring your mentor will use will be the one they are most comfortable with. There are two types of mentoring. One type is the structured mentor format where goals and expectations are clearly spelled out. In the structured format the results are measurable and there is accountability for personal improvement. The other is the unstructured type where the goals and expectations are not clearly specified. Results are rarely measured and minimal accountability is imposed, if at all.

In either type of mentoring, structured or unstructured, there are two styles that may be used. Formal style, with regular scheduled meetings to review progress and to move on to the next item in the plan. Informal style, where things are left very open to not having any regularly scheduled meetings, and an open plan to work on only items that are agreed upon.

The most benefit will come from a structured mentoring type with a formal style. This allows both the mentor and the mentored to know the exact expectations and assignments along with a deadline to accomplish the agreed upon plans. While some assignments might take a week or two to accomplish there are others that will take months, even years to accomplish. Speed is not as important as having a total understanding of what is being taught.

Throughout most of our lives we are mentored in an unstructured type through an informal style. We tend to observe others who we would like to be like. We try to figure out why some succeed and others do not. We find sound advice about how we can grow and develop as individuals and then we are left to our own devices. Though this process will have some results, it will take much longer and you may miss more opportunities than you may ever realize.

A mentor with a structured type of mentoring program using the formal style will be able to produce results much faster. As the mentor and mentored meet together they can discuss various opportunities and how they can be recognized and acted upon.

One of the most important lessons that can be taught is about culture and organization structures within the workplace. Those who learn how to work within the culture of the organization will advance much faster. Every organization will have at least a basic business model structure that is learned in undergraduate studies. Large complex organizations will have additional components in their structure that you must understand in order to move forward in your career.

The mentor is an important part of helping the mentored understand some of the structure of the organization and the culture of the organization. The mentor will also be able to share experiences and knowledge they have learned from others while on their own journey to where they are now in their life. In some cases a mentor is used to 'groom' the mentored one on a path to higher management and leadership positions. In this case, most of the mentoring will be structured and formal. Many organizations have a succession plan and they know what they want their managers and leaders to know. So there will be a plan to help the mentor guide the mentored to learn these things.

When a mentor is assigned by upper management to work with a junior manager or supervisor, the mentor might also be asked to evaluate and report about the mentored to see if they are progressing in their development. It is important to note that the mentor has specific duties as does the mentored.

In the following section the duties of the mentor will be presented.

## Section 5

# Duties Of The Mentor

While the mentor and mentored will have an agreed upon plan of what will be the objective, each will have different roles in the development of that plan. Both will also have duties or responsibilities that will be parallel, yet not necessarily the exact same thing. Think of a set of railroad tracks that run parallel in that they support the train en-route to its destination. If one or the other track fails to stick to its duty, the train derails. Both must be committed to ensuring that they will do their best to make the mentoring process work.

Surveys have been conducted over the years to find out what individuals think of the meaning of the word mentor. Many of these definitions have been presented earlier in this eBook. The mentor is known as being a trusted friend, a guide, one who can help with resources, one who listens, and one who will offer encouragement to help the mentored one move toward their goals.

Some of the qualities to look for in a mentor is one who is patient, listens carefully, dedicated to the mentored's plan, and available when needed. The mentor should also have a knowledge of the duties of a mentor and be willing to work within that scope. A good mentor knows that success is measured through a series of achievements culminating in accomplishing the object or purpose that will move the mentored in the direction they want to go.

There are some common expectations that all mentors should embrace. They must do all they can to start off by establishing a relationship with the mentored that is positive and personal. A mentor should not be neutral or distant in dealing with the mentored. There has to be a trust between the mentor and the mentored that begins with the mentor setting the tone. There also must be a mutual respect for each other. The mentor must make sure that regular meetings are held to have constructive discussions, review assignments, and check progress made before additional assignments can be given. The meetings should be fun and enjoyed by celebrating successes and gaining additional knowledge in a relaxed atmosphere.

The mentor is to help the mentored develop the skills they will need to help them in their career path. Each path taken by the mentored will be unique to that individual. There are some skills that will be learned or taught to help the mentored in areas of goal setting, financial prudence, conflict resolution and making hard decisions.

Mentors can also help the mentored in seeking out additional resources that will prove beneficial in meeting the objectives of the mentoring plan. The mentor is not a resource provider. They are aware of where the mentored can obtain the knowledge or skills needed so the mentored will learn to establish those contacts on their own. Perhaps the most difficult task for the mentor will be to help with self-confidence and social awareness issues. The mentor is to help the mentored become more aware and sensitive to various cultural differences, socioeconomic levels and racial bias that exists within our society. Respect should be shown to all cultures and races, no matter where they might be in the socioeconomic scale by not promoting the beliefs or values of one over another.

There should be some honest discussions about behaviors and the consequences of choices that individuals might make. No one is perfect, and to have a better understanding of the cultural and personal environmental factors will help the mentored be in a better position to deal with issues that might arise.

The mentoring process is about growth and development toward a stated goal or objective. Both the mentor and the mentored must have a clear understanding of the expectations. The mentor should adjust their style of teaching to that of the learning style of the mentored. There should be some flexibility in the mentoring program to make changes as needed or when conditions change. This is a working relationship and both have to be working together to see that the objective is achieved.

The best mentors come from those who have benefited from being mentored. They have seen the value and wisdom in this process and they are willing to give back what was given to them to help others. The future is made better through mentoring.

The next section will cover the duties of the mentored.

# Section 6

# Duties Of The Mentored

The mentored should realize that meetings are not just a 'chat' session. The mentored should view this as a productive process that has an objective. Every effort should be made by the mentored to stay organized, keep accurate records, and ask questions with a definite purpose. They should also have respect for the mentor and the knowledge and experience they will be sharing to help the mentored move toward the objective. The mentored will need to have a positive attitude, patience, and express gratitude for what they will be receiving from the mentor. They will also have to practice the assignments and demonstrate that they understand the application to real life situations. A good mentored individual will always want to take on more challenging assignments and tasks.

The mentoring process is to provide knowledge and experience through a systematic approach by using meetings to discuss the roles, behaviors, and proper interactions that will result in career advancement. The meetings are not just to sit and talk about current events or about the mentored's problems they are having at work. The mentor will initially take charge to set a pattern to how the meetings should be structured. The mentored should be prepared to give the mentor some biographical information on their education and work experience so the mentor will know what both will be dealing with in establishing the objectives and goals of the mentoring experience.

From the very first meeting the mentored should be organized. This means they have come prepared to establish a plan to reach an objective that will advance them in their chosen career. While both the mentor and mentored are expected to take accurate notes on the discussions, assignments, and the results of those assignments, the mentored is charged to keep these records. In the following section the importance of the initial meeting will be presented. It should be noted that the mentored needs to be proactive in this process and not just a spectator.

Questions should be asked with a purpose to increase understanding. The mentored should show respect to the mentor for any feedback that is given. Sometimes it is hard to hear some criticism that might 'sting' us momentarily, yet growth comes by making the changes suggested. The mentored must understand that some behaviors brought to the table are not acceptable in the workplace and they must be changed if one expects to move to a higher level within the organization or industry.

Patience is also a very good trait for the mentored to practice. Behaviors are acquired over long periods of time, and to change behaviors will also take some time to replace those undesirable ones. Another valuable trait would be one of being humble. Don't think you know better or more than your mentor. They will learn from you some things, but you should learn plenty more from them since they have been where you are now.

Keep a positive attitude about the mentoring process. If you are completing your assignments on time, spending more time listening to what is being taught, and putting into practice what you are learning, you will be moving quickly to where it is you want to be in the future. Don't settle for simple or easy tasks. Ask for and demand that your assignments be challenging so you will be able to grow and develop faster.

Once you have completed the objectives and have finished the mentoring plan you had established, think about 'paying-it-forward' by helping someone else who needs a mentor. The mentoring process is rewarding for both the mentor and the mentored. You can still be mentored for the next level in your career development while mentoring someone who is just starting out. It is a great feeling to give back and share what others have done for you.

The next section will present some of the objectives that should be considered as part of a mentoring plan that begins with the initial meeting between the mentor and the mentored.

# Section 7

# Objectives

The objective of the mentoring process should be tailored to the mentored's career goals. Most mentors are selected because they have accomplished and experienced what has led to their success in life. Sometimes however, the mentor selected will not be the best one suited for the mentored. This could be for any number of reasons. If in the initial meeting there seems to be a sense that the mentor and the mentored are not going to be able to work together they should seek a solution or find a mentor that will be better suited to work with the mentored. The objectives should be clearly understood by both the mentor and the mentored. They should be written in simple terms so there is no ambiguity of what the objective is or the path that will be taken to reach the objective.

The mentored is the one that is seeking to learn, accumulate knowledge, and to move forward in their career. So it is important that before the initial meeting, the mentored will have some idea of what and where it is that they want to be doing in the future. The mentored is not to use the mentor as a career counselor to help them find what they want to do in the future. It has to be assumed that the mentored has the educational experience and the desire to move toward the objective. The mentor's time will be wasted if he has to wait four years for the mentored to complete a degree program. If the mentored is working on a graduate degree that is in the current career path a mentor will have some value. The most value comes from the mentor when all the educational expectations have been met by the mentored so the 'grooming' can move toward the objective without competing for time and opportunity for the specialized learning through the mentoring process.

Most mentors will be able to help the mentored with writing the objectives, duties, and time frames based on their experience. The mentor is not to write a plan or the objective for the mentored. The mentor's role is to assist the mentored in creating the outline and finalizing the objective and plan. Some objectives might take only a couple of meetings and discussions to complete. The complete plan can take up to a year or more to achieve. The objectives are the pieces that will make up the plan. The overall plan should have a focus with each objective leading to accomplishing the plan. This is similar to goal setting where you have a goal that is made up of several action steps that lead to the accomplishment of the goal.

The plan might be to become a vice president or senior manager in five to seven years. The objectives might be to obtain various behaviors and experiences needed in order to be considered for promotions that would lead toward a position as a vice president or senior manager. The objectives within the plan will be dependent upon what level of skills and experience the mentored has at the time when the plan is being written.

While this might seem to be a process for those who are in management or seeking upper level positions, the mentoring process can be tailored to the entry level individual as well. Those who seek to change careers can also benefit from the mentoring process by learning what it might take to make the change from someone who has been there. Mentoring is a development process that should result in the growth of knowledge and experience to prepare one for the future they seek. There are plenty of opportunities for mentoring those who are working in entry level jobs who seek to move into a more stable and career-oriented employment. This process can take as few as two or three months to a year or more, depending on what the mentored needs to do to move forward. Mentoring could be summed up as creating the opportunity for an individual to increase their value and marketability in the job market. This could be to get that entry level job, move from one career to another, or move up the corporate ladder in their current organization or within another in the industry.

No matter what the objective or the plan is, it must be reasonable. It should be achieved within a stated time frame, and tailored to the mentored's appropriate and current career stage. Objectives should be short-term, medium-term, or long-term. They should be reviewed at each meeting to make sure that the objectives are being met and accomplished, moving the mentored toward the plan's goal. The overall plan should not be drastically revised or rewritten unless circumstances so dictate. The objective is to help the mentored grow and develop to prepare them for the future position desired. This is accomplished with a well-written plan that is comfortable for both the mentor and the mentored. Successes and achievements should be celebrated. They are the proof that the process is working.

The initial meeting between the mentor and mentored is important. It is within this meeting that the two become acquainted as individuals. The mentoring process will work best when each participant knows and understands the other's role. This initial meeting will have several parts to it. Getting to know each other is essential to the success of this process. Various objectives and plans will be discussed and then written down. Finally, there will be an agreement as to what plan and objectives have been selected, with a commitment from both the mentor and mentored to do all they can to make sure that success will be achieved at the completion of the plan.

The mentored should bring to this meeting the perceived career path and plan they have. They will need to share this information with the mentor so a productive discussion can lead to the proper plan being adopted. With a clear understanding of where the mentored wants to be in the future, it will be easier to see what steps must be taken to accomplish the objectives and in the time frame required.

The resulting plan should list the objectives in a reasonable order that clearly define what will need to be done in order to successfully complete the plan. Once the plan and the objectives have been established there should be an agreement by the mentor and mentored when the next meeting will be held and what expectations should be met by that time. There should be a purpose for each meeting with a discussion to review each objective or assignment that was given in the last meeting. Questions should be asked and answered to determine if the learning experience was achieved and how it was applied in a 'real life' situation.

New assignments should be discussed so that all expectations are fully understood. A review of what has been accomplished and a discussion how the new assignment will further add to the knowledge and experience. A chart could be made to show how much progress has been made toward the plan's completion as each objective is accomplished. It is also a good time to review if the plan or any objectives might need to be revised or modified due to circumstances that might have come up. This process is a relationship that is focused on accomplishing the plan agreed to. It should not be an attempt to place one ego above the other.

The next section will be about accountability.

# Section 8

# Accountability

Who is to be held accountable? Both the mentor and the mentored are to be held accountable for the objectives, plan, and progress made. The mentor is to help set the expectations of what is to be accomplished through the mentoring process. The mentored is to meet those expectations that are agreed upon. This accountability begins with the initial meeting and the writing of the plan along with the objectives that move the mentored forward. Measuring success is accomplished by having written objectives that are clear, concise, and reasonable.

The mentor is to set the tone of the mentoring process. The mentored has to bring what it is they wish to accomplish by having an understanding of the purpose of the process. If the mentored has no idea of what it is they wish to get out of the process then this could be a waste of time for both the mentor and the mentored. With a clear idea of what is to be accomplished by the mentoring process, both the mentor and mentored will be able to make this a productive relationship. It can only be a productive relationship if there is measurement and accountability for progress toward the objective or plan.

The mentor is accountable to the mentored to keep focus and to help the mentored move forward. The mentor is also accountable to make sure that the meetings are productive and held on a regular basis. They are also accountable to encourage and support the mentored in what it is they are seeking to get out of this relationship. A mentor is accountable to the mentored in making sure that the process is complete in that it will achieve all the objectives of the plan.

The mentored is accountable to make sure they use their time and the time of the mentor to the best possible advantage. The mentored must be accountable for completing the assignments on time or before. They must actively participate in the discussions and ask questions if they don't understand what is being presented. The mentored is accountable to the mentor to be making progress on the plan and accomplishing the objectives. The mentored must account for their personal development.

Both the mentor and mentored are accountable to participate actively during the entire plan until it is completed. They both should be willing to make this experience positive. Accountability also includes keeping the trust and confidentiality of the discussions and never compromising the integrity of the program. The mentor and mentored should hold each other accountable for their respective roles and actions taken.

The next section will discuss why mentors mentor.

# Section 9

# Why Mentors Mentor

The answer is very simple. Mentors mentor because they wish to give back that which was given to them by their mentor or mentors. Their mentor could have been a personal mentor, a curriculum mentor, or a combination of the two. Many of us have been exposed to mentoring without being formally involved with the process. This could have been done by association, exposure, or by assignment.

Mentors are a valuable resource to society. They teach, inspire, and encourage others to grow and develop to be able to reach their potential in various facets of life. Mentors can share their knowledge and experiences in a way to help reduce the time it would take an individual to learn on their own. Mentors help guide an individual through the intricate maze of the business world through discussions and assignments to help the mentored better understand how and why things are the way they are. Mentors work with their mentees so they will be able to quickly learn the lessons, and experience how interaction with others is so vital to the success of both the individual and the organization.

Mentors gain a sense of pride in helping others achieve their dreams and goals. They know the sweet taste of success and have the desire to have others experience that taste. Mentors give the credit for the success to the mentored, for they are the ones who have to make the achievements. The mentor is a willing participant who seeks no gain or praise for what the mentored accomplishes as a result of the relationship.

The mentor is not concerned with credit or glory. They derive the satisfaction of helping others and seeing that their knowledge and lessons learned are being passed on to the next generation. This allows a better foundation on which the future can be built faster. Knowledge and experience are the basis for the value one has in marketing themselves to prospective employers. How fast an individual can gain the knowledge and experience will determine how fast they can advance on their career path. Mentors understand that by helping those who desire to advance they can make that path easier for them to reach their objective or goal.

One of the best benefits of being a mentor is seeing the change that takes place with the mentored. As changes are made the mentor can see just where the mentored is going, even if the mentored has not yet been able to visualize the progress made or understand the direction they are moving. The mentor has the duty to explain how the changes are necessary to move from where the mentored is now to where they want to be. Then, as the changes are made, discussing how much progress has been made toward accomplishing the plan.

Sometimes we are so close to the forest we cannot see the trees. That is why a mentor can see things from a global perspective. They have the advantage of knowledge and experience to know what is actually being accomplished. The mentor should allow enough 'space' for the mentored to have the experience of self-discovery and for them to see the opportunities that will come into focus because of their efforts and dedication to the mentoring process. Seeing an individual grow and develop into what they want to be is the reward for being a mentor.

Many mentors and mentees will remain in contact long after the mentoring process has been completed. There are lasting friendships where future achievements can be discussed that have been as a direct result of the mentoring process shared. Mentors give back so others may prosper.

The next section is the conclusion and review followed by the Mentoring Plan Form and Objective Form.

# Section 10

# Conclusion And Review

The mentoring process has been around since the beginning of time. There is some confusion between a mentor and a coach, which on one level is similar in wanting to help others reach their potential. Mentoring is about developing experience, knowledge, and behaviors required to move forward in a facet of life. Coaching is related to performance, tasks, and expected outcomes relative to production.

The name mentor comes to us from Homer's poem *The Odyssey*. Mentor, who was Homer's trusted friend, was asked to take care of Homer's household while he was off to fight the Trojans to secure the return of Helen to her husband Menelaus the King of Sparta. Mentor was charged with the education of Telemachus, Homer's son, to prepare him to replace Homer as the King of Ithaca after his death.

There have been several other books and essays written about the mentoring process since the writing of *The Odyssey*. Each has, in some measure, been based on what Mentor was charged with regarding Telemachus. They have also further refined the definition of the term to what we now consider to be an acceptable mentoring process.

In the United States the mentoring process developed more focus on career orientation, while in Europe it took on a developmental or well-rounded approach to life. Today the lines between the two schools of thought are blurred. Both are used independently or in a combination of the two. This will depend upon the plan, objectives, and goals of the mentored, or to some extent the style of mentoring provided by the mentor.

Look for a mentor that can be of benefit to what you want to achieve. The personal mentor is preferred with a structured type using a formal style of mentoring. This has proven to be the most successful approach to the mentoring process.

When you understand the duties of the mentor and the mentored you will appreciate how the mentoring process works. A shared duty is to write a plan with objectives that will lead toward the accomplishment of that plan. During the initial meeting the plan and objectives should be clearly defined with a mutual agreement and understanding of what is to be achieved through this process.

As results are measured there is accountability for the progress made or the lack thereof. Both the mentor and the mentored are accountable for making sure the relationship is producing the desired results in a timely manner. **(See Appendix - Mentoring Plan form and Objective Form)**

Mentors mentor for personal reasons. Mainly for the satisfaction of being able to give back what was given to them by sharing their knowledge and experience. This is done so others will be able to take advantage of learning from someone who has been there and found success in their life.

The mentoring process is truly rewarding for both the mentor and the mentored. There are many individuals who have sought out mentors in various stages of their careers. Because they realized the value of the mentoring process, they took the opportunity to become a mentor to help others achieve more in their lives.

No matter what career stage you are in, be it entry level employment, a change of career, or upward movement within an organization, the mentoring process can be just the advantage you need to find the success you seek.

We hope that you enjoyed the **Mentor Plate Special** and will take the time to look at our other menu items at the **Job Seekers Café.**

*Thank you and come back soon!*

# Chapter 5

# Application Pizza

# Chapter 5
# Application Pizza

Put individuality into a personal master application, topped with the complete information of your job history, education, job skills, and other important details. Fill out applications much faster. Includes a master application form.

## Section Table of Contents

Introduction .......................................... 135

Job Posting Scams ................................ 137

Be Aware Of Job Posting Scams .......... 141

Social Security Number ...................... 143

Job Application Surveys ...................... 145

Personality Testing .............................. 147

The Application Process ...................... 149

Parts Of The Application .................... 151

The Master Job Application ................ 153

Conclusion And Review ...................... 157

# Section 1

# Introduction

Welcome to the **Job Seekers Café.** This menu item is entitled **Application Pizza.** You will find this pizza topped with information about the job application form and process. With today's technology being used by job seekers to apply for a job online or on a kiosk at the job location, you will need to know and understand how things have changed recently. While online or computer applications are now considered the norm, there are some things you should be aware of before you use this option. Many organizations will direct you to go to their website to complete the application. Others will recommend you post it to an online job recruiting site for any subscribing member organization who will have access to and can review your application.

As with most pizzas you can order it with the toppings you like. We will try to provide you with enough information so you can make your pizza to suit your individual taste. The Application Pizza is made with the best and freshest information. Enjoy the great taste of success in obtaining a job by making sure your job application is complete and representative of your skills, talents, and experiences.

You will notice that on the outer margins of this and most other pages there are Scholar Margins where you can make notes or comments about what impressed you when reading the material. Perhaps you might have a question and you will put a question mark to remind you that you need to find clarification of the text and the concept presented.

This eBook will take you through a few more things than just filling out a job application. It will touch on what to watch out for when job searching online. There are many scams that are being posted online about jobs in your local area where you can 'make' outrageous income for very little work. These scams are real and you should watch out for them. Some might only want to send you ads for other job postings, while others are looking to steal your personal identity.

There has been much discussion about whether you should give out your social security number or not. Some sources will say it is not legal for a company or organization to request it with the job application, while others say just give it to the prospective employer. This eBook will give you some information so you can make an informed decision on when you should and shouldn't give out this information your social security number.

You must be totally honest with the information you put on your job applications. Don't think that 'shading' it slightly won't make a difference. You might get the job and after a few days be called in to the manager's office to explain why the information you provided is not matching up with the results of a background check. Most of the time this is cause for immediate termination and some organizations won't listen to any excuses.

If there is something in your past that you feel you must explain, you have the choice of writing a cover letter that can address the issue, or you can state on the application you would like the opportunity to discuss the issue in a pre-interview. If you have the qualifications for the position let the organization know. A background check (which can now include criminal, credit, or financial information) may turn up some information that you would consider very personal. If the information is obtained from public records, credit bureaus, or government agencies it might harm your chances to get certain jobs.

Many of the online job applications will have additional parts that might be a job survey or a personality test. Some organizations might require you to complete them in order for them to accept your application. Others might make them optional at this time, yet may require them before a job offer is made.

Reference will be made throughout this eBook about concepts that can be found in some of the other **Job Seekers Café** menu items. While each eBook is a standalone publication about a given subject, the entire collection of menu items has been prepared to help a job seeker be totally prepared to reduce the time it takes to get a job.

# Section 2

# Job Posting Scams

We feel it important to begin this eBook by giving you some information about the job posting scams that are on the Internet. With fewer jobs available than the number of job seekers, competition for the jobs posted has become brutal. Unfortunately, this brings out the 'scammers' who want to take advantage of those who are frustrated or desperate to obtain employment. Scam artists might be taking money for services that do not exist or collecting personal information in order to steal your identity. Be alert and do your due diligence to make sure the job offer is legitimate by checking out the company.

The following information was obtained from the Federal Trade Commission Consumer Information at www.consumer.ftc.gov/articles/0243-job-scams. Be sure to read this information so you can avoid becoming a victim of a job posting scam. We have included some hyperlinks found in the original document. Some links may not be current or have been moved on the sites.

## JOB SCAMS

Scammers know that finding a job can be tough. To trick people looking for honest work, scammers advertise where real employers and job placement firms do. They also make upbeat promises about your chances of employment, and virtually all of them ask you to pay them for their services before you get a job. But the promise of a job isn't the same thing as a job. If you have to pay for the promise, it's likely a scam.

- Signs of a Job Scam
- Job Placement Services
- Where to Look for Jobs

- Report a Job Scam

## Signs of a Job Scam

Scammers advertise jobs where legitimate employers do—online, in newspapers, and even on TV and radio. Here's how to tell whether a job lead may be a scam:

### You need to pay to get the job

They may say they've got a job waiting, or guarantee to place you in a job, if you just pay a fee for certification, training materials, or their expenses placing you with a company. But after you pay, the job doesn't materialize. Employers and employment firms shouldn't ask you to pay for the promise of a job.

### You need to supply your credit card or bank account information

Don't give out your credit card or bank account information over the phone to a company unless you're familiar with them and have agreed to pay for something. Anyone who has your account information can use it.

### The ad is for "previously undisclosed" federal government jobs

Information about available federal jobs is free. And all federal positions are announced to the public on usajobs.gov. Don't believe anyone who promises you a federal or postal job.

## Job Placement Services

Many job placement services are legitimate. But others lie about what they'll do for you, promote outdated or fake job openings, or charge up-front fees for services that may not lead to a job. In fact, they might not even return your calls once you pay.

### Before you enlist a company's help:

### Check with the hiring company

If a company or organization is mentioned in an ad or interview, contact that company to find out if the company is really hiring through the service.

### Get details — in writing

What's the cost, what will you get, and who pays—you or the company that hires you? What happens if the service doesn't find a job for you or any real leads? If they're reluctant to answer your questions, or give confusing answers, you should be reluctant to work with them.

Get a copy of the contract with the placement firm, and read it carefully. A legitimate company will give you time to read the contract and decide, not pressure you into signing then and there. Make sure any promises—including refund promises—are in writing. Some listing services and "consultants" write ads to sound like jobs, but that's just a marketing trick: They're really selling general information about getting a job—information you can find for free on your own.

**Know whether it's a job placement or job counseling**

Executive or career counseling services help people with career directions and decisions. They may offer services like skills identification and self-evaluation, resume preparation, letter writing, and interview techniques, and general information about companies or organizations in a particular location or job field.

But job placement isn't guaranteed. Fees can be as high as thousands of dollars, and you often have to pay first.

The National Career Development Association (NCDA) offers some tips on finding and choosing a career counselor, and explains the different types of counselors active in the field.

**Check for complaints**

Your local consumer protection agency, state Attorney General's Office, and the Better Business Bureau can tell you whether any complaints have been filed about the company. Just keep in mind that a lack of complaints doesn't mean the business is on the up-and-up. You may want to do an Internet search with the name of the company and words like review, scam, or complaint. Look through several pages of search results. And check out articles about the company in newspapers, magazines, or online, as well.

## Where to Look for Jobs

You've read the many resume and interview tips from respected sources available for free online, and scoured online job boards and newspaper classifieds. Some other places to look for leads in your job search include:

### CareerOneStop

Sponsored by the U.S. Department of Labor, CareerOneStop lists hundreds of thousands of jobs. It also links to employment and training programs in each state, including programs for people with disabilities, minorities, older workers, veterans, welfare recipients, and young people. For federal jobs, all open positions are announced to the public on usajobs.gov.

### State and county offices

Your state's Department of Labor may have job listings or be able to point you to local job offices that offer counseling and referrals. Local and county human resources offices provide some placement assistance, too. They can give you the names of other groups that may be helpful, such as labor unions or federally-funded vocational programs.

### College career service offices

Whether it's a four-year university or community college, see what help yours can offer. If you're not a current or former student, some may let you look at their job listings.

### Your library

Ask if they can point you to information on writing a resume, interviewing, or compiling a list of companies and organizations to contact about job openings.

### Report a Job Scam

If you've been targeted by a job scam, file a complaint with the FTC.

For problems with an employment-service firm, contact the appropriate state licensing board (if these firms must be licensed in your state), your state Attorney General, and your local consumer protection agency.

To learn about credit and background checks when you're looking for a job, read What to Know When You Look For a Job.

October 2013

In the next section we will show you how to be aware of job posting scams.

# Section 3

# Be Aware Of Job Posting Scams

In the previous section you were given an overview of job posting scams and some of the things you should be aware of to avoid becoming a victim. In this section we will go a bit deeper into some of the various scams that are out there. Some articles about job scams claim that there are as many job scams as there are legitimate real jobs being posted. Finding a good job is just that much harder because of the job scams being promoted. Take a cautious approach to each job posting you look at. Make sure you put the job posting to the test to eliminate those that can possibly be considered a scam.

Some of the warning signs that a job posting might be a possible scam are:

- They are offering you a job without an application, resume, or an interview. They insist that you deal with them and they will not tell you the name of the company they represent unless you pay them a fee in advance.

- The company requires a credit card or a wire transfer of funds before they can work with you.

- The company requires your social security number or driver's license number.

- The income range is not in line with the amount of work or responsibility described.

- The wages are not clear for the position you are seeking. They are quoting a wage range that is not making any sense.

- There is no experience required or necessary. No company wants to train you how to work. They hire based on experience and education, unless the job only requires manual labor.

- You will have to pay for training for the position. If you are qualified you will not have to pay for training.

- You are given an offer for the job without talking to the hiring manager or visiting the company's location.

- Emails begin to arrive from non-business addresses. If the company name is not at the end of the email, such as a name@gmail.com or name@aol.com, then it might not be a viable email from a legitimate company. One like name@appleone.com would have more credibility as a real job posting.

- The job posting or ad is poorly written. This can be due to several typos, poor sentence structure, or misuse of proper grammar.

- The company wants you to do an interview through instant messaging or via text on your cell phone.

- The company is asking for you to pay them a fee for the interview, the background check, credit check, and drug testing that will be required before you will be offered the job.

Human resource managers, hiring managers, and 'real' companies offering jobs will not contact you off normal business hours unless you have requested them to do so. These will still be within an acceptable window of time that might be within a hour or so of the normal business hours. If you are getting calls (or emails) between 9:00 pm and 6:00 am chances are this is not going to be a real company.

Many of the job posting sites are doing all they can to weed out job posting scams. Once they are discovered and removed, they will 'rise again' in another form somewhere on the same site as a different company. You must do your due diligence to keep you and your information safe and out of the hands of job scammers. You have to check out the company, visit their website, check with the Better Business Bureau, or do an Internet search to get more information about the company. Some of the scammers are really slick and will do all they can to gain your trust. They will make promises that are just what you want to hear. Take the time and check them out. It will be worth the time and trouble to do your research to avoid a scam. If you are a victim of a job posting scam you should report it to the proper authorities. Change all your bank accounts, credit and debit cards, or other accounts that may have been compromised. It is even recommended to change to another bank or financial institution to avoid the scammer trying to get back into your accounts with all your personal information.

In the next section social security numbers will be discussed.

**Section 4**

# Social Security Number

There seems to be much confusion about whether a company if can or cannot ask for your social security number. In most states there is no law against a company requesting your social security number. However, it is normally done later in the job selection process when you have been determined to be a viable candidate for the position being offered.

If you are filling out a job application online and you know you are on the company's website (not a third party website), you can feel more comfortable about giving them your number. Never put your social security number on a third party website. You will never know who will have access to it or how they might use it.

Scammers will tell you that they need your social security number to verify who you are and that you are legally eligible to work in the United States. They will then ask you for more information about your birth date, home address, phone numbers, and email addresses. Your marital status and spouse's name are required for emergency contact if something happens to you. They might even ask about your bank account so they can contact the bank as a reference about you. Never send your social security number in an email or over a social media network. Be careful with your personal information.

There are some employers that require you to provide your social security number when you are initially going through the job application process. These will include government agencies, state or federal hiring agencies, or if the position you are applying for deals with national security or defense. Even so, make sure you are giving it to them at the appropriate time and place when you are a serious candidate being considered for the position. If you are in personal contact with the hiring manager and have some reservations about providing the number, express your concern and let them know that you will provide them the information at the proper time.

Normally after an interview you are called back to meet with the hiring manager, and they will request your Social Security information so they can order a background check and/or credit check. Some states have restrictions about a credit check for employment purposes and how this can be handled. If you are applying for a position in a financial institution (bank, stock exchange, credit union, or other financial service provider) the organization may need the information prior to offering you a job. Most organizations are trying to balance your right to privacy and their right to make sure they don't hire an individual who is now or can become a liability in the future.

If you have any concerns about providing your social security number be sure to contact the hiring manager at the company and ask them about their policy and what protections they have in place to keep your information secure. Any legitimate organization will understand your concern and will be more than happy to explain their policy and how the information will be used. They will share the information they receive back by telling you things were fine or who you can contact if the information was adverse.

You are the first line of defense in protecting your personal information. Know who you are giving the information to and how it will be used. Some applications may not be considered if you don't put your social security number on them. Contact the company and ask about their policy regarding at what stage of the job application and consideration for employment the number will actually be required.

In the next section we will discuss surveys found on job applications.

# Section 5

# Job Application Surveys

With more job applications being requested to be completed online there is also opportunity to get some survey questions integrated into the process. These range from some standard interview questions to more 'profiling' inquiries. It is just another way to speed up the selection process to get to the best candidates possible. While this is not really a new thing it seems to be growing more popular to help employers screen applicants.

Some will ask multiple choice questions while others will ask the more traditional 'standard' interview questions. The best advice we can offer is to be honest in your answers. Some of the questions are very similar yet the answers must be consistent to the actual question being asked. You should carefully read each question and ponder for a moment what it is they are asking.

Most of the job application will be a 'survey' of your work history, education, and experience, as well as skills, talents, and abilities you possess that will set you apart from the rest of the applicants. Usually this is a 'just the facts' without any embellishments. Your resume, on the other hand, is a statement of facts of what you have accomplished and achieved in a written dialog.

The additional questions that might be asked will come in an open-ended question that must be answered with enough detail to demonstrate that you have adequate writing skills. There could be multiple choice questions that will ask you to select which answer would best describe you. No matter what you might think of these additional questions, they are now part of the application process.

Prospective employers want to know as much as they can about each applicant. They will have your job application and resume and now they want to know a bit more about you as an individual. If they like what they see they will take it to the next level of setting up an interview. It is at this point you become a candidate for the position.

Some organizations will review hundreds of applications and resumes and select ten candidates for an interview for each position that is open. Anything that can help narrow down the field at the earliest stages of the process is welcomed. Remember, the organization has in mind the kind of employee they want to hire. The candidate must also be able to fit into the culture of the organization. Some companies demand very high standards while others might be a little too relaxed for certain personalities. Your knowledge and experience are the two main areas that will get you an interview. How well you do in the interview will demonstrate your personality and ability to 'sell' yourself to the hiring manager.

The next section will deal with personality testing.

# Section 6

# Personality Testing

Personality testing has been around for a long time. It is well documented and has proven over the years to be somewhat reliable in helping to screen individuals for various personality traits. For many years only a few of the candidates for a position would be selected to participate in the personality testing. Since this was normally a subscribed or paid-for testing conducted by a third party, most organizations would be careful who was tested.

With technology today, some forms of personality testing are now becoming common with completing an application just like the job application surveys presented in the previous section. As the name implies this is a test to find out about your personality. Some of the questions will reveal your honesty and ethics. There are some limitations to doing a personality test as part of the job application. When you are questioned by a trained personality tester, they can 'sense' or make a judgment about your answers. If you are doing well the test will move on with more intense questions. The process can take an hour or longer. If the test interviewer senses that you are not suited for the position, lack the skills, or don't have enough knowledge about the position, the interview will be over much sooner.

There are a few candidates that feel they can fool the system by giving the answers they think the live interviewer wants to hear. A well-trained interviewer can detect someone fairly easily who is trying to 'outsmart' or 'game' the system. Most candidates just want to get past this testing and get an offer for employment. There are several personality testing companies out there and each has their own set of questions and methodology for determining the results they report.

Most of these personality tests will ask a question or make a statement and then ask you to select how you feel. Your choices will be strongly disagree, somewhat disagree, neutral, somewhat agree, or strongly agree. Some might only have disagree, neutral, or agree answers allowed. This could be argued as being too restrictive to really understand the individual. Having the five possible answers to choose from will build a better profile of the individual's personality.

A majority of the questions will deal with personality behaviors and your answers will indicate where you feel you stand with regard to that particular behavior. These questions are based on sound psychological principles through years of testing and following up on individuals to validate the results. Some individuals feel they are above reproach yet they fail to understand it is someone else who will be making the decision about their personality.

There are many companies that are now doing personality testing in-house. If the organization is large enough to afford the position, training, and certification of an individual or department to do the personality testing they may have quicker test results. Many of the tests are broken down into scales of which an individual might be able to fake. They can't, however, fake the entire profile.

The best way to handle the personality test is to relax and be honest in your answers. Don't waste your time trying to think of the 'politically' correct answer. Give your own honest answer. Organizations want honest employees and the personality test results can help find the most honest candidates.

Remember, by the time you get to the interview and the personality test you have cleared most of the hurdles. What will remain is how you compare to the other candidates and what differentiates the best overall qualified one. You can find more information online about personality tests and how they are used.

The next section will be about the application process and how it works.

# Section 7

# The Application Process

Those new to the job market might think that the application process is overrated. Once you have been a supervisor, manager, or an owner you will have a great deal of respect for the process. Time is money and money is what makes things work. If a company had to interview everyone who wants a job that has been posted, the line would be miles long. It just makes sense to have a screening process that simplifies the hiring process.

Your job application will become part of your permanent file with an employer. It will be there to locate your contact information. It will be used to help fill out all the legal documents concerning your employment. It will be used as a reference document for your supervisors and managers to review to make sure you have the required education, experience, and knowledge to do the job they are offering. Normally, the hiring manager is just one individual of many who will be involved in the hiring process. This is one reason the job application is so important.

The more complete the application, the more information will be available to be digested. Remember, you are not the only one who will be seeking the position. All those who you will be reporting to, if you are hired, will also be asked about their opinion and they may only be looking at your application and resume. This may be due to the amount of time they have available in managing their departments.

Many companies will have a target date to have the position filled by. They will post the position that needs to be filled and begin to accept applications and resumes. After they have received enough applications to establish a good pool of applicants, they may cease to accept any more applications unless there are no viable applicants within the pool.

Even during the period of time that the applications are being accepted they will be screened and the best applicants will be moved to a pile for further consideration. Once there are enough acceptable applicants the next screening step begins. This might involve a committee of managers to review the applications and resumes and to give each applicant a score. Those applicants with the highest scores will move on to the next screening level which might include an informal 'meet and greet' meeting to explain the position and review with the applicant their qualifications for the position. This gives the organization a chance to see you in person and get to know a little more about you. This might be done in order to further screen applicants to get to a number who will get a 'full' job interview.

Once you have been selected for a job interview, your job application and resume will be reviewed again for qualifications, education, and experience. The actual interview might be conducted by a hiring manager, a human resource manager, or some other designated individual. No matter who will be doing the interview they will have read both the job application and resume and you will be asked several questions to verify and confirm what you have stated on those documents.

Getting to the interview means you are in the 'running' to be considered for the position. Very few, if any, organizations will waste the time to interview someone who they know they will not hire due to lack of qualifications or lack of education. They don't have the time to waste.

The interview is to see how you interact with others and present yourself. Dress standards and grooming are also part of the interview process. How well you display confidence and take ownership of your accomplishments will also be considered. There may be ten others who will be interviewed and you will not know their work history or experiences. So you have to do your best.

The process works and accomplishes its purpose. All of the documents you provide to a prospective employer should be neat, clean, and easy to read. Don't make them have to try to figure out what you have done or can do. Make things easier for them by telling them.

The next section will be about the parts of the application.

# Section 8

# Parts Of The Application

The job application form has several major parts that are requesting to know more about you. Some job applications may not ask for all the items as the **Master Job Application Form (See Appendix - Master Job Application Form)**. We have provided a copy for your use at the end of this eBook. It is better to have more information available when completing job applications online or in person. This way you do not have to think about the answers you are being asked. Just write in what you have on the **Master Job Application Form**.

Please keep in mind that not all job application forms will have the parts in the same order as the **Master Job Application Form** we are providing.

The first part of the job application is general information about you and your contact information.

The second part of the job application will want to know what position you are applying for and your availability to start if an offer is made for employment. It might also include the desired wage or salary you want.

The third part is about your education and training for the position. This may include any military service you have completed or are currently serving and any additional languages you might speak, read, and write.

The fourth part will ask for you to list any special skills, talents, or abilities you have that might be beneficial to the organization or to the position.

The fifth part will want a list of your previous employers, starting with the most recent one first. This list will give the prospective employer a chance to see your work history and see what you may have accomplished or achieved in other positions with other employers.

Besides having all your job application items listed, the **Master Job**

**Application Form** is a foundational document to write your resume, power statements, and Me In Thirty Seconds (elevator speech). This will help you keep continuity through the documents you provide and the answers to the interview questions that will be asked later. Companies like to have employees who are organized and can present themselves with confidence. Stumbling for answers about yourself can leave a negative impression. You should know yourself better than anyone else. Know what you have written down on your job application and resume. If asked a question about something you have provided in a document you have given them, you should have the same answer as your job application and resume.

Some job applications will ask about your non-work activities such as any hobbies or special interests you have. If you have a gap in employment you should fill it in with any volunteer work you have done or a valid reason for not being in the workforce for that period of time. It might be to recover from an accident, or that you returned to school to obtain the skills and knowledge for the position you are seeking.

For certain positions you may have to provide a driving record. If there are certain days or shifts you will not be able to work, let them know up front. Don't wait to get the job and then start to negotiate what conditions you are willing to work under. Be honest in the beginning or you may never gain back the trust you will lose.

A note about references: Some applications will ask you to provide three or more references that they can contact. You should let anyone you feel will give you a good reference know in advance that you are seeking an initial job, a career change, or just a change in employment. You can have a separate list that you can offer at the time when you are actually being considered for the position. This way your references will not be contacted by everyone you have given the list to. You may tell the interviewer or the hiring manager you respect the time of your references and don't want them to be contacted until a job offer is ready to be made.

If you have any certificates, licenses, diplomas, etc., be prepared to have copies available for inspection. Don't say you have something that you don't have. Once found out you will be out of the running or terminated if you were given the position.

The next section will be about completing the **Master Job Application Form**.

# Section 9

# The Master Job Application

The **Master Job Application Form** is one of the most important forms or documents you will need to apply for employment. It is also the foundation for your resume, power statements, and your Me In Thirty Seconds (elevator speech). You might consider it a sales or advertising piece that sells your qualifications for the position you are applying for in your absence, since most job applications and resumes are read in private without you.

It is important that you list the correct dates where any dates are required. List all education, training, certifications, or skills in detail. A sloppy job application is normally not even considered. Make sure your job application is neat and clean. You want to make a great first impression and this job application is just the thing to do that for you.

Within this section we have provided a sample **Master Job Application Form** for you to see how it is to be completed. You will see that in the general information part all the areas are neatly filled in. Make sure you have an appropriate email address. Don't use something like: partyanimal457@mynet.com. You will have to create another email address to be more professional looking such as the one used on the sample provided.

Be clear about the position you are applying for. It should be stated as it was posted by the company. As for the salary desired, you should have done your research to know what the general range of pay is for the position offered. It is always safe to say 'open' so you don't lock yourself into a lesser amount than what the organization is willing to pay.

Be honest with your date of availability. Some companies will require that you give your previous employer a two week notice. Other companies might want to fill the position by a certain date. If you are currently unemployed then you can start as soon as they complete any background or physical exams that might be required as a condition of employment. Some positions might take a few months before you may be able to start and you could ask them if they have any other position that you can be placed into or if there is any education or course you could take to prepare for the position while you wait.

If you are the best qualified candidate they will not want you to look elsewhere if you can't wait until they are ready. Be open to discuss options that will work for both parties. Don't demand that you start immediately. If you are available now, let them know you are anxious to get started as soon as you can. If you have any doctor or dental appointments scheduled in the next ninety days or so, let them know. If you have a family wedding to attend and need to take a couple of days off within the first ninety days discuss this with them. Don't spring it on them a week before. Be honest and up front with them and they will do the same for you.

When completing the special skills part of the job application, put down everything you can think of that will increase your chances over the other applicants. You might have just that one more thing they want that the others failed to write down.

When it comes to your work history, be sure to list your positions, accomplishments, and experiences. If you supervised others, give quantitative numbers, not just a 'group of workers'. List all the functions of your job so they can see that you have experience that can be used in the new position. Bring as much as you can to the table so they will know that you are the best qualified candidate for the position.

Carefully review the following two pages. They are the sample **Master Job Application Form** and how it is to be completed. You will note at the bottom of the second page (or the back of the form) there is a checklist to make sure that you have properly prepared yourself for job searching. We have also provided a **Job Search Checklist (See Appendix - Job Search Checlklist)** or it can be downloaded from our website at and a **Job Search Activity Log (See Appendix - Job Search Activity Log)**, that can also be downloaded from our website at.

The additional forms are provided to help you stay organized so you can track your job search efforts. These forms will help you know what you need to do and where you have left job applications and resumes so you can follow up about the job.

Following the two pages of the sample **Master Job Application Form** will be the conclusion and review section.

Chapter 5 - Application Pizza

# MASTER JOB APPLICATION FORM

This generic Master Job Application Form complies with federal and state laws against discrimination; however, the user must exercise caution by checking local laws that might have additional restrictions. This form when filled out will contain personal information that you might wish to keep confidential.

## GENERAL INFORMATION

| Name (Last) | (First) | (Middle Initial) | Home Telephone |
|---|---|---|---|
| Smith | Jessica | A | (818) 555-1212 |

| Address (Mailing Address) | (City) | (State) | (Zip Code) | Other Telephone |
|---|---|---|---|---|
| 1332 E. Main St. | Homeville | CA | 90026 | (818) 555-3579 |

| E-Mail Address | Are you legally entitled to work in the U.S.? |
|---|---|
| jasmith123@mynet.com | ☒ Yes  ☐ No |

## Position

| Position or Type of Employment Desired | Will Accept: | Shift: |
|---|---|---|
| Assistant Clerical Supervisor | ☒ Part-Time<br>☒ Full-Time<br>☐ Temporary | ☒ Day<br>☐ Swing<br>☐ Graveyard<br>☐ Rotating |

Are you able to perform the essential functions of the job you are applying for, with or without reasonable accommodation? ☒ Yes  ☐ No

| Salary Desired | Date Available |
|---|---|
| Open | 3-31-14 |

## Education and Training

High School Graduate or General Education (GED) Test Passed? ☒ Yes  ☐ No
If no, list the highest grade completed:

### College, Business School, Military (Most recent first)

| Name and Location | Dates Attended Month/Year | Credits Earned Quarterly or Semester Hours | Credits Earned Other (Specify) | Graduate? | Degree And Year | Major or Subject |
|---|---|---|---|---|---|---|
| Homeville College<br>Homeville, CA | From 09/08<br>To 06/12 | 134 | | ☒ Yes<br>☐ No | BA<br>2010 | Business Admin. |
| | From<br>To | | | ☐ Yes<br>☐ No | | |
| | From<br>To | | | ☐ Yes<br>☐ No | | |

**Sample Master Job Application Form**

| Occupational License, Certificate or Registration | Number | Where Issued | Expiration Date |
|---|---|---|---|
| | | | |
| | | | |
| | | | |

| Languages Read, Written or Spoken Fluently Other Than English |
|---|
| Spanish |

## VETERAN INFORMATION (Most recent)

| Branch of Service | Date of Entry | Date of Discharge |
|---|---|---|
| | | |

## SPECIAL SKILLS (List all pertinent skills and equipment that you can operate)

MSWord, Excel, PowerPoint, Access, Outlook, Adobe InDesign, Adobe Illustrator, Photoshop, Windows

Page 155

## WORK EXPERIENCE (Most Recent First)   (Include voluntary work and military experience)

| | |
|---|---|
| **Employer:** Homeville Hardware | **Telephone Number:** ( 818 ) 555 - 1776 |
| **Address:** 145 N. State Street, Homeville, CA 90026 | **From (Month/Year):** 7/2010 |
| **Job Title:** Office Supervisor | **To (Month/Year):** 3/2014 |
| **Number Employees Supervised:** 3 | **Hours Per Week:** 40 |
| **Specific Duties:** Handled purchase orders, invoices, accounts payable and receivable, assisted with payroll, and helped with customer service when needed in the store. | **Last Salary:** $14.75 hour |
| | **Supervisor:** Jack Johnson |
| **Reason For Leaving:** Owners were retiring and closed business. | **May We Contact This Employer?** ☒ Yes  ☐ No |

| | |
|---|---|
| **Employer:** Ron's Cafe & Diner | **Telephone Number:** ( 818 ) 555 - 9120 |
| **Address:** 1483 Hwy 29, Homeville, CA 90026 | **From (Month/Year):** 6/2007 |
| **Job Title:** Shift Supervisor & Waitress | **To (Month/Year):** 7/2010 |
| **Number Employees Supervised:** 6 | **Hours Per Week:** 30 |
| **Specific Duties:** Made shift schedules for peak customer demands and helped with the inventory, receiving, and ordering of food and supplies as needed. | **Last Salary:** $11.35 hour |
| | **Supervisor:** Ron Ortega |
| **Reason For Leaving:** Finished my degree, wanted an office job. | **May We Contact This Employer?** ☒ Yes  ☐ No |

*Sample Master Job Application Form*

## Check List

- ☒ Correct contact information & phone number
- ☒ All addresses are correct
- ☒ All dates have been verified
- ☒ All education is correctly listed
- ☒ Resume complete
- ☐ Me In Thirty Seconds complete
- ☐ Power Statements complete
- ☐ Job Search Activity Log entries made as contacted

# Section 10

# Conclusion And Review

Today there are many things that you need to know about job searching. This includes knowing about job posting scams and how to avoid them. With the job market as competitive as it is, scammers are working hard to get your money and personal information. Look carefully at each job posting and what it says about the job. Are they just promising you a job only if you will pay them for the information? Watch for the warning signs of a job posting scam. Avoid becoming a victim by wasting money or losing your personal identity.

Your social security number is very important to you. You must provide it when and where it is appropriate to give it to an employer. If it falls into the wrong hands it can ruin your credit, wipe out your bank accounts, and even put you into debt that you did not seek.

Some of the online job applications will contain a survey that will request more information about you. These will be basic job interview questions to see if you might be considered for a full interview. Be honest and don't think that you can 'game' the system. Similarly, some applications will also contain personality testing. Personality testing is used to determine some of your behaviors and personal character traits. Again, don't think that by answering the 'politically correct' way you will improve your chances of getting the job. You might be able to 'fake' your way through a scale or two, but you can't 'fake' the entire profile.

The application process has been around for a long time. Over the years it has been refined and modified to meet the needs of the employer and the laws, regulations, and policies imposed by the government. It works for the purpose of what it is intended to accomplish. It is a system that lets the employer find and select the best possible candidate to fill the position for the company.

There are some basic parts to the job application. Not all parts will be on every application. Some applications might even contain additional boxes wanting more information about you. Keep in mind that many online job applications are timed. If the application is not completed within a standard period of time, the application will be automatically rejected. This is one reason to have a master job application form on hand so you will not be wasting time trying to remember where you have worked and those dates of employment. The master job application is a very important document since it is foundational for several other job search preparation items.

The job application is the first place you start. Sometimes it will be accompanied with a copy of your resume, which is usually the second document you will provide to a prospective employer. Your power statements and Me In Thirty Seconds (elevator speech) will be written from the information contained on your master job application form. The power statements could be used on your resume to support your qualifications or in an interview to answer a question. The Me In Thirty Seconds will be used when you are asked, "Tell me something about yourself." It will also be part of your networking 'script' to gather information about where there might be job opportunities available for someone with your qualifications.

Remember to keep your job application neat and clean. Take care in making a good impression with all your written documents that you submit to any organization. In your absence, it will be 'selling' you. Make sure the application is complete in every possible detail. If you have more to say or would like the prospective employer to know about you, you can put that information in a cover letter. This might be more information about classes you are still attending, certificates you will be completing soon, or any special information that you were not able to include on your job application.

No matter what job you are seeking, be it an entry level job, a career change, or moving upward in your current organization, you should always keep an up-to-date master job application and resume on hand. You never know when you might find yourself back on the street for any number of reasons looking for employment.

We hope that you enjoyed the **Application Pizza** and will take the time to look at our other menu items at the **Job Seekers Café.**

*Thank you and come back soon!*

# Chapter 6

# Sampler Plate

# Chapter 6
# Sampler Plate

Find out how your contacts can help you find a job by building your own personal network. Learn how to find opportunities others miss by not making these important connections. Served with a network contact form to help keep you organized.

## Section Table of Contents

| | |
|---|---|
| Introduction | 163 |
| Network Tracking | 165 |
| Scripting | 167 |
| Informal Networking | 171 |
| Formal Networking | 173 |
| Networking Letters | 175 |
| Job Fairs | 179 |
| Social Networking | 183 |
| Conclusion And Review | 187 |

# Section 1

# Introduction

Welcome to the **Job Seekers Café**. This menu item is entitled **Sampler Plate.** This menu item will give you a sample of several different flavors of networking to find employment. Combining each of these samples will help to satisfy your hunger for obtaining a job. Each one will help you to understand more about the networking process and how you can use each one to your advantage.

Tracking your networking activities is important. If you don't track the efforts you are making, how can you know who you talked to, sent an application or resume, and who you need to follow up with? Many job seekers after a week or two can't remember who they contacted, where they were located, and what the job position was that was posted. Then, if the organization did call back to set up an interview, the job seeker may not know who called or where they are located. You don't want to start calling everyone who you think you have contacted and ask them if they called about an interview. Just a bit tacky.

You will notice that on the outer margins of this and most other pages there are Scholar Margins where you can make notes or comments about what impressed you when reading the material. Perhaps you might have a question and you will put a question mark to remind you that you need to find clarification of the text and the concept presented.

One of the first samples we will be addressing is scripting. No, you are not going to be writing a Hollywood blockbuster movie script. This will be a script that you will be writing to help you stay focused on what you will be telling and asking others while you are building your network and resource list. Then you will be given some samples of informal and formal network contact lists and how to engage or interact with your contacts.

Next you will be served up a taste of the use of and preparation of networking letters for various scenarios. Then, we will discuss job fairs and how these can help you move forward on your quest for employment. Afterwards you will be served up some information about how social networks have become an important part of job searching today.

In the fast-paced world we live in today, the more you know and the more you do, your chances of finding a job will hinge on your ability to properly network. More jobs are now found due to personal networking efforts than any other avenue you might consider to pursue. The final pages of this eBook will be copies of the Network And Resource List form and the Scripting Form.

There will be many things covered within this eBook. Some you will find very comfortable, while others things might be a bit out of your comfort zone. This is the time to leave your comfort zone and meet the world head on. Take a deep breath, muster up all the confidence you have within, and then charge forward.

Reference will be made throughout this eBook about concepts that can be found in some of the other **Job Seekers Café** menu items. While each eBook is a standalone publication about a given subject, the entire collection of menu items has been prepared to help a job seeker be totally prepared to reduce the time it takes to get a job.

# Section 2

# Network Tracking

It is important to track each contact you make and each referral you are given. You can use the **Job Search Activities Log (See Appendix - Job Search Activities Log)** to record your contacting dates and information as you do your job search activities, which includes building and working on your **Network And Resource List**. You will need to have the **Network And Resource List (See Appendix - Network And Resource List)**. Use this to list your contacts and referrals so you will have a list of resources to contact each day.

The network you will be building will begin with a list of those you know who will be able to help you find out where there are job opportunities. Begin with your family, neighbors, relatives, church members, club members, and friends that will be able to help you locate the resources you will need. Once you have the names listed on the Network And Resource List, begin writing in the contact information and then giving each resource a priority score. Each one should have an 'A' if they will be able to help you directly, 'B' if they might be able to help you directly, and 'C' if they might be able to indirectly help you with referrals. This list should have ten to fifteen individuals listed with all contact information, and should take less than fifteen minutes to complete.

Next, add on more names of individuals or organizations that you feel might be able to help you find the information you need. Be sure to have all the contact information and priority scores completed. Now you should have a minimum of thirty names of contacts and resources to work on. As you make contact with each one, work your script (we will discuss scripting in the next section). Be sure to ask the three networking questions so you can add two names for each contact you make. In a short amount of time you will have a very large list.

Make sure that you begin to contact all your 'A' priority scored resources first. They should be the ones that will offer you the most help with the least amount of effort. Besides, your family and friends will be a great place to practice your networking script. You want to work the script until it sounds like your natural voice and not a 'canned' sales pitch.

It is important that you get referrals with every contact you make. If you don't, you will soon be out of resources to contact. By increasing your list daily, you will soon have a list longer than your ability to contact. Nevertheless, keep building your network and resource list, if for no other reason than you might be able to help someone else in building their personal list.

As you make contact with the people or organizations on your list, place a check mark (✓) to show that you have contacted them. If they were able to provide you with valuable information that might help you, place a star (★) next to the check mark. If you need to follow up with a resource you can place a circle next to the check mark (◯) and once you have followed up place a dot in the circle (⊙). If the resource did not provide or was unable to provide you with anything useful, put a minus (−) sign next to the check mark. This will be your way of visually knowing who you have contacted and where you have received help and where you did not.

## Network And Resource List

| No. | Name Of Resource | Contact Information (phone number, address, email) | Priority |
|---|---|---|---|
| 1. | Bill Jones | 555-2786    1232 N. First St., Homeville<br>bill.jones@mynet.com | A |
| 2. | Tom Stanton | 555-8951    1275 N. First St., Homeville<br>StantonT@mynet.com | A |
| 3. | George Larsen | 555-6585    326 E. Poplar Ave., Homeville<br>georgelarsen23@mynet.com | A |
| 4. | Cindy Allen | 555-3467    254... | B |
| 5. | Joyce Brighten |  ...lle | B |
| 6. | Rex Knox |  | A |
| 7. | Jill Howell | 268 N. Third St., Homeville<br>howelljill@mynet.com | A |
| 8. | Sam Paterson | 555-1456    674 N. Pine St., Homeville<br>sampaterson@mynet.com | B |

**Sample Network And Resource List Form**

In the next section you will learn about scripting and how to network.

# Section 3

# Scripting

(NOTE: This section on Scripting is copied from the Basic Breakfast Plate eBook, another eBook in this series.)

Have you ever answered the phone and immediately been able to tell that the one who was calling you was reading from a script? "Hello. My name is ... and I am calling to tell you how you can save some money. Would you like to save some money? Great, let me tell you how ..." Many times these calls are made without passion or sincerity. They will sound artificial which makes you begin to question why they are calling you. Many of these callers are working in a 'boiler room' and there is a great deal of pressure to get you to use the service or buy the product they are selling.

Your script will not be selling anything. The script you will use will be one for those you have on your networking and resource list. You are trying to gather information from those on your list about any jobs or opportunities they might know of that could be of help to you. You will find that most people like to help others. This will not cost them more than just a few minutes of their time and they will feel good that they were able to be of some help to you.

There are three basic scripts that you will need. One will be used with someone you know. This will be the easiest one to create and use. The second one will be for those who were referred to you by someone else. Being a referral, these will also be easy to use. The third one will be to someone that you do not know. This is not as hard as you might think. Once you have contacted those you know and several of the referrals, calling those who you don't know will be a little easier. The more people you call the easier it will become to call on almost anyone on your network and resource list.

Every script you write should have six basic components:

1. A greeting

2. A quick question regarding if this is a good time to talk

3. Explanation of why you are calling

4. Use of your Me In Thirty Seconds or a couple of power statements

5. Asking the three networking questions

6. Closing by thanking them for their time

Each script will use the basic script model with only a few differences in what questions will be asked. No matter what script you are using there are a few things that you must do exactly the same. These include asking the three standard networking questions.

The three networking questions are:

1. Do you know of any job openings in your company that might fit my qualifications?

2. Can you recommend anyone who hires or manages people who do what I do?

3. Do you know two people who work in my field of experience who might be able to assist me?

Creating a script is not hard. By using the **Scripting Form (See Appendix - Scripting Form)** you can write your scripts. The scripting form is also available on our website. The purpose of writing a script is to keep you focused on the purpose of your call. The purpose of your call is to network, not to ask for a job. By having a written script you will be able to get your questions asked and answered quickly so you won't take too much of the other person's time.

Although we are talking about having a script it is important that you practice it over and over until your natural voice takes over. This way you will sound more confident and will have removed some of the roughness of the script.

The script will sound more natural when you use the proper greeting. When the individual answers the phone say, "Hello, _____ (name of contact), this is _____ (your name). Is this a good time for you to talk to me for a minute or two?" This lets you identify with the contact and lets them know your name. Asking them if this is a good time to talk with you is showing respect for the contact's time. They might be in a meeting or just leaving to visit a customer. You are giving them an opportunity to talk with you now or at a later time when it is more convenient. This will let them know how important you consider their time. If it is not a good time you should ask them when would be a good time and make arrangements to contact them later at that time.

If this is a good time to talk to them, continue with your explanation of why you are calling them. This should take less than ten seconds. Then give one of your Me In Thirty Seconds or a couple of power statements. This will give them information about you that they will need to be better prepared to point you in the right direction. Now you will ask the three networking questions and take note of the answers they give you.

You will close the call with a sincere 'thank you' for the time and any names or referrals they gave to you. Remember, you might have to contact this individual again later and you want them to have a positive feeling toward you. Their time is valuable to them and if you express your appreciation they will be open in the future if you should ever need to call them again.

If you were referred to someone your greeting will be slightly different. You would say, "Hello, _____ (contact name), my name is _____ and _____ (name of who gave you the referral) suggested that I call you. Is this a good time to talk to me for a minute or two?" Then continue as you would for a call to someone you know.

The main difference here is that if they answer 'yes' to first of the three networking questions and you are talking to the manager or interviewer, you can ask to set up an interview. Ask them when it would be convenient for them to have you come in for an interview. If the answer is 'no' then continue to ask the second and third networking questions. Again, thank them for the time they spent with you and if you were able to set up an interview you can repeat back the time and date and state that you are looking forward to meeting with them. Then keep the appointment.

If you are calling someone you do not know or were not referred to then you would ask the person who answered the phone for the name of the manager or hiring manager. Then you would say, "Thank you. May I speak to _____ (name of manager) please?" When connected to the manager you say, "Hello, _____ (name of manager), my name is _____. Is this a good time to talk to me for a minute or two?" Then continue as you would for a referred contact.

Remember, the purpose of scripting is to keep you focused on what you need to be asking to build your network and resource list. It is not to be asking for a job. If you do happen to get a 'yes' to one of the three networking questions, that's great. However, you should ask for two referrals that you can add to your network and resource list in case you can't secure an interview at this time with this contact.

Scripting is a part of the overall job-seeking package. If you don't get all the other parts it will be much harder for you to find a job. Take the time to prepare for your job search activities. Practice your scripts until you are feeling confident that they are in your natural voice and not as if you are reading a 'canned' script. The more natural you sound the better.

In the next section we will discuss informal networking.

# Section 4

# Informal Networking

In the networking sphere there are two types of networks. One we call informal and the other formal. Your social network contacts will fall into one of these two types of networks. In this section we will discuss the informal network. Both networking types are important and there may be some contacts that might be safe to put in any network type. Here we will try to explain the informal network and how you can use it to your advantage.

The informal network group of contacts will primarily consist of your family, close friends, church members, neighbors, friends of friends, your barber or hair stylist, and those you strike up with a casual conversation. Your family will want to see you succeed in life and they are willing to help you find work if you are in need of a job. Your in-laws will be happy to help you since they don't have any room in their home for you to live in. Good friends also want to see you succeed and they can be asked for help also. You spend time with your barber or hair stylist who have their 'ear to the ground' and know what is going on in the community. They can be a very helpful source of information.

The informal network is your primary network for a couple of good reasons. For one, they will work with you by reading your resume and giving you feedback on it. They will listen to your Me In Thirty Seconds (elevator speech) and power statements until you get them to sound natural. These are the ones in your corner and they don't want you to make a mistake when you start calling your formal network contacts. Practice with those on your informal network contact list. They will be the most forgiving.

The informal network contacts should be the first ones you write on your network and resource list. Consider these names as 'assets' and treat them as if they were (they really are) gold. Their value is actually worth more than you realize. Respect what they have to say to you. Some feedback might be a bit harsh, but accept it as a need to change something that will make you better than you are currently.

Your informal list will be your first calls to practice your script and to see if you can find some leads. You will gain confidence and will be able to refine your 'script' with each call you make. It is important to practice, practice, practice. Get your script to be in your natural voice. Make it flow so smooth that no one can tell that it was originally a written script. Once you get it down smooth you will be able to 'work it' as the situation demands without missing a beat. You don't want to be so attached to the script that you forget to listen to the other person. Sounding like you are reading a script will come off like you have little if any confidence in yourself.

Although we call it an informal network, you still must take it seriously. You will be surprised at the number of referrals, job opportunities, and the growth of your personal network. You don't have to be 'pushy' about finding where job opportunities exist. Just strike up a casual conversation and let the other individual know that you are in the job market and give them your Me In Thirty Seconds speech. You are not looking for them to offer you a job, only to provide information about any job opportunities they are aware of at this time that meet your qualifications.

Sharpen your skills with your informal network. Then use those skills with confidence to get the information you need to secure the job you want. Once you get into making those network contacts you will be surprised to see just how much is out there.

In the next section we will discuss formal networking.

# Section 5

# Formal Networking

Your formal network is an important part of your network and resource list. The difference is how you will make your approach when you contact those on the formal list. These are the 'professionals' who know the people, know the opportunities, or can you refer you to the where you will find what you are looking for. These can be temp agencies, employment agencies, recruiters, and organizations who sponsor job and career fairs.

With your formal network you have to be on your game. These are the ones who you will have opportunity to demonstrate your self-confidence and tell about your qualifications. These are your 'power brokers', who, if you can impress them will do what they can to help you. At this point you should be using your 'script' in such a natural voice that they will listen to every word. Even on the phone you will sound like you are organized and enthusiastic about this opportunity to talk with them.

Where will you find your formal network contacts? These can be those who you do not know or were referred to. They can be members of a service organization, chamber of commerce, or a trade association. These are those who mingle with others who have a keen sense about the job market in the local area or can refer you to someone they know who will be able to help you. These may be industrial insiders who know where businesses are growing or moving to.

If you are attending a job or career fair, you will consider these to contacts to be on you formal network list. This is because your first contact will be in person, face-to-face. You will be observed on how you present yourself, the way you dress for the event, and your level of self-confidence. These things, along with your enthusiasm, will tell them more than what you have on your resume.

Even at the job or career fair, you should be exchanging business cards, noting the date and time you spoke to the individual on the card. Add any comments you feel important and when you get home, add them and any referrals they gave you to your network and resource list.

Also, after you get home from the event you should send them a thank you note expressing your gratitude for taking the time to help you. This will make a very good impression and might make the difference in you getting a call for an interview.

When you are networking your informal or formal network contacts, you will use the opportunity to find out if the contact knows of any employment opportunities for which you are qualified. Always ask the three networking questions and be sure to write down any referrals with name, phone number, address, and email address.

In the following section we will review networking letters and correspondence.

# Section 6

# Networking Letters

This section will cover networking letters and correspondence. This can be one of the most important things you can do to make a positive impression when trying to set up an appointment or get information from someone who is some distance from your location. If you are unable to contact them by telephone it is fine to send a letter. It will lend a personal touch that can only be conveyed by a personal letter to the recipient.

In today's world of instant communication, while fast can be good, taking the time to send a letter or note to someone through the postal system can have a very 'tangible' impact. There seems to be more thought given when we write something rather than just saying what we are thinking. It's just more personal since someone had to find the paper and pen (or turn on the word processing program), write the note or letter, address the envelope, and then mail it. It is nice to talk to the grandchildren on the telephone, but that drawing and note they send gets read several times and ends up on the refrigerator door. It just becomes more personal when we take the time to do something special for someone and it is remembered long after a phone call. This example applies to our business correspondence and communication as well.

The time invested in writing a thank you note to someone who took the time to talk with you or helped you will be some of the most valuable time you will have invested in building a stronger personal relationship. As with all communication we engage in, there should be a specific purpose. Make sure in the note or letter you detail something that they did for you or how you appreciated the encouragement they gave you. This way it becomes more personal and not just a 'form' letter or note. Make it personal and meaningful. You probably know that great feeling you get when you receive a personal note of appreciation from someone.

There is a section later in this eBook that will be covering job fairs. You should consider a job fair as a way to build your network outside of the traditional method of making phone calls. Here you will get to meet face-to-face many representatives from several companies and organizations in a single location. It is important that you send a thank you note to those who you spoke with that gave you some useful information or referrals. Make sure you get a business card from each individual you talk to. This way you will have all the contact information and the correct spelling of the individual's name.

Here is a sample thank you note for someone you called on your list:

> Dear Mrs. Stevens,
>
> I really appreciated the time you took on Wednesday at the Homeville Job Fair to talk to me and provide me with the two referrals and the job lead. I contacted the lead you referred yesterday and they requested a copy of my resume.
>
> I will be contacting those who you referred me to on Friday to see if they know of any job opportunities that might fit my qualifications.
>
> Thank you again for your time and assistance.
>
> Mary Johnson

Here is a sample thank you note for someone you met at a job fair:

> Dear Mr. Newton,
>
> It was a pleasure to meet you last Tuesday at the Job Fair held at the Convention Center in Homeville. I really appreciated the time you spent with me explaining the positions available at Omega Industries.
>
> There were a couple of positions that you mentioned that I feel I am qualified to fill. Your company seems like a great place to work based on what you told me.
>
> My resume is attached for your review. I am looking forward to meeting you again and discussing my qualifications. You can contact me at (555) 555-5555.
>
> Thank you again for your time and assistance.
>
> Michael Barns

If you want to handwrite the notes that is fine, just make sure your handwriting is legible.

There are two types of network letters you can send. One applies to a recent graduate looking for information about job opportunities for someone who has a degree in a specific field of study. The other is to an individual in an organization to whom you have been referred or perhaps you might know. Both are similar with some subtle differences.

Here is a sample networking letter from a recent (or soon to be) graduate:

---

George Planter
1421 N. Capital Street
Homeville, California 90026
(323) 555-9012 - gplanter@mynet.com

Mr. Robert T. Vance
President
Vance Technologies, Inc.
9873 W. Lincoln Ave.
Homeville, CA 90026

April 12, 2013

Dear Mr. Vance,

    I am a senior at Homeville University and found your contact information on the Alumni Network. I am hoping that you might be able to help me learn more about the technology field. I have been taking courses in IT, programing, and business management. The career counselors at the university have encouraged me to consider making a career in the technology field.

    I would be interested in hearing why, how, and what made you decide to go into the technology field, and, if you feel that an internship after my graduation might be appropriate for me to gain some actual experience in the technology industry.

    I really appreciate you being willing to give me some of your time and will contact you next week to arrange an informational interview to see if this will be the career path I will follow. I want to thank you in advance for any assistance you will be able to give me.

Sincerely,


George Planter

**Here is a sample networking letter to a referral or someone you know:**

Grace Beebe
276 E. State Street
Homeville, California 90026
(323) 555-8901 - gracebb@mynet.com

Mr. Jeff Reynolds
Vice President
Dart Cord Company
123 S. Madison Ave.
Homeville, CA 90026

July 23, 2013

Dear Mr. Reynolds,

    I was referred to you by Beverly Hart from the Jones Fabric Company of Newtown, CA. She felt you would be a great contact for information on the local textile trade and business in Homeville.

    My objective is to find employment in the textile industry. I would like your advice on what career opportunities there are, how I might be able to job search in this field, and where I can find job leads in the Homeville area. I have a bachelor's degree in Business Administration from Homeville University.

    Thank you in advance for any information and advice you will be able to share with me. I look forward to contacting you next week to set up an informational telephone interview. Again, thank you for your assistance.

Sincerely,


Grace Beebe

In the next section we will discuss job fairs, career fairs, and how you can get the most out of the experience by attending them.

# Section 7

# Job Fairs

To go or not to go, this is the question. Job fairs and career fairs certainly have a place for those searching for employment. There are some who claim that a fair is over-crowded, fast paced, and too busy to be of any real value. Others claim they are a great place to meet many representatives from many different organizations all in one place. Here is where you can get many contact names and lots of company information in a short amount of time. The difference of perspective is only the individual's attitude in going.

Sure there will be plenty of people competing for even just a moment of time with a representative. If you are prepared and have a plan you will be able to come away having met those who can help you get to where you want to go. If for no other reason, you should go to a job fair and use it as a 'training ground' for your self-confidence and to practice delivering your Me In Thirty Seconds speech. Even if you don't say it to perfection, the representative probably won't even remember what you said. They will have met so many people that they won't have time to remember who was who.

Most job fairs are open to the public as a whole with a very diversified listing of those organizations participating in the event. They are generally open for those who are seeking an entry level position, a change in employer, or for those seeking a career change. A career fair is more geared to a college or university setting where participating organizations have a much narrower focus on specific fields of study. It might be technology, medical, agricultural, or engineering graduating students that are being targeted for specific jobs in specific industries.

You should know what to expect at a job fair. Job fairs are usually published well in advance to 'cast a net' over a very large area. You will be able to go online and at least find a list of what companies will be participating in the event. From the list you should be able to recognize names of several major employers that you might be comfortable working for. Do some research on those companies and be prepared to ask responsible questions of their representatives. Never ask, "What does your company do?" If you have a purposeful question it shows that you are a bit more serious because you at least took the time to do some research on their organization.

Once your have 'worked the room' on those who you had selected, take some time and visit some of the 'less engaged' participating employers. Properly introduce yourself, proceed with your Me In Thirty Seconds speech, and then ask if they have any positions for someone with your qualifications. If they don't currently have any openings, ask if they might know of some other organization that might have something you are qualified to fill. You have nothing to lose and everything to gain. Either way, you get another chance to practice your introduction and Me In Thirty Seconds speech. Always be sure to thank them for talking with you and for any information or encouragement they might give you. You never know what might happen in the future if you do make a favorable impression.

With most job and career fairs you will be required to register prior to the event. Some will even ask that you forward your resume online before the start of the fair. Others will want you to hand a hard copy of your resume at the door of the event. This is done so all the organizations attending will have access to a database provided by the event organizers, and allows them to review all resumes after the event. Still, you should carry with you several copies of your resume to hand directly to any representative who might ask for it.

Many assume that every organization will be represented by a hiring manager. This is not always the case. There may be a representative from the company who is there only to take information or act as a 'recruiter' for the organization. Those they feel meet the qualifications they are looking for will be referred to the hiring manager to contact at a later date.

Since these fairs are a busy place, there is not much hiring 'on-the-spot' going on. If you do have the qualifications they are looking for, or they feel you can fit into their organization, they may take your name and resume and set it aside so they can contact you later for a job interview. Don't think that you will be getting job offers from every participating organization. This is not the purpose of the event. A well-qualified candidate might be pulled aside and given a bit more personal attention. With all the numbers in attendance there usually is not a lot of time for such individual consideration.

Some fairs might be less attended and you will be able to meet and talk with representatives from many organizations. Other fairs will have strict crowd control so that you will be let in when there is room for you. There will be others where it is everybody for themselves. Be mentally prepared for each case scenario and just go with the flow. Keep a positive attitude at all times.

How should you prepare for a job or career fair? The first thing you should find out is if the fair will have organizations that will be looking for someone with your qualifications or education. Some fairs are industry specific and if you are looking for an entry level-position in the technology field you wouldn't want to be attending the Culinary Arts job fair for professional chefs. Research the fair to make sure that it is worth your time to go to it.

Always arrive early so you can find a parking space. This will also allow you some extra time to review who you want to see at the fair. Practice your Me In Thirty Seconds speech several more times before getting out of your vehicle. If you are lucky enough to be one of the first to enter the fair you will not have to wait as long to speak to the organizations you are targeting.

What to wear? How you dress is important. This is not the 'county fair' with farm animals. This is a business environment and looking professional is the order of the day. Make sure you wear comfortable shoes since you will be standing most of the time. You will be making an impression by how you are dressed, in the confidence you display, and in the organizational skills that you use. The representative will be using visual, verbal, and kinesthetic (physical) senses in forming an impression of who you are. In other words they will be looking at you, listening to you, and noticing how firm of a handshake you have. You might even be talking with one individual while another is doing the observation. No matter how you show up, wear your best smile throughout the event. It can really make a difference.

Be prepared to ask purposeful questions. Don't be asking about breaks, vacations, or allowed sick days. This information will be given at the proper time, usually during an orientation after you have been offered and have accepted a job. The most important questions you can ask after you have told them your qualifications is if they have any open position that you might be able to fill. If not, ask if they know someone else who you could contact that might have such information.

Job and career fairs should be part of any job seeker's networking plan. Since you do have a plan for job searching (you had better have a plan), there are a few things you will need to include in your plan to take to a fair. A well-written resume that highlights your qualifications and accomplishments is one of the most important things you can take with you. Have some 'business contact' cards printed with your correct contact information. You can have them printed professionally or just do it in a word processing program. Keep it neat and easy to read so they can find the information to contact you. Avoid excess 'artwork' on the card. Keep it basic and to the point. Leave plenty of white space so there is room for writing notes or comments. When you ask a representative for their business card be sure to offer your card in return. This demonstrates that you have some knowledge of business etiquette and customs.

If you have contacted the companies you have targeted, you might just walk the floor and listen in on what others are saying. You will be able to see the good ones and learn from their presentation. You can let others be asking some of those questions you shouldn't be asking. This is how you can gather more information about the organization and what they are doing.

One of the most important parts of attending any fair is timely follow-up. You should make some form of contact by phone, email, or a note within a week. Large organizations will prefer a note rather than a phone call. Don't go to a job or career fair and then take a three-week vacation before following up. Those who made the effort to make contact within a week will have the advantage over you. Stay relaxed and calm. Show your enthusiasm by maintaining proper eye contact when you speak to a representative. If you don't show interest in them or their organization, they might not be interested in giving you an interview later.

Here is a quick checklist of what you should take to a job or career fair. Take a friend who will make you more comfortable at the event so you don't feel alone. Bring some 'business contact' cards to pass along to those who you talk to. Take several copies of a well-written resume that will 'showcase' your qualifications for the position you are seeking. Have a well-prepared Me In Thirty Seconds speech that will grab their attention and make a positive impression. Finally, have a good attitude and enjoy the experience. You will find the time worth it if you are prepared.

In the next section, social media networking will be presented.

# Section 8

# Social Networking

Social networking is growing in popularity. It has really caught on in the last several years. There are some great things that this new avenue of networking has to offer, and there are some things that you should be aware of that might cause you some harm. In this section we will try to give you the information on how you can get the most out this technology to improve your networking efforts. We will also discuss some of the warning signs you should be watching for so you can keep your personal information safe.

Online you will find plenty of social media sites that all claim to offer something for everyone. There are about a dozen that are popular in the United States. There are plenty more here in America and around the world. We will touch on a few of the more popular ones at the time of this writing. Some social media sites are being bought out or merged into some of the larger ones. It is a very fluid and ever-changing environment. There will always be new start-up companies that might even have better service and offerings than those referenced in this section. Which one or how many you choose to use is up to you. The further you cast your net the more chance you have of making the right connection and finding the job you want.

For business purposes, LinkedIn has some valuable features to help a job seeker. LinkedIn has more professional individuals in influential positions that can help the job seeker. The next one to consider is Twitter. It has a more casual approach to connect with other individuals who are in a similar situation as you currently find yourself. Facebook is the largest of the social media sites in terms of numbers of users. It also has a place for the job seeker. Google+ also allows you to join in groups or communities to network with others regarding job search activities.

Some of the sites will also allow you as a subscriber to follow many companies and organizations where you can get additional information about job opportunities before they are posted on the Internet. If you are lucky enough to be among the first to see these, you will have a slight advantage if you respond or make contact quickly with the company.

These social media sites are free to sign up for an account. Once you have the account you can begin to make posts and get your message out. You will have to do some work to help build your network. The larger your network the better your chances are of getting leads to where the job opportunities are located. On each social media site you will be required to create some sort of profile so others will be able to get to know something about you. Some of these profiles are private and others may be very public. Before you post your personal profile you had best know how your profile will be used.

Your email address and your social media identification (or 'handle') should also be professional. Any photo you post should make you look as professional as possible. You will have to use status updates to keep your network informed as to your ongoing situation. Just remember, budget the amount of time you will spend on working on your social media network. Don't be guilty of spending so much time on your social media networks that you begin to neglect your telephone calls to secure a job interview. You may think you have nothing but time to kill waiting for the job offers to arrive. Remember, sometimes you have to go out and get the offer yourself.

On any social media site you should be trying to add five or more new names or contacts to your networking list every day. This way your social media network will grow to a size that will make it viable in producing the results you want. You can ask those in your network to provide you with names they know who might be able to help you. There are plenty of 'hidden' jobs that only appear on social media sites. These jobs start off hidden from the general public and if not filled they will then be released to the public.

Each of the social media sites referenced above are continually improving their offerings to help their subscribers. You should visit each one and see if they are offering you something you need. Each has a vast list of categories to choose from that will help narrow down the search area.

Think about this; just as you are able to look at others on social media sites, someone can be looking at you. If you are doing everything you can to present a professional appearance you won't have anything to worry about. It is estimated that about 37% of employers use social networks to review job applicants. The information you have on your social media sites could cost you a job without you even knowing it. Many of the employers who do use social media sites report that they do use some of the information found to make a decision whether or not to hire someone.

There are estimates that almost half of the job seekers are now active on social media sites. Couple that with about a third of employers using those sites to screen potential employees. That is a large quantity of job seekers being evaluated in some measure by the way they present themselves. If you are planning to use social media to help you build a network to find out where the job opportunities are, we suggest that you first clean up any site you now have. This might mean abandoning it entirely if it might be damaging to the impression you want to make to a prospective employer. This means you might have to create a new social media account with a new profile, photo, and tone to what you post.

The information you post should allow any employer to evaluate if you will be a good fit into the company's culture. Your grammar, the words you choose, and how your communication skills are displayed will also be very telling about you. What you want to have posted is information about what you have accomplished in your current, or most recent, job. You want to highlight your qualifications for the job you are seeking. You will also want to post things about your interests in moving upward in your career.

Social media is just that, you have to be social to get any value out of it. You will need to participate by making comments, posts, and working with those in your network if you expect to see any positive results from your efforts. Create a blog or website that readers of your social media site can be directed to for more information. You certainly will have more room for information on a blog or website than you will ever have on a social media site. Post photos that have relevance to what you are trying to do. Make sure all who visit your site leave with a good feeling for having been there.

Being online on any social media site will give you an advantage over those who are not. You are your 'product' and you should promote yourself by all means available. You will need the search ability and visibility so prospective employers can find you and be able to learn something about you that might make them interested in contacting you.

When you do find an opportunity on your social media site, try contacting those in your network or find others out there who might have a direct connection to the organization and see if they will be able to help you. The worst thing is they say no, or nothing at all. You only need one with the right connection to change your life forever. You are the one who needs to do the work. You will have to create the network and work the network. Be careful not to let it consume all your time. This is just another tool to use in your job searching efforts. Use it wisely and you will find it complements all your other efforts.

Above all else, keep your private information secure. Don't post your social security number, bank accounts, or contact information on a public social media site. Share them only with those you know who will not misuse them. Your are the first line of defense in protecting your identity.

Online you will be able to find more information about using social media to build a job search network. Take the time to carefully look into what each vendor has to offer and decide if they have what will help you. Some sites are very social and less job-search related. Others will have more job search resources that will be of benefit to you.

The next section is the conclusion and review of this section, followed by some networking and resource list forms and a scripting form.

# Section 9

# Conclusion And Review

Today, having a personal network to help you in your job search efforts is one of the most important things you can have. More jobs are found through networking than all other avenues of job searching combined. In order to make use of the value of your network and resource list you have to work it. This means making calls to find out who knows of job opportunities that you might be qualified to fill. Before calling though, you have to work out your calling script. The purpose of the script is to keep you on focus by following the six steps of the script. You should know your script and practice it until it becomes your natural voice.

There are two main types of networks. One is referred to as your informal network and the other is your formal network. Your informal network consists of those whom you know such as family, relatives, neighbors, church members, and others that you know well enough to strike up a casual conversation when you see them. These are your first contacts, so you can practice your script, Me In Thirty Seconds, and power statements. They will also be willing to help you write and review your resume to make sure that it is complete and highlights your qualifications for the job you are seeking.

Your formal network list consists more of the professional individuals you know, temp agencies, employment agencies, career counselors at school, or members of any organization you belong to. When you talk with your formal network contacts you want to have your script and Me In Thirty Seconds polished and be able to deliver it with a sense of confidence.

There are going to be times when you will need to write a note or a letter to someone you have contacted thanking them for their assistance. If you attend a job or career fair you should send a note to those you spoke to in order to establish a more personal relationship. You may have to contact them in the future and you want them to have a good opinion of you. Letters and notes do not take much effort to write and send off. But rewards can be great for such a small gesture, letting them know you appreciated the time they spent with you and any information or referrals they gave to you.

Job fairs are held all the time. You can find them on the Internet or look for their postings at your public library. These can be a bit intimidating if you do not know what to expect. Know what you want to accomplish at the fair, what organizations you want to contact, and how you will use the information you get. Job fairs usually have a mix of companies and organizations from different industries. The representatives are normally there to meet individuals and review their qualifications for various positions that they have now or will have in the near future. It gives the attendees a chance to meet and get to know about some companies and discuss their qualifications with a representative. Normally, a job offer is not made at a job fair. There are too many things going on and it is hard to keep track of everyone they meet. When going to a job fair make sure you are prepared with proper dress for the event, extra copies of your resume, and some 'business contact' cards to exchange with those you talk to.

Career fairs are normally held on a college or university campus and are more focused on career paths that the students are prepared to pursue. There may be a limited number of organizations or companies participating and they are looking for individuals with degrees in areas that they need to hire in. There will be more focus on students who have the education in a given field who meet the qualifications for any job that is open.

Both job and career fairs are well worth attending. They can be a great investment of your time if you go with a purpose. When you work the fair properly you will be able to add more to your network and resource list. The more contacts you have, the faster you will be able to find the job you want.

Social media is now a major part of networking. You can draw from a larger circle of contacts and even follow companies and organizations that are looking for your particular qualifications. Don't get so caught up in the social media network that you forget to actually work on your network list. Budget your time so you can still be setting up interviews and working your contact pool on your network list.

We hope that you enjoyed the **Sampler Plate** and will take the time to look at our other menu items at the **Job Seekers Café.**

*Thank you and come back soon!*

# Chapter 7

# Rock Solid Resume

# Chapter 7
# Rock Solid Resume

Prepared just right using proven principles to get attention and the results you want to achieve. Select a resume to suit your taste and individual requirements. Includes information about improving your resume so it will be read.

## Section Table of Contents

| | |
|---|---|
| Introduction | 193 |
| What Is A Resume? | 195 |
| Resume Myths And Other Lies | 197 |
| Objective vs Branding | 201 |
| Mistakes That Kill | 203 |
| Gappers | 205 |
| Changing Locale | 207 |
| Checklist For A Resume | 209 |
| Resume Checklist Form | 211 |
| Types, Styles, Formats | 213 |
| Words That Have Power | 221 |
| Forwarding Your Resume | 229 |
| Conclusion And Review | 233 |

# Section 1

# Introduction

Welcome to the **Job Seekers Café**. This menu item is entitled **Rock Solid Resume.** Nothing else can satisfy your job search hunger as much as a well-written resume. A resume that highlights your qualifications and experience so it will stand out above all the other resumes that are being submitted.

In this eBook you will be shown how to write a resume that will get results. If you are new to the job market, changing jobs, or seeking a career move this menu item will be able to help you prepare the correct resume. You will be shown what to put into your resume and what you should leave out. On average a resume gets only 15 to 30 seconds of reading time. If you can't grab and hold the hiring manager's attention within that time you won't be getting a call for an interview.

You will notice that on the outer margins of this and most other pages there are Scholar Margins, where you can make notes or comments about what impressed you when reading the material. Perhaps you might have a question and you will put a question mark to remind you that you need to find clarification of the text and the concept presented.

There are keywords that you should use in your resume, and there are other words that you should avoid. This eBook will give you plenty of useful keywords. If used correctly they will get your resume some additional reading time. You will have to be careful and not use some of the overused, outdated, and passive words that are no longer acceptable on a resume. There will be some new words that you will learn that will help your message stand out above the other applicants.

Resume types and styles have a great deal of impact if you use the right one. If you use the wrong type or style it won't get the results you are after. We will show you various types and styles with examples so you can see how they are formatted. At the back of this eBook there will be a resume worksheet that will help you write your resume. Resumes do take some time to write, edit, proof, rewrite, reedit, reproof, etc. You want the information to flow from the page to reader's eyes so they can immediately see all your information. Don't make them read through several paragraphs of hype and fluff trying to find your information.

Your resume is your advertisement that is trying to sell you to a prospective employer. What they see will have them making some judgments about you. If you send out a resume with poor spelling or grammar they will assume that you do not have the communication skills they expect every employee to have. If your resume is not presented in an organized layout they might think you lack organizational skills. A resume could be considered to be the key to getting an appointment for an interview. Make sure your key is capable of opening that door.

Reference will be made throughout this eBook about concepts that can be found in some of the other **Job Seekers Café** menu items. While each eBook is a standalone publication about a given subject, the entire collection of menu items has been prepared to help a job seeker be totally prepared to reduce the time it takes to get a job.

# Section 2

# What Is A Resume?

A resume is a document that speaks on your behalf detailing your work and education history to let a prospective employer know if your qualifications might fit a job opening within their organization. Resumes are generally one page in length and can be up to two pages. This depends on the number of years and how much relevant experience is required to convey your qualifications. A resume is the most common format when applying for employment in the vast majority of industries within the United States.

A Curriculum Vitae, or CV, is similar and is used when you apply for a job in a foreign country or in the education, scientific, academic, and research fields. They are often used when applying for grants or fellowships. The CV is usually longer than two pages and will contain much more detailed information. It will list your education, research experience, and affiliations. They will also contain a list of honors, awards, and publications you have been involved with.

There are many similarities between the resume and the curriculum vitae. Both should be specifically tailored for the position you are applying for. In most cases there is not a one-size-fits-all template that can be used generically. The main difference is that the resume is a concise document focused on brevity, whereas the curriculum vitae is a longer and very detailed summary. Industry hiring managers are normally not going to spend the time required to read a curriculum vitae. There is just too much information that is not needed for them to make a judgment about your qualifications to do the job they are looking to fill.

A question is often asked whether a cover letter should be sent with a resume. The answer is yes. It should include information specific to a particular industry or organization. In this cover letter you can express your thoughts on why you are applying for the position with this organization. Your cover letter should also use some of your power statements to reinforce your qualifications for the position. It should be neat and easy to read. This is also a demonstration of your communication and organizational skills.

You may have filled out a job application online and were then given instructions on how to forward a copy of your resume. Think about it, so far you have only submitted blindly who you are and what you have done. It is only the documents that are speaking for you at this point. If you have a good resume and your application was acceptable, your chances are getting better for being invited for a face-to-face interview with a live person. If the organization requested that you send them a copy of your resume you have the opportunity to use a cover letter to let them see a bit more of your skills. When you email your resume you could still send a letter that is similar to a cover letter in the body of an email. Indicate to the hiring manager you have submitted your job application and resume online and wanted to know if they have received them. Be sure to provide all your contact information so they can respond if they did not receive them or there was an issue created during the transmission of the email so you can resend them if requested.

How you write your resume is critical to it being able to secure an interview. In the following sections you will learn about the proper way to write, format, and create a resume that will be read and get you closer to the results you are seeking. The resume is a very important part of your job search activities. If you don't have a good (actually great) resume you may never get a chance to be interviewed.

Over the years there have been many individuals asking for help in writing their resumes. There are usually five or more drafts written, edited, and proofed before one shows any promise of being a good resume to submit. Don't try to wing it with the first draft only. After wasting a couple of months without success you will realize that your resume is not working for you, but against you. Take the time necessary to get it right. It will save you time in the long run.

In the next section we will cover resume myths and other lies that might cost you a chance at the job you are looking for.

# Section 3

# Resume Myths And Other Lies

How strange it is that there are so many things in life that have unwritten rules that must be followed explicitly or else. Writing a resume is no exception to having some unwritten rules that if not completely adopted could cost you a job. We will have to place these rules in the proper category of being a myth or a lie. True, many years ago they may have been the convention to follow even when they were not really rules, just urban myths, that were continued to be accepted.

**Myth 1.** You should include only experience where you were paid for your services.

**Not true.** Volunteer service or an unpaid internship demonstrates that you have experience and you should be given credit for it. Those just entering the job market after high school, even some college graduates, and those who have been unemployed for some length of time should list what they have done even if they were not paid. Many organizations are now showing more community involvement and like to see that prospective employees have a sense of community pride in helping others as a volunteer. Sometimes you can gain experience and skills only as a volunteer where you can develop and put into practice your leadership and organizational abilities.

**Myth 2.** You cannot have any gaps in your employment history.

**Not true.** Mothers often leave the workforce to take time to raise their children. Some have been sidelined due to an illness or accident. Others have been asked to take care of aging parents. A few lucky ones have been able to step out of the workforce and spend some time traveling around the world. They attend seminars about gourmet cooking, or are now directing their personal investment portfolios. Any gaps should be easily explained with valid documentation.

**Myth 3.** You can only submit a one-page resume.

**Not true.** Although most resumes can be written on one page, there is no rule that states a two-page resume will be rejected. A resume for an entry-level job, or for someone with little or no experience, should only be one page. Most mid-level or above applicants will have more experience and accomplishments and will therefore be expected to provide more information regarding their qualifications and what they will be able to bring to the position if they are hired. Long-winded resumes where there is no substance will be rejected quickly. Be concise and to the point.

**Myth 4.** You should write one generic resume and use it for every job or position you want.

**Not true.** You may have the qualifications for several jobs being offered at several different organizations. Therefore, you must have a resume that targets a particular position at each company. Even at a hundred yards you can get a bullseye with a rifle, yet you might not hit the target with a shotgun. Focus closely on each position separately so you will have a better chance of getting an interview and a job offer. You might even get multiple interviews and offers.

**Myth 5.** You have to use bullet points to show your qualifications.

**Not true.** If a hiring manager looks at a single resume and it only contained bullet points it might not matter. However, if they are looking at hundreds or more and they all contain bullet points, their eyes will glaze over and they will not be able to see what was written. For some hiring managers the use of bullet points are an indication that the applicant found a resume online and just cut and pasted the bullet points because it was easier than taking the time to make a factual statement about their qualifications. Use statements in sentence form to show what results were obtained by your personal efforts and contributions to support your qualifications.

**Myth 6.** You have to tell them about your duties and responsibilities.

**Not true.** Most organizations are interested in filling a position with an individual who has the qualifications and can bring something that will be of additional value to the company. The organization is concerned with their needs, not yours. You are better served by finding out the details of the position and then writing about your experiences and accomplishments that will define you as the best qualified applicant for that particular job.

Now that we have busted some of these old and outdated myths, the next few sections will begin to focus on the proper ways to prepare your resume for success. Will you have an objective or a branding statement? You can decide after you read the next section.

# Section 4

# Objective vs Branding

Is it not obvious that every applicant's objective is to get a job? Many job applicants are making a "What I want" or "my real career" objective statement at the top of their resume. What the hiring manager is looking for is a branding statement of what value you have to offer the organization. While many applicants will write an objective statement, it still comes across as what they want and not what the organization needs. This is where the distinction between an objective statement and a branding statement is made. Most applicants want a lot of things that the prospective employer couldn't care less about. On the other hand, the organization is more interested in how much value and experience you can bring to the position and company.

If you really want to make an objective statement you can include it in the cover letter you send with your resume. Just make sure you write it in a way that shows your interest in helping out the organization. It may be hard for some individuals to grasp this concept, but remember you are not the only applicant that is competing for the position. You can place your career goals into a Qualifications Summary that references the position you are applying for. You can state that you are qualified for what would be a logical next step in your career development so you can continue to grow in your career.

Just what is a branding statement? It is a shortened and more concise version of your Me In Thirty Seconds speech. It is to the point, without any extra or meaningless words. One approach that seems to work for many job seekers is to write the resume without the branding statement at the top of the page. Review and read carefully the rest of the resume and make some notes on the key items that stand out about your value, attributes and uniqueness. Then take these items and craft them into your branding statement. Keep it brief and on point. Use power words that emphasize what value you can bring to the organization, then place it at the top of your resume just below your contact information and see how it reads.

Your personal branding statement should be unique to you, not a generic one that anyone can 'cut-and-paste' into their resume. The branding statement should have your personality all over it and no one else's. The words you use should be your own. Start with the personal attributes that make you who you are. Are you dedicated, creative, enthusiastic, respected, etc.? What value have you created as a result of your personal efforts such as having cut production time, cost savings, and increased customer satisfaction? What makes you unique and different from all the other applicants like how you approach an issue, things you have achieved, and what you have accomplished?

If you are into social media networking you should have an identifiable branding statement of who and what you are. With so many hiring managers and employers looking at potential candidates for a limited number of job openings, they are increasing the amount of time they spend in reviewing an applicant's online presence and how they are branding themselves. Make sure you protect your brand. It is an image that you will be creating that must match up with all your other documents and communications such as your resume, cover letter, and online networks.

Some articles suggest that a branding statement be less than fifteen words, while others say keep it to one or two sentences. No matter what, make sure that it describes you in a professional way that will prompt hiring managers to want to contact you. There is a big difference between starting off your resume with a statement of: "Looking for a good job" and "Dedicated sales professional with a track record of increasing sales and customer satisfaction."

Write and rewrite your branding statement. Ask those who know you for their opinion of what you are stating. They may be able to help you polish it and make it even better. You need to differentiate yourself from all the other applicants and having a branding statement might make the difference that will get you noticed. You may find many other articles on the subject of branding statements online or in business magazines. There you may also find many samples that will help give you some ideas of why some are more effective than others.

The next section will give you information on the resume mistakes that can kill your chances for any additional consideration.

# Section 5

# Mistakes That Kill

Hiring managers, or other managers, will be reviewing job applications first to determine if the applicants have the needed skills to meet the job position qualifications. If they feel that the minimum standards have been met, then they will be looking for resumes that show an applicant's communication skills. Will the resume be neat and properly formatted, or will it contain some resume killers?

If your resume is poorly formatted with odd indentations or extra spaces you may be in trouble. Don't use unusual type fonts. They are hard to read and won't add anything to what you have to say. Adding a cartoon caricature or photo on the resume can speak of immaturity regarding the applicant. If you feel like you need to use a template for your resume, use it only as an outline to make sure that you have all the information you want to say. Then type it out in your own format that doesn't say you were too lazy to put any thought into creating it on your own.

Don't be sneaky about items such as gaps in your time line. Use dates when you started and when you left. Don't think that a hiring manager will not be able to detect when a job applicant is being sneaky. If you have been unemployed then state it. Don't hide it. It may be discovered at a later date and it could cost you your job for not being totally honest about your situation. Many good employees have lost jobs because of things they didn't want known, and then it showed up later. With the current job climate, many hiring managers expect many of the applicants to have been unemployed at some time. Some hiring managers expect to have a cover letter come with the resume; if not, it might be tossed into the trash.

Some applicants will fail to focus on expectations and results. They will instead list all the responsibilities for their last job. Be sure to emphasize your achievements and what you did to accomplish them. Keywords are great if they are used in moderation. Too many keywords can give the impression that you are trying to over-inflate your accomplishments. Keep focused on your experiences and achievements and state them honestly.

Spelling and grammar, if not correct, can sink a resume very quickly. Read it over, edit it, and then have someone else read it. Just before you send it out, read it again just for insurance. Keep to the relevant things and do not go off into the irrelevant zone where resumes go and never come back.

Another issue that irritates a hiring manager is looking at an unprofessional email address or social media handle. Anyone can get an email address for free. Why would you take the chance on an unprofessional email address? Make sure you use a professional-appearing social media handle.

Ever try to read a whole lot of small type in one solid block? Use a proper font size so your message can be easily read. Don't get too personal with your information. Such as your marital status, social security number, and such personal information like your age or any disability that you might have. These items can be discussed at the proper place and time and will be requested once you accept the offer the organization presents to you. Avoid using the term "transferable" when referring to your skills and abilities. Use terms like "skills", "skill sets", or "ability to" in making your point. Avoid using a phrase like "utilized my skills" on your resume. Who's skill would they be if not yours?

Do you like being lied to? No! You don't and neither do hiring managers and the organizations they work for. Think you can get away with it? You will be found out and, even if it is several years later, you can be terminated when the lie is discovered. This can apply to previous jobs, positions, education, schools attended, or degrees earned. Even an omission is a lie if you should have been upfront with your employer about the issue. A half-truth is still not the truth. It is a lie no matter how you try to justify it. Don't take your position titles to a higher level than you actually had. If you were an assistant manager say you were the assistant manager. Position titles can be found out and if you stretch it to higher level, then you will be out.

The next section will deal with gaps in your time line and how you can explain them.

# Section 6

# Gappers

Many job applicants will have gaps in their job history time line. These could be caused by events and situations that they did not have any control over. Gaps are not necessarily bad if you have a good reason as to why they exist. Being unemployed for three years and saying you just got "out of the habit" of looking for work is not a good explanation for any gap.

How you use your time while not in the workforce is more important to the hiring manager than why you were out of it. Some women will leave the workforce in order to raise their children. Other individuals will take time off to care for aging or sick parents who require constant attention. There are still those who decide to go back to school or college full time to get the skills and knowledge they need to get a better job. Some will have been in an accident or had a medical condition that required many months to fully recover. A few will be lucky and travel the world or manage a large financial portfolio for awhile. There are many reasons why someone may remove themselves from the workforce. Serving in the military is still considered being in the workforce, while spending some time in prison is explainable, though painful to admit. Still, fill in the gap and explain it in person to the hiring manager. You wouldn't be the first one they dealt with regarding this or any other issue. Never stretch the dates of other jobs to cover any gaps. If you are found out, it is the same as lying and it can cost you now or in the future.

If you are currently unemployed, what are you doing to keep yourself busy? You could be volunteering to occupy your time. There are many community projects and events that need volunteers and you can take advantage of these opportunities. Spending some time taking job-related courses at an adult school or working part-time can give the impression that you are doing what you can to stay busy and not lose any skills that time can erode. Some individuals will freelance their talents and abilities to remain active. Become self-employed doing odd jobs for others. If you do photography you can take wedding photos or portraits of friends and family. If you own rental property you can list the time as being active in property management.

Students who are recent graduates should have some internship or other experience as a volunteer somewhere. It could be at the public library helping with adult reading and literacy improvement. It could be volunteering at a local hospital or nursing home helping to care for patients or helping their family members cope with the stress. You might even take advantage of the time being out of work to do a forced cleaning of your closet or garage and selling some of your treasures you have collected over the years. This way you could state that you were engaged in a marketing business. Just be careful not to make too much out of it other than stating that it kept you busy while working on your job search activities.

There can be as many valid reasons why someone has a gap in their work history time line as there are individuals with gaps. Don't hide them or try to deny them. What you have done is just that—what you have done.

Gaps are acceptable if there is a valid reason for them. In some cases you might be asked for some documentation to support your explanation. You should welcome the opportunity to provide it since this is an indication that they feel you have the qualifications and might fit into the organization's culture. No matter the outcome, be thankful and appreciative of the opportunity they extended to you for considering you for the position.

The next section will be some food for thought about relocating in order to secure the job.

# Section 7

# Changing Locale

You may find a job that is a dream come true. The only hitch is that you will have to relocate. This can be good, or it can be bad. This will depend on your point of view and that of any others who might be impacted by such a move. Perhaps you would like to return back home and you found the perfect job opportunity. You may have been wanting to return home for some time and this might be that opportunity. Your cover letter or resume may be the place to start.

You might be thinking you could use someone else's address until you get the job. This might not work out if you are across the country and they want to see you tomorrow morning. Now you have to explain that you live in New York and would like to work in Seattle and you were only using a relative's address on your resume. Be honest about where you currently reside and that you would be interested in relocating to another location if the opportunity arises. Some companies will pay relocating expenses, others may split the cost, and some will allow you the opportunity to pay the cost yourself. It doesn't hurt to ask and the worse case is that you will have to face the cost of moving on your own.

You can simply state on your job application, in a cover letter, or in your resume that you will be relocating to the new area by a certain date. You could just say you are willing to relocate ton a certain area or location if offered the job. This has nothing to do with your qualifications for the job, only your willingness to relocate to another area. Your spouse might not be able to relocate and having to sell your home can take too much time. To relocate is a major decision and should not be taken lightly. It can have a major impact on the family, especially if children are in school and the timing is not right.

In some cases this might be an opportunity to get into an organization and get the experience and make the connections you need for career advancement. If you have spent some time in a far off corner of the world you might get the opportunity for a promotion back at headquarters because you have the knowledge and experience to deal with the distant branches from first hand experience.

You may want to consider taking a week or two to be in the area of the job location making yourself available for job interviews. This can also be mentioned in your cover letter, in an email, or in a phone call to the hiring manager. If your job application and resume meets with their approval they should be flexible and consider your availability for an interview. If the opportunity for the job requires that you relocate and it is a step forward in your career path it might be worth it. If it is only a move to another organization to the same position that you currently have you might want to keep some options open. What if you don't like the location once you get there? What if you are not comfortable with that location's culture? Relocating is a serious matter and should not be taken lightly.

Relocation can have its upside also. A change of location, will bring new friends and new opportunities. Change is good and is part of moving out of your comfort zone. You might find yourself competing with locals for the position and your chances might be slim at best. Discuss this concern with the hiring manager before you commit yourself and your money to a move.

The next section will provide you a checklist for your resume—what you should have, and what not to have, in it.

# Section 8

# Checklist For A Resume

You have heard this many times, that a resume might get a 15 second look initially. If it doesn't pass, it goes into the trash. With so many resumes being submitted for a single job posting you have to ensure your resume gets a longer look and is put into the to-be-considered pile. You can accomplish this by writing a resume the proper way. This section will deal with using a checklist to make sure that your resume will be on target and get the full consideration it deserves.

Before we get to the checklist there are a few quick and easy tests that you can do on your resume.

1. Is my resume able to be read quickly?

    The answer needs to be yes because it is short and to the point. It is written in a standard font in the proper font size for a resume.

2. Do I have a well-written branding statement at the top?

    A branding statement is a more powerful tool written in a powerful voice, rather than an objective statement.

3. Are my sentences beginning with an action verb or a passive verb?

    Use words that imply action, accomplishment, or achievement.

4. Are all my words spelled correctly? Is my grammar correct? Is my syntax or tense correct for the words I have used?

    Make sure that you proof your resume for spelling, grammar, syntax, and the proper verb tense.

5. Am I telling them what I want, or informing them what I can do for them?

Remember, they have a need to fill a position and are looking for the best possible job candidate. Your needs are not important. What you can bring to the position is what is important to them.

6. Are all my dates for education, employment history, certificates and licenses, and military service correctly listed?

These items can be, and chances are very good they will be, verified. Make sure that you double check your dates, titles, etc. They must be correct before you send your resume out or post it online.

These are just a few of the things you should be aware of as you are preparing your resume. Your resume must have a visual presence that will let the reader know that you have a good command of the language and have good to great communication skills. Your resume will say more about you than just the words you use to describe your qualifications and what you think you have to offer the prospective employer. Remember, you will need more than one resume because you will be targeting your qualifications to the specific job posting.

The checklist is a tool that can help you craft a great resume. You can accept the suggestions, or ignore them. Time and thousands of resumes submitted support the premise for each suggestion offered. Many job seekers will find the easiest way to do a resume. They won't give a single thought about how it might be received by the hiring manager, let alone how it will compare with the other resumes that were given the proper attention to detail.

Remember, your resume is speaking for you normally before you ever get to see the hiring manager or a live body. If it doesn't speak well for you, don't expect an invitation for a job interview. Months will be wasted and you will still be waiting to get an interview. Someone might even ask you if you have a resume. This may imply that it is not working for you. If so, then you should consider rewriting a new resume that does follow today's conventions.

You should consider using the checklist as you write your resume. Then use the checklist after the first draft to make sure that you are getting things right. Do your revisions and then have a friend or relative use the checklist against the corrected resume to see if they find anything that might need some more consideration. This is not meant to be an exercise in writing. It is meant to be one of the steps you must take in order to perfect your resume to improve your chances of it being read and you being considered as a candidate for an interview.

On pages 225 and 226 you will find the **Resume Checklist Form**.

Following the checklist will be a section on types, styles, and formats for a resume.

Each of the questions or items presented on this checklist should be answered as **yes** or **no**. All of your final answers should be a resounding **yes**. Take the time to review your resume carefully. Let it have a powerful voice that can be heard and not just a whimper that gets ignored.

# Resume Checklist Form

| Yes | No | Checklist Items |
|---|---|---|
| | | Does it look like an original writing and not a cut-and-paste using an online template? |
| | | Does it have equal margins on all sides? |
| | | Is there balance with the white space and the text? |
| | | Does it have a professional and polished look to it? |
| | | Is the resume easy to read by sections that are clearly labeled so information can be found easily? |
| | | Is the work history listed in reverse order so that the most recent employment is listed first? |
| | | Is the font used a standard resume font style? |
| | | Is the spacing and use of fonts consistent throughout the resume? |
| | | Have you changed all bullet points into power sentences? |
| | | Does your branding statement make a powerful impression? |
| | | Is your resume aimed at a specific career path and job position? |
| | | Does your experience and qualifications meet or exceed the job position requirements? |

# Resume Checklist Form

| Yes | No | Checklist Items |
|---|---|---|
| | | Does the resume address the hiring manager's and the organization's requirements? |
| | | Does the resume list credible accomplishments? |
| | | Are all accomplishments presented in the Situation-Action-Results format with quantifying numbers? |
| | | Are all your quanitifying numbers in figure form rather than in spelled out words? (123, $, %) |
| | | Are all your statements regarding your accomplishments beginning with or using an action verb to grab attention? |
| | | Did you keep your responsibilities separate from your listed accomplishments? |
| | | Does your resume's content relate and support your career goals? |
| | | Have you listed all honors, awards, recognitions, or affiliations relative to your past employment? |
| | | Did you use power statements to support your qualifications and your accomplishments? |
| | | Is your resume in a conservative style and not on colored paper with unconventional fonts? |
| | | Have you taken the time to look at sample resumes or asked someone else to help you write your resume? |
| | | Have you proofed, edited, and rewritten your resume to improve it? |
| | | Do you feel that your resume is as perfect as you can possibly make it without any spelling, grammar, syntax, or tense errors? |

# Section 9

# Types, Styles, Formats

This is the section where you will be putting it all together. You will learn about the various types, styles, and formats used in writing a resume. This is not your life's story, it is your working life's story. So it will not be that long. You should write in words that you would normally use. Don't try to impress a hiring manager with some words you never use. They will come off as awkward and they will distract from what you are trying to say.

There are four basic types of resumes.

**1. Chronological Resume.** This is the one most preferred by hiring managers since it has everything they need to make an informed decision. It is used by job seekers who have work experience. It provides a reverse vocational history of your job experience, accomplishments, skills learned, education, and contributions made while working for your previous employers.

**2. Functional or Skills Resume.** This for those job seekers who are changing careers, have some large gaps in their time line, re-entering the workforce, or have changed jobs frequently. You will list your skills and experience that will emphasize your professional strengths in general that you feel to be of benefit for the position you are seeking. This type of resume is harder for a hiring manager to read in order to get the information he needs.

**3. Historical or Anecdotal Resume.** This is a blend of the chronological and functional resume. This can be used for the same reasons as the functional resume. This type of resume will let the hiring manager know some things about you, but not as much as you would want them to know by using the chronological resume. Usually this is a last resort type of resume. It can be the right one for some situations where the other types should not be used.

**4. Limited Experience or the Ready to Start Resume.** If you are entering the workforce for the first time or if your experience is very limited then this might be the best type of resume for you. Be careful not to overstate your skills or abilities. Don't be afraid to list some beneficial character traits you possess. This is a good resume for the individual who is new to the job market and it can only help if written correctly.

There are some basic parts that every resume should cover. Over the years the basic parts have been cut back due to privacy laws and the information not being relevant at this stage of the hiring process.

**Name, address, telephone contact numbers (home and cell), and email address.** Make sure you use your current information. Many job seekers will take an old resume and make a few changes in their job history and forget to change the old phone numbers or addresses.

**Title of the form.** "Resume" or "Resume of Working Experience" identifies the purpose of the form. In the past some have started with an objective statement to lead things off. Today this is being replaced with a branding statement that was discussed earlier in this eBook. The branding statement is more powerful and sets you apart from those whose objective is to get a job.

**Date listing.** The date for your employment should be month and year. If you are still currently working then you would put down the starting month/year and then just put "present" where you would normally put the ending month/year. Putting this information on the side allows the hiring manager to see this information without having to read through your whole resume.

**Job data.** List your last position with title and the name of the company or organization with their location (city, state).

**Job description.** This area is for you to highlight your accomplishments. Don't use it to list your job responsibilities. Hiring managers are not interested in your responsibilities, only what you accomplished that can be quantified or qualified.

**Education.** This area will list your education starting with your most recent degree or certificate. If you have a master's degree in business, chances are they are not interested in where you attended elementary school.

**Military service.** If you have served in the military you should list the branch, your highest rank, and any special skills that you acquired while serving.

**Other skills.** This area is where you would list any other languages you speak, the computer programs you know, and other items that might interest a hiring manager that relate to the job being offered.

You could add a line for references and state they will be provided upon request. Make sure you have them available on a separate sheet of paper in case they do request the information. As for any personal information such as marital status, children, hobbies, etc., don't put these items on your resume. They have nothing to do with your job qualifications for the job you are seeking. As for salary desired, just leave it off. Instead, ask them what they would normally pay someone with your qualifications in that position. Let them make the first offer so you will know if it might be close to what you would be willing to accept.

Make sure that you focus on your accomplishments made in your last job. Be sure to use numbers, percentages, and money figures to support your statements. Begin your statements with strong action verbs. Give the impression that you are an active employee and not just a clock puncher. Remember to write your qualifications to show what you can do for the organization. Avoid telling them what you expect from them.

Show your expertise in your career field by listing any trade associations or affiliations where you are a participating member. This shows the hiring manager that you are serious and passionate about your job. Stick to the relevant experience you have with the job you are applying for. Stay focused and don't waste your time going off on any tangents that will distract the hiring manager.

If you have recently graduated from college, or a technical school, make sure to list your academic highlights. This can also include any professional development, on-the-job training, internships, or continuing education classes. This lets them know that you are very aware of the importance to keep up with what is going on in your industry.

If it doesn't fit or sound right, leave it out. Don't add fluff to make it seem like you have done more than you have. Any interviewer can see through it with just a couple of questions. If it is apparent that you have added to your resume they might begin to wonder what you have added to your other documents. Keep your resume concise and to the point. Take time and review the following pages that will have examples of each of the resume types discussed in this section. Following the samples the concluding paragraphs will give you some more information on how to make your resume stand out above the others.

# Chronological Resume Sample

**Jane Jobseeker**
123 N. Main Street
Homeville, California 90026
(323) 555-1212 - janejobseeker@mynet.com

**Resume of Working Experience**

7/2007 to present     **Head Cashier, Ralph's Discount Store, Homeville, CA**
Trained new cashiers in proper register protocols and in customer service procedures. Created a customer service program that increased customer satisfaction by 28% during the first year. Scheduled work shifts and vacation time for 18 employees and worked with accounting to ensure payroll was accurate and produced on time.

3/2005 to 6/2007     **Waitress, Maria's Mexican Grill, Homeville, CA**
Served customers by recommending and explaining the various menu options. Built a loyal following of over 35 customers who made reservations to be seated at my tables.

7/2004 to 2/2005     **File Clerk, Homeville Hardware Store, Homeville, CA**
Filed invoices and purchase orders. Worked with sales manager to reduce 24% of the time in receiving the sales representative's paperwork. Improved the invoice payment cycle by 4 days by placing invoices in the accounts payable register as they arrived daily.

**Education**

Homeville College, Homeville, CA - 2 semesters of general education courses
Homeville High School, Homeville, CA - Graduated 6/2004

**Skills**

MSWord, Excel, PowerPoint, 10 Key, Windows XP, Vista, 7.

**References**

Available on request.

Type Font on sample: Adobe Garamond Pro (similar fonts: Century, Times, Palatino)

# Functional or Skills Resume Sample

**Robert Wannajob**
1830 N. State Street
Homeville, California 90026
(323) 555-2468 - bob.wannajob@mynet.com

**Experience and Accomplishments**

**Organization:** Reduced department costs by 32% through implementing an inventory control and purchasing program by removing duplication of items and the quantities ordered.

**Creative:** Established a team concept approach to better serve the clients that resulted in increasing from 7 out of 10 projects completed on time to 9 out of 10 projects finished before or on time. This resulted in an 18% increase in customer satisfaction.

**Supervision:** Managed 4 teams of 5 graphic artists each that served 12 clients that represented 39% of the company sales. Collaborated with the sales department and each team resulting in a 15% increase in sales over the previous year.

**Client Contact:** Worked jointly with the sales department to develop 19 more customers that added an additional $204,000.00 in sales in 1 year.

**Employment**

| | |
|---|---|
| 8/2003 to present | Account Supervisor, Highland Advertising Co., Homeville, CA |
| 1/1999 to 7/2003 | Sales Manager, York Publishing, Homeville, CA |
| 4/1996 to 12/1998 | Salesman, Sussex Printing Inc., Homeville, CA |
| 9/1993 to 3/1996 | Assistant Ad Sales Lead, Gene's Advertising, Homeville, CA |

**Education**

Bachelor's Degree in Business Management, Homeville College, Homeville, CA

**What I Can Do For You**

Strong communication skills, customer service abilities, sales experience, and professional contacts. I can hit the ground running.

Type Font on sample: Calibri (similar fonts: Arial, Myriad Pro, Tahoma)

# Historical or Anecdotal Resume Sample

**Betty Needwork**
4321 S. First Avenue
Homeville, California 90026
(323) 555-9876 - bettyn@mynet.com

20 March 2014

Mr. James Hyring
Human Resource Manager
Market Pros of Homeville
7632 N. Lincoln Avenue
Homeville, CA 90026

Dear Mr. Hyring,

    I am a marketing professional with eight years experience at a Fortune 1000 marketing company and I am responding to your job posting for a marketing assistant at Market Pros of Homeville. I have followed closely your fast-growing company and I am uniquely qualified to respond to the challenges of such growth. In my last job, the budgets of the marketing programs I worked on grew from $1,300,000.00 to over $10,800,000.00.

    I have directed a team of 12 marketing specialists that were able to meet client deadlines within budget over 98% of the time. I was also able to improved customer satisfaction by 16% in 1 year by developing a customer contact calendar. I oversaw the company's expansion and recruited 23 top marketing professionals into the Northeast that resulted in additional sales of over $750,000.00 in 12 months. I have successfully handled the launch of a major product line from one of our accounts that surpassed the anticipated sales goal for the first quarter by over 45%.

    I have a Bachelor's of Science degree in economics with a minor in finance.

    What can I do for Market Pros of Homeville? I can bring a professional track record of accomplishment in meeting deadlines, increasing sales, recruiting new talent, and improving customer satisfaction.

Sincerely,


Betty Needwork

---

Type Font on sample: Palatino (similar fonts: Garamond, Century, Times)

# Limited Experience or Ready to Start Resume Sample

**John Startnow**
711 W. Hope Road
Homeville, California 90026
(323) 555-7733 - startnow.john@mynet.com

**Resume**

7/2013 to present    Sales Associate, Bill's Mobile Phone Sales, Homeville, CA

Provided customer service by handling returns and sales. Helped to meet and beat store monthly sales goals by 22% on average monthly for 6 consecutive months. Reduced theft and shoplifting in the store by suggesting the doubling of sales associates' presence on the sales floor and thereby increased profit margins by 12% in 6 months.

**Education**

Currently enrolled in general education courses at Homeville College, Homeville, CA. Expected to achieve an Associate's Degree in business in the Spring of 2016.

Homeville High School, Homeville, CA. Graduated 2013.

**Skills**

Bilingual:            English and Spanish, read, write, and speak.
Computer Skills:      MS Word, Excel, Windows, and Internet
Typing:               30 words per minute

**What I Can Do for You**

Customer focused, dedicated to increasing business knowledge, goal oriented, and ready to move forward.

Type Font on sample: Arial (similar fonts: Calibri, Myriad Pro, Tahoma)

The samples were presented using various fonts so you can see how each might look on a resume. Those mentioned are easy to read and can be found in most word processing programs. Use the font's bold face for headlines and items you want to stand out. Italics are much harder to read and should be avoided when possible. It is possible to combine a serif faced font with a sans-serif faced font in moderation. Myriad Pro can be used in places where you would use a Garamond bold font, leaving the Garamond regular font for the body of text. A good rule of thumb is not to mix three or more fonts in a document.

No matter what resume type, style, or format you choose to use, make sure that you follow the suggestions contained within this eBook section. Time has proven these techniques to be effective in helping job seekers get to the interview part of the employment process. If you find that you are not getting any calls for an interview, check your resume and see if you have a weak spot that is costing you interview opportunities. It only takes just a little more effort to craft a well-written resume as it does to fill in a resume template that might not get you the interview.

Remember, if you address the needs of the organization you will have a much better chance of getting an interview. Think in terms of meeting what qualifications the organization is looking for. Then you can highlight your accomplishments that will show that you are qualified for the job.

There is a **Resume Worksheet (See Appendix - Resume Worksheet)** that you can use to help write and structure a proper resume.

In the next section you will learn about words that have power to attract attention and help define your accomplishments.

# Section 10

# Words That Have Power

Words have power. Action verbs have power that can help state what you are doing now or have done in the past. They can speak to ownership of your accomplishments and qualifications that can help you get an interview for the job you are seeking. There are many other verbs that can be used just as effectively as those presented here. Use the action verb that best describes your abilities to get things done and what you have accomplished. These words work best with the quantifiers and qualifiers you will use to support the results you have achieved.

You will find the power words arranged by association to a particular category. Notice that many of the power words can be used in a number of categories. There are many more power words that you could use. You are not limited to the power words that are listed in this section. As you write your power statements and sentences try using a different power word to see how it works. Some words will improve your message more than others. Choose the best word or words to express your qualifications and accomplishments. Get the hiring manager's attention by using power words.

The categories listed are a grouping of words that describe what you have accomplished or a qualification you possess. If one of your strengths or an accomplishment relates to your ability to communicate you can make a selection from the communication category.

# Communication

| | | | |
|---|---|---|---|
| Advertised | Developed | Instructed | Recruited |
| Addressed | Directed | Interpreted | Redirected |
| Arbitrated | Discussed | Lectured | Referred |
| Arranged | Displayed | Mediated | Related |
| Authored | Distributed | Moderated | Represented |
| Called | Drafted | Negotiated | Showed |
| Circulated | Edited | Oriented | Spoke |
| Coached | Emphasized | Persuaded | Translated |
| Collaborated | Enlisted | Presented | Transmitted |
| Communicated | Familiarized | Promoted | Tutored |
| Conferred | Formulated | Publicized | Wrote |
| Convinced | Influenced | Recommended | |
| Corresponded | Informed | Reconciled | |

If you have creative talent you should include a power statement of what you have accomplished. You can identify the project where you have used your talent and how that talent benefited the department or organization. Many hiring managers like to hire creative individuals. They tend to bring fresh ideas to the table which sparks more creative thinking.

# Creativity

| | | | |
|---|---|---|---|
| Acted | Developed | Initiated | Proposed |
| Adapted | Directed | Instituted | Researched |
| Authored | Established | Integrated | Revised |
| Composed | Estimated | Introduced | Revitalized |
| Conceived | Fashioned | Invented | Set up |
| Conceptualized | Forecasted | Investigated | Shaped |
| Created | Formulated | Originated | Studied |
| Customized | Founded | Performed | |
| Designed | Illustrated | Planned | |

If you are a self-starter or a take-charge sort of individual this is a display of initiative. Managers like employees who show initiative and don't have to be told what to do all the time. If this category fits your personality then be sure to use these words to show that you have the initiative to get the job done.

# Initiative

| | | | |
|---|---|---|---|
| Acted | Established | Inventoried | Reviewed |
| Attended | Examined | Maintained | Shipped |
| Automated | Expedited | Monitored | Solicited |
| Collected | Founded | Moved | Sorted |
| Compiled | Handled | Operated | Submitted |
| Considered | Implemented | Packaged | Systematized |
| Contemplated | Increased | Participated | Trained |
| Delivered | Induced | Performed | Utilized |
| Developed | Inspected | Processed | Verified |
| Discharged | Instituted | Provided | |
| Engaged | Insured | Received | |
| Engineered | Interviewed | Recruited | |

Most employers love to have workers who are organized. These are the individuals who can prioritize their work so they are always productive. If you are an organized person then be sure to use some of these words to describe yourself and your accomplishments.

# Organization

| | | | |
|---|---|---|---|
| Allocated | Coordinated | Guided | Reconciled |
| Analyzed | Delegated | Handled | Recorded |
| Arranged | Detailed | Headed | Reorganized |
| Assembled | Developed | Managed | Reported |
| Authored | Directed | Organized | Reviewed |
| Balanced | Evaluated | Outlined | Scheduled |
| Budgeted | Extracted | Oversaw | Structured |
| Calculated | Forecasted | Planned | Wrote |
| Calendared | Formed | Prepared | |
| Computed | Formulated | Prioritized | |
| Consolidated | Gathered | Projected | |
| Controlled | Generated | Purchased | |

How well you relate to others in the workplace is important. Do you work well with others? Do you share your time, talents, and knowledge with your co-workers? One thing the hiring manager is trying to assess beyond your qualifications is how well you might fit into the company's culture. Let them know that you are proud of the relationships you have built in the past.

# Relationships

| | | | |
|---|---|---|---|
| Accommodated | Contributed | Helpful | Reconciled |
| Adjusted | Cooperated | Inclusionary | Referred |
| Advised | Corresponded | Influenced | Rehabilitated |
| Advocated | Counselled | Joint effort | Related |
| Agreed | Demonstrated | Led | Represented |
| Arranged | Diagnosed | Mediated | Requested |
| Assessed | Educated | Mentored | Respected |
| Assisted | Encouraged | Moderated | Served |
| Authored | Enlisted | Modified | Shared |
| Clarified | Expedited | Motivated | Sharing |
| Coached | Facilitated | Negotiated | Sold |
| Collaborated | Familiarized | Personalized | Supportive |
| Common ground | Followed | Persuaded | Taught |
| Compassionate | Guided | Professionalism | Team player |
| Consulted | Harmonized | Provided | Trained |

Are you a leader or a follower? This category includes anyone who has ever supervised, managed, or led an organization. Some of the power words may not apply only to a supervisor, a manager, or the leader of a company. Many of the words can apply to almost any position you have ever held. Leadership and management are two separate concepts that share an overlap in duties and responsibilities.

Depending on the organization, some leaders will take a more prominent role in the day-to-day management of the organization. There are some organizations where the managers are expected to assume most of the leader's responsibilities. Normally, most organizations have a balance of power between the managers and the leaders. Managers usually know their boundaries and will manage their departments. This doesn't mean that they cannot be a leader also. Leaders usually do a better job at leading, having to deal with more visionary details of the business. There are plenty of words in the leadership category and you should use all that apply to your experience.

# Leadership

| | | | |
|---|---|---|---|
| Accomplished | Coordinated | Instructed | Regulated |
| Administered | Delegated | Led | Reported |
| Allocated | Designated | Managed | Represented |
| Analyzed | Developed | Marketed | Required |
| Appointed | Directed | Monitored | Researched |
| Appraised | Disapproved | Motivated | Resolved |
| Approved | Discharged | Negotiated | Retrieved |
| Assigned | Dispatched | Operated | Reviewed |
| Attained | Encouraged | Organized | Scheduled |
| Audited | Enforced | Overcame | Screened |
| Authorized | Evaluated | Oversaw | Secured |
| Awarded | Executed | Persuaded | Selected |
| Balanced | Forecasted | Planned | Set goals |
| Budgeted | Generated | Prepared | Specified |
| Calculated | Governed | Presided | Sponsored |
| Catalogued | Guided | Prioritized | Stipulated |
| Chaired | Headed | Processed | Strengthened |
| Classified | Hired | Produced | Supervised |
| Compiled | Implemented | Projected | Systemized |
| Computed | Improved | Purchased | Tabulated |
| Conducted | Increased | Recommended | Taught |
| Consolidated | Influenced | Recorded | Trained |
| Controlled | Inspected | Recruited | Validated |

The results you have achieved in the past are a fair indicator that you will continue to accomplish many more things in the future. This is the heart and soul of what you need to stress when you write your resume. Positive results are taken to the bank. Negative results can, and probably will, cost you your job. You may be a great communicator or be a very creative individual, however if you can't show any results for your efforts and have produced very little, why should the prospective employer think that you will suddenly change?

Results are what you have accomplished in your previous jobs. These are the results that you can identify exactly what you have contributed to the organization. The results should be stated in qualified and quantified terms to support your statements.

Pick the best word to begin describing your accomplishment and then support that statement.

# Results

| | | | |
|---|---|---|---|
| Accomplished | Customized | Helped | Reduced |
| Accounted | Demonstrated | Identified | Reinforced |
| Achieved | Designed | Illustrated | Repaired |
| Acquired | Developed | Improved | Replaced |
| Advanced | Directed | Increased | Resolved |
| Altered | Dismantled | Initiated | Restored |
| Answered | Doubled | Instituted | Revitalized |
| Attained | Earned | Integrated | Set up |
| Attracted | Eliminated | Invented | Shaped |
| Awarded | Enlarged | Manufactured | Solved |
| Benefited | Established | Marketed | Spearheaded |
| Built | Expanded | Obtained | Started |
| Changed | Fashioned | Originated | Strengthened |
| Clarified | Finished | Performed | Surpassed |
| Combined | Formed | Pioneered | Tested |
| Completed | Formulated | Planned | Transformed |
| Composed | Founded | Predicted | Tripled |
| Conceived | Fulfilled | Prevented | Turned around |
| Constructed | Generated | Produced | Upgraded |
| Created | Halved | Reconciled | Won |

You may wish to include some of your personal characteristics to your resume so the hiring manager will have a better idea of your personality. Here is a list of words that you can use. Never overstate your personal characteristics. They are more interested in your accomplishments and the results you have obtained over your working career.

# Personal Characteristics

| | | | |
|---|---|---|---|
| Accomplished | Demonstrative | Intellectual | Prudent |
| Active | Determined | Intelligent | Questioning |
| Adaptable | Diligent | Judicious | Quick-witted |
| Adventurous | Diplomatic | Knowledgeable | Rational |
| Analytical | Discreet | Level-headed | Reasonable |
| Approachable | Easygoing | Lively | Reflective |
| Artistic | Efficient | Logical | Relaxed |
| Astute | Empathetic | Loyal | Respectful |
| Attentive | Energetic | Mature | Responsive |
| Broadminded | Enthusiastic | Motivated | Sensitive |
| Business-like | Even-tempered | Non-judgmental | Serious |
| Careful | Fast learner | Objective | Sincere |
| Cheerful | Friendly | Open | Spontaneous |
| Committed | Generous | Optimistic | Stable |
| Competent | Good-natured | Organized | Sympathetic |
| Confident | Happy | Outgoing | Talented |
| Conscientious | Hardworking | Passionate | Thorough |
| Consistent | Helpful | Patient | Tolerant |
| Cooperative | Honest | Perceptive | Trainable |
| Courteous | Humorous | Persuasive | Trustworthy |
| Creative | Imaginative | Positive | Visionary |
| Credible | Impartial | Practical | Warm |
| Curious | Industrious | Proactive | Willing |
| Decisive | Innovative | Productive | |

The next section contains information about how to forward your resume to a prospective employer, and a sample cover letter you should send with every resume.

## Section 11

# Forwarding Your Resume

You may be asked to forward your resume as an attachment to the job application, an email attachment, or to post it to a particular website. Some organizations will request that you send it in the mail to the attention of an individual who will be involved with the decision regarding who to call in for an interview. You should always have a cover letter to go with your resume that should have some reinforcing statements of your qualifications for the job position being offered.

Most word processing programs can save a resume in a document file. Several of these word processing programs will also allow you to save the resume in a PDF file. Both the document file and PDF file can normally be attached to an email to be sent electronically. You should be given instructions on what type of file format you should use and how to use it.

If you are emailing your resume, you can put your cover letter in the body of the actual email. Make sure that you have identified the job position in which you have an interest. If you don't, you might get a call about another position that you wouldn't want and, in the meantime, the one you were interested in has now been filled. If you have been able to demonstrate that you have the qualifications to fill several open positions you might be asked if you would be interested in them also. This lets you know that you have some additional options with the organization and they liked what they saw and would like you to be part of their team.

On the next page you will find a sample cover letter. You will be able to see how the cover letter is composed and how things are to be stated. Like your resume it is important to highlight your accomplishments and show how relevant they are to the position you are interested in. Both the resume and cover letter should be written specifically for each position you are applying for. There is no one-size-fits-all resume or cover letter. Take the time to make them unique to the position that has been posted. It will be well worth the extra time you spend in targeting them to the position.

Following the sample cover letter will be the conclusion and review section. After that you will find the resume worksheet to help you prepare a powerful resume that will get the results you want.

# Cover Letter Sample

Joyce Brighton
367 Snow Springs Drive
Homeville, California 90026
(323) 555-5584
joycejohnbrighton@mynet.com

24 March 2014

Mr. Earl Krandal
President
Krandal Department Store
272 N. State Street
Homeville, CA 90026

Dear Mr. Krandal,

I recently saw a job posting in the Homeville Times classified section stating you are in need of an Assistant Manager for the housewares department. I have been in retail sales for over 9 years and I know that I have the qualifications you are looking for.

In the past year I developed a promotional campaign program that increased sales of our housewares by 65%. This was accomplished by matching products that are used at the same time while preparing meals. In collaboration with our vendors we were able to promote the campaign and increase our sales by $76,000.00 over a 3 month period and during this time the store customer traffic increased by 15%.

I took the lead in organizing product sales training classes to increase our sales staff's product knowledge which increased customer satisfaction by 43% in 6 months. Sales also showed an increase by $175,000.00 due to the acquired skills our sales staff had learned.

Based upon my experience and accomplishments I feel that I would be a perfect match for the qualifications you are looking for in an assistant manager. I have enclosed my resume to provide you with more information regarding my qualifications, abilities, and accomplishments. I look forward to hearing from you soon.

Sincerely,


Joyce Brighton

Type Font on sample: Times Roman (similar fonts: Garamond, Century, Palatino)

# Section 12

# Conclusion And Review

A resume is a document that speaks for you about your qualifications, accomplishments, work history, and education. It needs to be an accurate record so a prospective employer can see if you have what they are looking for in a job applicant to advance to the next level of the hiring process. Similar to a curriculum vitae (CV), it will have all the information required to determine if you are qualified for the position. The difference is that a resume is no more than two pages, while a curriculum vitae is no less than three pages. CV's are used for international job opportunities or for job offerings in the United States in the education, research, scientific, or academic fields.

A cover letter should be sent together with every resume you send out that is written specifically for the position being advertised. The resume should also target a particular position and not try to be a one-size-fits-all. There are many myths or lies circulating around about what should be on a resume and some off-the-wall unwritten rules that must be followed. There are some general conventions about what should be covered in a resume, however there are no firm and fast rules that they must be exact or else. To the contrary, if your resume is not in a proper format it may be rejected, but not necessarily.

In times past, one would state at the top of the resume an objective. All applicants have the objective of getting a job. The best way to differentiate you from all the other applicants is to have your own personal branding statement that identifies what you have to offer the employer to meet their needs. It is about what they want that counts. Not what you want.

Your resume should be a document free of any errors. This includes spelling and grammar. Use the proper tense for the words you choose. Be careful to make sure the format you use is easy to read and find the information the hiring manager needs to make an informed decision. Keep your writing on point and don't add fluff just to make it look bigger. You need to show the results you accomplished. The hiring manager is not interested in your daily duties or what you were responsible for. They want to see how you accomplished what you did and how the results contributed to the organization.

Many individuals now have gaps in their work history time lines. This is not that bad if you can provide information on what you did while out of the workforce. Did you volunteer to help others? Did you return to school? Did you have to take care of a sick child or aging parents? There are many valid reasons for gaps in employment. Just taking a break from working is not considered to be a valid reason for not working for three years.

If the position for which you are applying will require you to relocate, be sure to think it out and consult with those who's lives will be impacted by your decision. There are good points to consider and there are some not so good points. Whatever you decide, make sure you are doing it for the right reasons. Don't just take it so you will be employed. If it doesn't work out you will be back to the starting gate once again, in a different location no less.

You should consider using a resume checklist to make sure that you have all the information required and that it is in the proper context. Use a type and style in the format that hiring managers expect. Above all else, keep it neat and clean so it can be easily read. Be sure to use power words to state your qualifications and the accomplishments you achieved.

Forward your resume in the prescribed manner that the organization has requested. It will be in your best interest to follow their procedures and policies rather than think they will accept yours.

Write, edit, proof, rewrite, reproof, etc. Do this again and again until it is flawless. What you send out is a reflection of you as an individual. If it is sloppy and disorganized, they will make the same judgment about you as an individual.

This eBook was written to help you write a powerful resume and we hope that you found it informative and that it will benefit you when you prepare your resume.

We hope that you enjoyed the **Rock Solid Resume** and will take the time to look at our other menu items at the **Job Seekers Café**.

*Thank you and come back soon!*

# Chapter 8

# The Power Burger

# Chapter 8
# The Power Burger

Build your own power statements to leave a lasting impression. Set yourself apart with this powerful ability to state your qualifications with confidence. Satisfy your interviewer's hunger for a well-spoken job candidate. Includes worksheets.

## Section Table of Contents

| | |
|---|---|
| Introduction | 239 |
| Power Statement Basics | 241 |
| Words That Have Power | 243 |
| Ownership Statements | 245 |
| Qualification Statements | 247 |
| Personality Statements | 249 |
| Branding Statements | 251 |
| Conclusion And Review | 253 |

# Section 1

# Introduction

Welcome to the **Job Seekers Café**. This menu item is entitled **The Power Burger**. This is a menu item that you will be able to use over and over throughout your job search activities. Power statements are what you will use to respond to questions, state your qualifications, and to take ownership of your accomplishments on your resume. They will also emphasize what you are bringing to the table when you deliver your Me In Thirty Seconds.

When used properly, your power statements will state your case by projecting and demonstrating self-confidence. In this eBook you will learn how to craft your power statements using power words that will have a lasting impression on a hiring manager. You will also learn how to put power statements into your resume, your Me In Thirty Seconds, and how to use them in responding to interview questions.

You will notice that on the outer margins of this and most other pages there are Scholar Margins, where you can make notes or comments about what impressed you when reading the material. Perhaps you might have a question and you will put a question mark to remind you that you need to find clarification of the text and the concept presented.

With an 'arsenal' of power statements you will be able to 'fire' back the best response to any inquiry. Once you have created and perfected a dozen or so power statements you should be able to 'craft' them on the fly to be more focused on your reply.

In this eBook you will find a list of power words that you can use to describe your personality, skills, abilities, and accomplishments. Resumes and answers to questions that sound like they have been a cut and paste of generic online documents will actually cause more harm to your chances of getting the interview you will need to get hired. Be original and put some thought behind what you are stating. Seek help from others and use a 'collective' mind to polish your words and presentations.

Power statements are now being used as a branding statement. It is important to use them on your cover letters and while working on your network and resource list. Make sure that your power words that you are using are in the active voice and not the passive voice. When you speak or write in the passive voice you are projecting an impression that you are lacking some self-confidence. Your active voice will signal clearly that you are taking ownership of your statements and you are confident of your qualifications for the position.

This eBook might be one of the smallest in the series. However, page for page it has more power within it to help you get to an interview and a job offer than any of the other eBooks. Many will try to be 'natural' and just answer questions as they are asked, write statements they think that the hiring manager wants to hear, and not differentiate themselves from all the other applicants.

Take the time to prepare and practice using many power statements so you will be able to quickly respond and reinforce your qualifications every chance you get. They do not take that long to write, read, and perfect as you might think. Take a challenge after you have finished reading this eBook by taking 15 minutes and writing 5 power statements about your skills, abilities, personal traits, and accomplishments. Once you have some experience in writing them, you will only have to modify them to suit any particular situation.

Reference will be made throughout this eBook about concepts that can be found in some of the other **Job Seekers Café** menu items. While each eBook is a standalone publication about a given subject, the entire collection of menu items has been prepared to help a job seeker be totally prepared to reduce the time it takes to get a job.

# Section 2

# Power Statement Basics

Power statements are simple, concise, and to the point. There is no room for any fluff or unnecessary words. Their power comes from the words you choose to define and describe who you are, what you have accomplished, and your experiences, with authority and self-confidence.

There are two popular styles of power statements. Both styles are very similar in that they have three parts or components that make up the power statement. The difference between them is that one is often spoken while the other is often in a document such as a resume, cover letter, or in a script that is used for building your personal network and resource list.

The ownership power statement style is used mostly during a 'face-to-face' or 'over-the-phone' interaction when you are supporting your qualifications, your experience, or your accomplishments. These power statements begin with **"I am ..."**, **"I have ..."**, or **"I can ..."** when making statements to support your claims. After you have made the 'announcement' that you own the following information, you will provide an example of what you are claiming. In the next part of the power statement you will state the actions you took and then qualify or quantify the results you achieved.

The 'situation-action-results' power statement style is more often used in written communications such as resumes, branding statements, and cover letters. Here you will identify a situation, what action was taken by you, and the results you accomplished. In this style you will have to rely on the words you choose to 'speak' for you. Know the power words that will best 'speak' in your absence.

With both styles of power statements you have the same objective. Start with a 'bold' opening using key or power words to grab a listener's or reader's attention and draw them in so they will want to know more. As they listen to you speak or read your documentation, you will be providing them with positive qualifying or quantifying support to your key or power words.

When writing your power statements you must use an active voice. Don't be guilty of using a passive voice that will have you eliminated. The hiring manager is also making an evaluation on your communication skills. If you fail to demonstrate that you have a good command of the language they will stop listening to what you are saying. When they stop listening to you they will not hear how you have the qualifications they are asking for in the position posted.

In the following sections of this eBook you will be given examples of various power statements as they can be applied to your qualifications, experiences, and your personality. Power statements are a very powerful part of your job search preparation. The better prepared you are the quicker you will be able to get a job. Power statements are also a great tool to use to make that differentiation between all the applicants. Those who make the best use of the power statements are the ones who get the job offers.

In the next section you will be presented with lists of power words and the association they have to areas of experience, qualifications, and personality.

# Section 3

# Words That Have Power

Rather than reprint the entire section found beginning on page 235 in Chaper 7 of this book, we will refer you to turn back to that part of this book.

We hope that you were able to use the lword lists presented. Many of the words can be used in other categories. The lists are not to be considered as a limitation on what words you may choose to use. Just use an appropriate word to describe what it is in your message.

Try avoid many of the overused and 'beat-to-death' words that have seemed to have lost their impact. There are many words to choose from. Take the time to try several words to see what sounds and describes best what you are trying to convey.

In the next section we will cover ownership statements and learn why they are so powerful.

# Section 4

# Ownership Statements

Ownership power statements show that you are not afraid to take ownership and claim responsibility for what you have accomplished or what results were achieved due to your personal involvement. You begin your ownership statements with: **"I am ..."**, **"I have ..."**, or **"I can ..."** which says you own this statement and no one else can claim it. It is a great way to start off a conversation by demonstrating self-confidence with both the words you choose and the tone in which you deliver your message.

Your ownership power statements will have a key or power word that you will support by finishing your statement with quantifying and qualifying facts of the results achieved. You must write your own power statements using actual facts. (These are not to be a work of fiction.) You have many things that you have done in your current or most recent job. You will be able to refer to those things and back them by what you did and what results were achieved due in part to your leadership or participation as a team member.

The power statements you use should be relevant to the position you are applying for. If you are applying for a selling position you don't need to talk about a job you had as a security guard. It would be better to use a power statement about how you 'sold' someone on helping out as a volunteer for a worthy cause that you were engaged in. This at least would demonstrate your ability to 'sell' an idea or concept to someone else.

The following power statements are examples of ownership statements. Be careful not to copy or use them unless they fit your exact experience. It is time to be Joe Friday and just give the facts and nothing but the facts. If you go overboard, you will talk yourself right out of the job. The more you can individualize you own personal power statements the better. They should be unique to you and you alone. Avoid any power statement that sounds too generic. For one thing, you will diminish your credibility, giving the impression that you are not unique or the perfect fit for the position.

*'I am very dependable. I have only used one sick day in the past three years. I take great pride in being to work on time and getting my work done so others who depend on my completing my part can do their's in a timely manner. Thus our customers benefited by us delivering their projects on time."*

*'I have been a project manager for 15 years. I made it a point to select team members who could get the job done by using the individual's unique skills for various parts of the project. Each team member was able to provide input regarding all decisions and by having an open line of communication we as a team always completed our projects on time and under budget. We had a 95% customer satisfaction rating in an industry that has less than 65% customer satisfaction overall. I work with my team and they work with me.'*

*'I can handle customer complaints. In my last position I was always asked to get involved immediately if a customer had an issue with our products or service. I would listen to the customer and try to understand the underlying issue. Together we would come to a reasonable solution that was fair to the customer and to our company. Almost 95% of those who had a complaint continued to do business with us because I took the time to listen to them.'*

You can state your facts without shouting them. State them confidently and with conviction and they will be remembered. The hiring manager will be interviewing several candidates for the position and you want to make a favorable impression with your ownership power statements.

The next section will be about qualification power statements.

# Section 5

# Qualification Statements

Qualification power statements can be about your education in a specific area or your past experience that relates to the job position being offered. Just like the ownership power statements you are presenting the facts as to why you are the most qualified candidate. There will be other candidates that will be discussing their qualifications. However, they may not be making qualification power statements that will sum up their qualifications in a single statement. They might just ramble on about their qualifications trying to wear down the hiring manager or the interviewer. Be concise, be confident, and be to the point. This will demonstrate your organizational and communication skills which is what the interviewer is looking for in a candidate.

Your qualification power statements will also use key or power words to help you state more accurately your qualifications. Choose these words carefully so you will sound confident. Back up your qualifications with actual facts. It might be a degree you have earned in a particular discipline, a technical training certificate earned, or on-the-job experience you have accumulated over several years working in the industry. You might have some volunteer experience that will help support your qualifications for the position. Be sure that it is directly related to the job position being offered.

The following examples of qualification power statements will give you a better idea how you might be able to write your unique qualification power statements. Like the ownership power statements the qualification power statements must fit you individually. Don't try to take a qualification power statement off the Internet and be the eighteenth individual to use it applying for the same position. You are unique and you should present yourself as being such by making your qualification power statements fit you as an individual.

*'I supervised a department of 12 service technicians. Some had many years of*

*experience while there were a few who had less experience. I would review the service orders and would send the best qualified technician with one less experienced so the qualified technician could help train the other technician on how to best address the customer's issue. Not only were the customers pleased with the quality of service, they also noticed that we took pride in training all our technicians. Our retention of qualified technicians reduced our turnover in our service department by 84%.'*

*'As the accounts receivable manager I brought my team together to seek a solution to how we could reduce the time from sale to payment. We discussed several options and came up with a plan to work closer with our customers and keep in contact with them so we could better understand their particular situation. What resulted was an increase in sales by 27% in six months. Our sales department was kept informed of what we were doing and with their cooperation we reduced the payment time from 45 days to an average of 32 days in less than 4 months.'*

*'I have a doctoral degree in psychology with 12 years of private practice. I have worked with individuals from simple depression to multiple personalities. I am board certified and licensed to practice psychology in three states. I am the past president of the Nevada State Psychologist Association and have over 20 articles published in various trade journals distributed nationally.'*

Sometimes your qualification power statements will get a bit long. Not to worry, since they can be used as a Me In Thirty Seconds (also known as an Elevator Speech). You could modify the longer ones by shortening them to a specific topic or item. As a qualification power statement keep it less than thirty seconds if you can. Once you go over thirty seconds the hiring manager might begin to 'tune' you out.

We are all unique and each of us has qualifications that employers are looking for. Use qualification power statements to get the interviewer's attention and deliver an unforgettable message.

In the next section we will present personality power statements.

# Section 6

# Personality Statements

We each have our own unique and individual personality that makes us who we are. No two of us are exactly the same and the difference between each of us might be what separates one of us from further consideration as a job candidate. That doesn't mean that there is not a job out there where your personality will be accepted. It only means that you will have to keep looking until you find the right opportunity by finding an organization where you will make a perfect fit.

Think about all the various personalities that you see in your circle of friends. Some are timid, some are bold, some are daring, and others just go with the flow. What a hiring manager is trying to discover is the personality traits of the individual who will best fit in with the organizational culture. You see some companies where everyone is loud and aggressive. Others will be more subdued and will look for ways to help you find the product or service that will meet your requirements.

In writing or creating your personality power statements you have to be honest. Don't stretch the truth to make you seem something different than you are. If you are quiet and reserved that is not a problem, just try to tie in another personality trait that the hiring manager will find of greater value. For example, you are quiet and reserved yet you take time to study the situation so you have a better understanding on how to proceed, keeping mistakes to a minimum.

Review the following examples and see how they might provide you with a foundation to write your own unique personality power statements.

*'I am a quiet individual who is always looking for better ways to improve customer relations. I am a good listener and want to really know the issue before making a decision that would not be in the best interest of the customer and the company. In my previous jobs many customers knew that I would listen to them*

*and as a result they would seek me out and I would help them understand which product would best suit their requirements.'*

*'I am proactive in greeting customers as soon as they come into my department. I know how I like to be treated and I make it point to treat my customers even better.'*

*'I am known as the happy one wherever I have worked. I always look at the brighter side of life. I know that it has influenced those around me to take a more optimistic view about life being good. Sure we all have down days and most of that can be attributed to our attitude. A happy attitude is contagious, and perfectly fine to spread around.'*

Personality power statements will not normally use any qualifying or quantifying support. The support given to the statement is how you present it. Do you state it with confidence and assurance? If not, it will not sound credible. Don't be afraid to stand up for yourself and who you are. Personality is important and if you have the personality that will work well with the culture of the organization then you have a good chance of getting the job.

Look at the personal characteristics section on page 10 of this eBook. Find as many of the traits listed that you feel best will describe who you are in regards to your personality. Write as many personality power statements as you can. Practice them until you can state them with total confidence.

The next section covers branding statements.

# Section 7

# Branding Statements

Branding statements are condensed power statements that will normally be found at the top of a resume or in a cover letter stating what you have to offer a prospective employer. Branding statements are powerful because they are very concise and only list the important key points about what you have to offer.

There are branding statements that have been created by just reviewing your other power statements and taking the important facts and putting them into a very condensed sentence or list of attributes. Don't try to write your life's history as your branding statement. It will not get read and it might just cause the hiring manager to move to the next resume and job candidate.

Some hiring managers might ask you to describe yourself in only five words. Which five words would you use? If you have written a good branding statement you could pick five words from it to respond to the request. This will also show consistency in your words, both spoken and in your written documents. Consistency is a good thing.

Branding statements have replaced the objective statements once used on resumes or cover letters. It is a given that your objective is to get a job. So why state the obvious? Using a branding statement will differentiate you from all the other candidates. In just a few words or lines you will be able to say so much more about your qualifications and what you can bring to the job.

The following are examples of branding statements. You will see there are several ways in which they can be written. Here again, you want to be factual so you can offer support if asked for more information. Don't just put things down that you think sound good. They are only good if you can give support to the claim you are making. Remember to keep your branding statements relative to the position you are applying for or else they will confuse the hiring manager.

*Dedicated sales professional with a track record of increasing sales and customer satisfaction.*

*Strong communication skills, customer service abilities, sales experience, professional contacts.*

*Professional, a track record of meeting deadlines, increasing sales, recruiting new talent, improving customer satisfaction.*

*Customer focused, dedicated to increasing business knowledge, goal oriented, and ready to move forward.*

*Currently licensed as a professional insurance agent, bonded, loyal customer following, dedicated to providing five-star service to my customers.*

*Current teaching certificate, bilingual, creative, thoughtful, patient with children.*

*Master's degree in business management, domestic and global logistical support experience, willing to relocate.*

*Cashier certified, trained supervisor, detail oriented, provides exceptional customer service.*

Keep your branding statements simple, concise, and relative to the job position being offered. Be selective in the words you choose to use. You can also add to the branding statement items, like if you are willing to relocate or willing to travel. Just be careful that you don't put yourself in a corner and regret making a branding statement you can't or won't be able to support.

You may want to use the **Power Statement Worksheet (See Appendix - Power Statement Worksheet)** to write your power statements. Write as many as you can and be creative using different power words. You will be surprised at how a change of a word can make a big difference.

The next section is the conclusion and review for this chapter. Following that section.

# Section 8

# Conclusion And Review

Your communication skills are demonstrated with every method you employ to inform others about your qualifications, experiences, and what you have to offer a prospective employer. The words you choose, in writing or speaking, will be perceived as a reflection on your ability to communicate effectively. Use the best choice of words to give power to your statements along with a sense of confidence. By taking ownership of those statements you will make a positive impression on any hiring manager.

This eBook has been presented so you will be able to understand the importance of the power of the words you use. It should help you begin to think in terms of how you want to construct your statements and replies to interview questions. Being prepared by having written down your own answers to interview questions or in answering any inquiry about you will show that you are taking your job search activities seriously. Nothing is more annoying to a hiring manager than to have a prospective candidate stumbling around trying to think of an answer to a simple question.

Prospective job candidates that demonstrate their ability to communicate orally and in writing, answering questions promptly, succinctly, and with authority, will have a measurable advantage over the other less-prepared candidates. Most interviews are less than an hour. You must however, spend enough time to thoughtfully work on your power statements so they will be well crafted and be delivered to get the results you are seeking. You must have enough power statements to cover a range of situations and responses to demonstrate that you can be direct and to the point. The more power statements you have in your 'arsenal' the better you will have to draw from to properly respond to an inquiry. You will also discover that you will have the ability, due to being familiar with the concept of power statements, to formulate them 'on-the-spot' for any question you might be asked.

To demonstrate that you take ownership of your statements you can begin each one with one of the following introductory phrases: *"I am ..."*, *"I have ..."*, or *"I can ..."*. You will then present support to what you have done, accomplished, and the results of your efforts. Be careful not to come off as not being a team player. If your results were because of a team effort, give credit to the team for the results. Just be sure to highlight your involvement as having played a significant role in obtaining those results. You should write your power statements in the 'situation-action-results' style that will give background, what was done, and what results were achieved.

Power statements should begin with some powerful keywords that will grab attention. Once you have their attention give support to what claim you are making. Use an active voice in the choice of words you will use.

In this eBook you have been given a section, Words That Have Power, to help you use specific words to help you state your case. While they have been presented in various groupings, many of the words can be used in nearly every category. Try different words until you find the one that will best convey your message.

Practice writing and speaking your power statements until they sound natural and not like a 'canned' response. Make them specific and individualize them to you. Make sure that you are making statements that will convince the hiring manager that you are the best qualified candidate for the position.

We hope that you enjoyed reading **The Power Burger** and will take the time to look at our other menu items at the **Job Seekers Café**.

*Thank you and come back soon!*

# Chapter 9

# Thirty Second Sandwich

# Chapter 9
# Thirty Second Sandwich

Get an interviewer's full attention with this confident and powerful 'elevator' speech. Get right to the point to make a solid presentation about your qualifications for the job. Learn how to select the right words for any given situation.

## Section Table of Contents

| | |
|---|---|
| Introduction | 259 |
| Me In Thirty Seconds - Defined | 261 |
| Where To Begin | 263 |
| Putting The Pieces Together | 265 |
| Adapting Your Speech | 269 |
| Engaging Your Speech | 271 |
| Taking Your Elevator To The Next Level | 273 |
| Speeches For All Occasions | 275 |
| Conclusion And Review | 279 |

# Section 1

# Introduction

Welcome to the **Job Seekers Café**. This menu item is entitled **Thirty Second Sandwich.** This menu item will certainly hit the spot, and can be used in multiple job search activities. Your Me In Thirty Seconds (Elevator) speech can be used when you are networking to build a list of contacts that can help you learn where job opportunities exist. You can also use it during interviews or when asked to speak about your qualifications or who you are. A Me In Thirty Seconds speech is nothing more than a thirty second 'spot' commercial that is trying to sell who you are and what you can do for an organization.

Those who learn to master the Me In Thirty Seconds speech certainly have an advantage over other job candidates. A well-written Me In Thirty Seconds speech will speak for itself in allowing the hiring manager or interviewer to see and hear your organizational and communication skills. When delivered with confidence it will be long remembered and become the standard by which all other candidates will be measured.

You will notice that on the right side of this and most other pages there are Scholar Margins, where you can make notes or comments about what impressed you when reading the material. Perhaps you might have a question and you will put a question mark to remind you that you need to find clarification of the text and the concept presented.

There are several types of Me In Thirty Seconds speeches that you will want to prepare and have at the ready to respond to the questions you will be asked. You should have several prepared to answer inquiries about your work related experience and qualifications. Others you might want to have prepared in advance are a few about you personally and what positive character traits you possess.

In the sections that follow you will be given information on how to write your Me In Thirty Seconds speech, how to modify them 'on-the-fly', and how to create one to fit the request being asked. They are easy once you understand the basic structure and the order in which to present the contents. When written properly they are very powerful tools to have on hand.

At the end of this eBook is a Me In Thirty Seconds Worksheet that you can use to create and craft your message. By the time you have read through this eBook you will be more than qualified to write and deliver a well-crafted Me In Thirty Seconds speech that will grab the attention of the hiring manager. This will take some effort on your part to write, rewrite, and revise your Me In Thirty Seconds speech several times. What you want is a polished presentation that you can deliver with confidence, full of all the information required to determine that you are the ideal job candidate for the position.

You will begin by learning what is a Me In Thirty Seconds speech. Then you will be shown how you can adapt your message to various situations and how certain key or power words can strengthen your message. This will be followed by the various places you will be able to use your Me In Thirty Seconds speech. Finally, you will learn how to take your Me In Thirty Seconds speech to the next level.

This eBook has been written to help those who have never heard of a Me In Thirty Seconds speech, as well as those who have used them in the past and are looking for ways to update and improve their message. No matter what level you are at, you should learn something that will help you create a very powerful Me In Thirty Seconds. This will get you recognized as being organized and a great communicator by making an impression on the interviewer.

Reference will be made throughout this eBook about concepts that can be found in some of the other **Job Seekers Café** menu items. While each eBook is a standalone publication about a given subject, the entire collection of menu items has been prepared to help a job seeker be totally prepared to reduce the time it takes to get a job.

# Section 2

# Me In Thrity Seconds - Defined

The Me In Thirty Seconds speech is also known as an Elevator Speech, so named because you are able to deliver the message in about the time it takes for an elevator to travel several floors. One important point about the Me In Thirty Seconds speech is when you use it you are now in control of the conversation or the interview. This is one reason that you have to perfect your speech so it will have staying power with the listener. An engaging Me In Thirty Seconds speech presented with confidence and authority will long be remembered.

Who uses a Me In Thirty Seconds speech and why? There are many opportunities to use a Me In Thirty Seconds speech. They are used by job seekers while networking, attending job fairs, and during job interviews. Salespeople will use them when meeting prospective customers in order to make a quick and informative introduction about themselves or their organization. The purpose of a Me In Thirty Seconds speech is to convey a specific message in a short period of time. If it is much longer than thirty seconds you will begin to lose your listener's attention.

When we are forced to fit our message into thirty seconds, we have to choose our words carefully. Picking the correct words can also make your message more powerful. There is magic in brevity. It can grab attention and say so much more with fewer words. This is why so many commercials you see on television and hear on the radio are about thirty seconds long. They know that you will tune them out if they go beyond a certain amount of time.

A Me In Thirty Seconds is used to identify your interests, experiences, strengths, accomplishments, or goals when used in a job-seeking environment. In a business setting it will let the prospective customer know about you, the organization you work for, and what products or services you can provide to help them accomplish their goals and objectives.

There are several styles or types of Me In Thirty Seconds that you can use. Be sure to use the appropriate one that applies to the situation. When asked in a job interview to *'Tell me something about yourself'*, you will need to steer your answer so it relates to the position being offered. It will still need to include some personality traits that you can bring to the table that will benefit the organization. If asked to *'Describe how your background and experience makes you qualified for the position'*, you will need to have a different Me In Thirty Seconds ready to go that will give 'facts' why you think you are qualified for the position. Don't try to give opinions why you feel you are qualified. Facts go to the bank, opinions are tossed out. Another request might be asked to *'Tell me about your education and how it relates to the position'*. Here is where you want to make sure that your speech is in line with whatever educational requirements were posted regarding the position.

Each situation will require a slightly different Me In Thirty Seconds speech, so you will need to be prepared. Perhaps the interviewer wants to see how you react under pressure and how quick you can think on your feet. If you are prepared for several different scenarios, you can modify them 'on-the-fly' to respond to almost any request made of you. Some interviewers might ask questions regarding your goals or future plans. Many a job candidate forgot to think about their goals. You must show how well prepared you are and how serious you have taken your job search activities by being able to answer this request.

If you are networking to find out where job opportunities exist, then you will have an introduction of who you are to start the Me In Thirty Seconds speech and at the end ask some networking questions. Everything in between will be a normal Me In Thirty Seconds speech. This is also the same for working job fairs or career days.

In a business sales situation you will also have an introduction of who you are unless you have already established a business relationship with the individual you are calling on.

Many things can be learned from a Me In Thirty Seconds speech. The interviewer will have a sense of your ability to communicate, your command of the language, and your degree of self-confidence. You may be a little nervous; that is to be expected. You are however, expected to be prepared and to be able to deliver your Me In Thirty Seconds in a professional, business-like manner.

The next section is about where you will need to begin.

# Section 3

# Where To Begin

You should begin with some lists that reflect the skills, abilities, talents, and personality characteristics that you feel will best describe who you are. The next set of lists should have what you have accomplished and what you did to achieve those results. Make another list of your qualifications which you have obtained through education, certified technical training, or on-the-job experience. A good place to start would be to review your power statements and your resume for some ideas. After all, a Me In Thirty Seconds speech is just a longer version of a power statement. Be careful not to make your Me In Thirty Seconds a rehash of your resume. They have read your resume. Bring in some new information for them to hear about you.

You will want to put some sort of 'hook' in the beginning of your speech to grab the listener's attention. Then state your message clearly and succinctly. Avoid rambling on and getting off track. Know what you want to say by preparing your Me In Thirty Seconds speech in advance. Practice it enough times so you let it flow in your natural voice. Don't let it come out like a 'canned' or 'scripted' message. Relax and be yourself. If you have practiced it enough times you will have no trouble sounding confident. If you are not prepared you will sound unsure of yourself.

Here is some good advice that few job seekers take. It takes a bit of extra research on your part, but it might make the difference between just getting an interview and getting the job. Find out what the organization is trying to accomplish with this position and find a way to tie in your experience and qualifications to set you apart from the other applicants. By putting this into your Me In Thirty Seconds they will be able to hear what you can do for them. Remember, you don't have to shout to be heard. Let the message flow with your confidence. You have their attention, so don't waste the opportunity.

You can also make a stronger impression if you can show how your 'hard' skills make you qualified for the position, and how your 'soft' skills show your ability to work as a team player, be a compassionate person, or your ability to take it to the next level. Most of the other job candidates have similar qualifications and experience by the time you get to the interview process. What you need to do is show your uniqueness and how you can bring more to the position.

Many employers are looking for individuals who recognize that personal growth and improvement are essential in moving forward. Organizations have goals and so do managers. People in the organization have both work-associated goals and personal goals. Both are important and should be in balance so they are not in conflict.

By now you should have some of the pieces of the Me In Thirty Seconds puzzle. Now is the time to start putting them together so they will make the picture whole. Begin with your lists and start with one work-related Me In Thirty Seconds speech. Since you are looking for a job this is a good place to start. Once you understand the construction of the Me In Thirty Seconds speech you will find it easier to write those about your personality traits, qualifications, education, experience, and goals.

In the next section you will begin to put the pieces together.

# Section 4

# Putting The Pieces Together

Begin putting your thoughts on paper. You can type them into the computer or you can go 'old-school' with pencil and paper. You will write, review, edit, rewrite, and proof it again and again before you have it perfected. Don't be discouraged because your first, second, third, or tenth draft is not perfect. Each draft will get you closer to where you want it to be.

Here is a good example of a Me In Thirty Seconds speech that would be used in a job interview situation (they have previously been introduced so there is no need to re-introduce themselves):

*'I began working in the construction business with my father when I was 16 years old. I later went to a community college to study drafting and then on to a four-year university to earn a bachelors degree in architecture. My qualifications come from having worked in construction, learning drafting, and earning a degree in architecture. I am uniquely qualified by my experience and education on how to build a single house to a major shopping center. From what I know about your company's goals, I can bring my experience and education to help you expand your business.'*

In this example the job candidate states his experience, qualifications, and education that identifies with the needs of the organization.

If you wanted to use this for networking to find opportunities for employment, you would add an introduction and make some changes to the last line.

*'Hello, my name is John Clayton and I began working in the construction business with my father when I was 16 years old. I later went to a community college to study drafting and then on to a four-year university to earn a bachelor's degree in architecture. My qualifications come from having worked in construction, learning drafting, and earning a degree in architecture. I am uniquely qualified*

by my experience and education on how to build a single house to a major shopping center. I feel that my education and experience make me uniquely qualified for a position in the construction industry.'

This Me In Thirty Seconds should be followed up with the three networking questions:

1. 'Do you know of any open positions in your company that might fit my qualifications?'

2. 'Can you recommend anyone who might hire or manage individuals who do what I do?'

3. 'Do you know two people who are employed in my field of experience who might be able to help me locate some job opportunities?

By asking these questions you will be able to increase your networking list and be able to practice your Me In Thirty Seconds speech several more times.

When writing your Me In Thirty Seconds speech you should use present tense action verbs. Your choice of power words is also important to grab attention.

If you are in a salesperson's position and wanted to use a Me In Thirty Seconds speech to secure an appointment to present your products and services, you would only have some slight modifications to make.

'Hello, I am David Brown with Impact Sales Corporation. Mr. Jefferies of your head office suggested that I meet with you and give you some information regarding some of our products and services. I have some brochures and information that you might find helpful in training your sales force in sales presentations, follow-up tracking, and after-the-sale-support. Mr. Jefferies has used our services and products for the past five years and reports that sales have been increased by 15% year over year by using our products in the home office. Would you be available next Wednesday morning for about 45 minutes?'

This could be used as a phone lead or even used at a business convention to introduce yourself and your organization to a prospective customer. The referral gives you credibility if you have been referred. If you have not been referred, don't say you were. Best to revise it to:

'Hello, I am David Brown with Impact Sales Corporation. I have some brochures and information that you might find helpful in training your sales force in sales presentations, follow-up tracking, and after-the-sale-support. Mr. Jefferies *from your home office has used our services and products for the past five years and reports that sales have been increased by 15% year over year by using our products. Would you be available next Wednesday morning for about 45 minutes?'*

Your Me In Thirty Seconds speech should be able to be revised and adjusted to fit the situation you find yourself in. You will only have to change a couple of words usually. Seldom do you have to go back to the drawing board and start all over. At the end of this eBook you will find a Me In Thirty Seconds Worksheet to help you write your messages. You can also find it online on our website, along with our other job seeker's forms that you can download for free. **(See Appendix - Me In Thirty Seconds Form)**

When you write your initial drafts, just write them out. Then go back and start to polish your message by changing words and descriptions. Be sure to give quantitative results of your accomplishments. Make sure to have a strong beginning with an attention-getting statement, backed up by the situation, the action taken, and the results obtained. End on a high note that will 'book-end' your message. Writing is only half the job. How you deliver it is just as important. The best-written Me In Thirty Seconds speech can be killed off by a poor presentation. A poorly written Me In Thirty Seconds speech is doomed before you can even present it.

Don't be afraid to ask for help. If you feel you are in over your head, then get some help. There are plenty of individuals out there who can and will help you prepare your Me In Thirty Seconds speech. Take advantage of this help so you can get the interview and the job.

You will have to practice reading out loud your Me In Thirty Seconds speech. You will have to time it to make sure that you are at or close to thirty seconds. If you are too short don't try to speak slowly to fill the time. If too long, don't try to speak faster. You want to deliver your message in a relaxed, confident, and natural voice.

Make sure that you are making statements you can back up with results. Don't make claims and leave them there hanging in the breeze. Interviewers have heard this many times before and can tell when someone is making a claim or a supportive statement.

Here are some examples to consider:

Claim: *'At my last job I was responsible for the entire sales for the company.'*

Statement: *'At my last job I was directly involved in increasing my sales by 25% over my goal, helping the company to achieve sales over the previous year by over 18%.'*

The statement quantifies the results of the action taken. You could use some qualitative statement, which would have less impact, to tell of awards, performance evaluations, education, or skills you have. The reason qualitative statements have less impact is that quantitative numbers is how business and results are measured. They are best describing results in quantitative terms like numbers, dollars, and percentages.

If you are new to the workforce you may not have many quantitative results to list. So you would use a qualitative statement such as:

*'I earned my bachelor's degree and was listed among those as having earned it with the highest of honors.'*

*'In my last job I was trained and certified to safely operate a forklift.'*

*'I currently use the Microsoft Office Suite of programs and I am skilled at using Adobe's InDesign and Photoshop. Do you use these programs here in your offices?'*

The last qualitative statement ends with a question. If they answer yes, then you have some skills they would be interested in having. If they answer no, they know you have the ability to learn computer programs and would still consider you as a possible candidate for the position.

The above examples are of sentences that you might be able to use. By themselves, they are not long enough to be considered a Me In Thirty Seconds speech. You could combine two or more with additional information that would build up to a Me In Thirty Seconds speech.

In the next section we will discuss adapting your speech to the situation.

# Section 5

# Adapting Your Speech

Once you have an idea how to structure your Me In Thirty Seconds speech you will find that there will be times when you have to adapt it to a particular situation. This is very easy when you understand up front that you might be faced with this possibility in a job interview. This is one reason you should have several Me In Thirty Seconds speeches written and ready to go when needed. There will be times when you will just have to modify it on the spot and we will help you understand how to do this.

You should note that your Me In Thirty Seconds speech is your own personal 'commercial' message. Each speech you write should be unique to you and you alone. Don't use someone else's. It won't sound like you and match up with other documentation and statements you have provided or made. You can use the format or the style, or maybe some of the verbiage, but you must still make it yours. You own this statement. You shouldn't want to use one that belongs to someone else. It might sound great, but it won't be yours.

During an interview you might be asked to explain how you handled a particular situation, or asked how you might handle a hypothetical scenario. Your answer could come in the form of a Me In Thirty Seconds speech that you would adapt to the request, tying in a strength you have or relating it to a similar situation that you actually experienced.

For example, say you were asked what you would do in a hypothetical scenario where your manager was not treating everyone fairly. Perhaps you had worked within a similar situation and could relate a story about how it was handled, or you could bring up your ability to tactfully approach the manager about the issue.

"Tell me how you would handle a scenario where your manager was not treating everyone fairly in your department."

*'In a previous job I had a manager who was treating some workers unfairly. Those he liked got the simpler projects. It would look like they were completing more work than the others. Then when performance reviews were held, higher marks went to those who completed the most projects. It finally came out in a staff meeting where several of those getting the lower marks spoke out about the work being unfairly assigned. I made a suggestion that work should be distributed based on project completion, thus getting the next project scheduled. Then it would be more luck of the draw and fairer.'*

The above example is good if you had experienced something similar in your past employment. If you did not have such an experience, the following example might give you some ideas how to respond to the request.

*'Fortunately I have never experienced a manager being unfair. If I were to have one, I believe I would be able to openly discuss my concerns in private with my manager, express my feelings, and perhaps offer some suggestions how project assignments could be made in the future. I am sure being more fair in assigning projects would result in improved productivity and morale within the department. I would want my manager to know that I am thinking about what is best for the customer and the company.'*

There is a certain rhythm and tone to writing a Me In Thirty Seconds speech. The more you write, the better you will be at adapting to the questions being asked. Sometimes it might be very hard to quantify your statements, but you can always qualify them drawing from your experiences. You can tell how your personality traits would help in finding a reasonable resolution of the situation.

The next section will be about engaging your speech.

# Section 6

# Engaging Your Speech

In this section you will be shown how to engage your speech so it will have the maximum impact. You have an important message to share and how you share it will determine the results you obtain. You have spent hours working on drafting your Me In Thirty Seconds speeches. Now is the time to have a critical review of them. Proofing is fine, but you will have to put in some time to edit the words to have the ability to engage your listener with your message.

Here are a couple of examples where you can see a first draft that is good, but how you can improve it to really engage your interviewer. In this example we will see how a retail sales associate can improve their message to engage in a conversation rather than giving 'flat' responses or answers to the questions.

*'I have five years of retail sales experience. I have supervised many associates and increased sales through my ability to make others feel comfortable. I listen to those I supervise and to my customers. This way I can see their side and see if together we can find a solution to the issue at hand. I keep my manager aware of how things are going and ask for advice when needed. I feel that I can be a great benefit to your company, if you will give me a chance.'*

There are many things being said in the above example, but they seem to be disjointed. By taking this first draft we can craft it to flow better, put the information in a logical thread, and engage the interviewer with a powerful closing sentence.

*'I have been in retail sales for five years. During this time I have been able to cultivate a loyal customer following because I listen to my customers. Because of my customer service skills I have been able to increase my personal sales by 27% in one year. I have supervised a staff of 12 sales associates and I used my skills of listening to help them achieve their work and store's goals. By working with those I supervise and training them in product knowledge there has been an increase in store sales by*

*31% in one year. My manager was always involved and helped me stay focused. Is this what you are looking for in the candidate who will fill this position?'*

As you can see, the second one has more engagement in how the information is presented. It engages the listener to show what results have been achieved and how they were obtained. At the end, a question is asked to get feedback from the interviewer. If this sort of performance is not wanted, then the hiring manager will have a tough time filling the position. This example is engaging because it reveals qualifications and results that have been quantified. It also asks for confirmation that you have met or exceeded the requirements of the job position to be filled.

When writing your Me In Thirty Seconds speeches be sure to make them engaging. They should grab and hold the interviewer's attention to every word, and every sentence, so they will listen intently for what you will say next. Get them involved in a conversation by asking a question when appropriate. By being conversational you will be relaxed and appear more confident. Conversation will allow you to be remembered more than those who give direct answers and nothing more.

The next section will cover how you can take your elevator to the next level.

# Section 7

# Taking Your Elevator To The Next Level

In this section we will show you how to elevate your Me In Thirty Seconds speech to the next level. Taking your speech to the next level is about using dialogue. We are not asking you to write a novel or a screenplay. We will show you how writing your speech's dialogue can increase your chances of moving you to the front of the 'candidate consideration' line. Some of this information may be new to you or perhaps you have taken some writing courses that spent some time on writing dialogue. In any case, we hope that this section will be of value to you in taking your speeches to the next level.

When considering how dialogue is used in writing novels or screenplays it is through the dialogue that the words will move the storyline. The same can be said about using dialogue to move your message. In writing a story that is moved by the dialogue, you must first know what it is you want to say. Then write your dialogue to keep the reader's (or in this case—the listener's) interest and have themon the edge of their seat to see what comes next.

Your Me In Thirty Seconds speech is 'your' story—or at least a small part of your life's story. Its purpose is to convey the message that you are qualified for the position being offered because of your education, experiences, and qualifications. You can also insert some of your positive character traits to help differentiate yourself from all the other candidates. You will have a limited amount of time to tell your story so you had best write and deliver your story so it will make an impression on anyone who hears it.

Your dialogue will be in the first person. Since you are talking about yourself this is understood that you will speak from your point of view. You are not doing a narrative about someone else. So make your words come from your life experiences. You can even place a first person voice to a hypothetical question if you are prepared. Just don't get creative and take credit for what you 'did' in the scenario. Nothing happened since it is only a hypothetical situation. You can, however, relate how a personality trait would guide you to find a solution. This can be by building a consensus from a group trying to seek resolution to an issue, or how you might demonstrate leadership by getting to know the situation and issues so you would have a better understanding. Once armed with the facts you would be able to propose an intelligent suggestion.

You are, in effect, writing a script that you will be delivering to an audience that will be making a judgment about you. You want to choose your words, tone, diction, and delivery carefully so that your message is received properly. Too many individuals will try to 'wing it' in an interview and end up stumbling over what they want to say. Their message is never delivered and so it is never heard. Practice (rehearse) as many times as you can until your message is delivered in your natural voice. Sound confident when you speak so the interviewer knows you are qualified.

It is important to remember that how you punctuate your Me In Thirty Seconds speech will also have an impact. Make sure that you don't run your words together so there is not enough time to let them sink in. Over the years there have been those who have tried to 'spit' it out so fast that their message was never heard.

For those who feel they can weave a story into their Me In Thirty Seconds speech be careful not to make the story overshadow your qualifications. You can tell your qualifications in a story form as long as it stays within the boundaries of a Me In Thirty Seconds. Don't take it to mean that you can tell a ten-minute story of something that happened at your last job. No matter how entertaining it might be, it is not relevant to the purpose of your Me In Thirty Seconds speech.

Remember that when you write your Me In Thirty Seconds speech, punctuate it so you can catch your breath and allow what was just said to be absorbed. Next, take the time to highlight those words that will need to be emphasized so they will stand out. Yes, it will seem a bit awkward in the beginning to say your Me In Thirty Seconds speech out loud, but the more you work on it by rewriting, editing, and emphasizing key words, it will be worth all the effort.

The next section will cover speeches for all occasions.

# Section 8

# Speeches For All Occasions

In this section we will show how a single Me In Thirty Seconds speech can be modified to be used in several situations. We would suggest that you take a Me In Thirty Seconds speech that you have written and practice modifying it to suit several situations. By doing this you will be better at modifying on the fly if you have to 'bend' your response to properly answer the request made.

We are going to take one of the examples used earlier in this eBook and see how we can modify it to suit several different inquiries. First, we will look at the Me In Thirty Seconds speech as it was presented.

*'I began working in the construction business with my father when I was 16 years old. I later went to a community college to study drafting and then on to a four-year university to earn a bachelor's degree in architecture. My qualifications come from having worked in construction, learning drafting, and earning a degree in architecture. I am uniquely qualified by my experience and education on how to build a single house to a major shopping center. From what I know about your company's goals, I can bring my experience and education to help you expand your business.'*

Now we want to take that same Me In Thirty Seconds speech and modify it to be elevated to the next level by creating some dialogue. It should sound more natural and conversational.

*'I was sixteen when I starting working in my father's construction business. He taught me the basics and suggested that I attend community college and study drafting. I continued with my education by earning a bachelor's degree in architecture. During the summer months I would work on houses, small commercial buildings, and major shopping centers. What I learned on the job combined with what I learned in the classroom makes me qualified for the position of assistant project manager. I know there is plenty of value that I can bring to your company.'*

The above example tends to show a more relaxed and confident tone. Both examples are basically stating the same thing. Even though the first example was a rewrite of the original first draft, you can see it is possible to continue to refine and improve your Me In Thirty Seconds speech. What words you will choose to emphasize will also help to make this more conversational and not a 'straight' reading of a press release.

Next we will see how to change from a job interview Me In Thirty Seconds speech to one about your personality. Some interviewers like to ask about your job qualifications and then about your personality. You might think that they are trying to mess with your mind, and maybe so. Don't use the same Me In Thirty Seconds speech. Change things up enough so they sound like you have more than one speech and can respond without hesitation. Both will highlight qualifications for the job. The personality traits you want to tell them are those that will show that you are a team player and that you get along with your fellow workers.

*'I have spent the past eight years working as an accounts payable manager. During this time I have supervised eleven accountants. I worked directly with the five largest suppliers to make sure our bills were paid on time and appropriate discounts taken when allowed. As a result the company was able to save over two percent on our purchases which generated a savings of over $50,000.00 each year. I enjoyed having a personal and professional working relationship with our suppliers.'*

The above Me In Thirty Seconds speech states several work-related qualifications and mentions the personal relationships she cultivated with the suppliers. Now let's look at how this could be transformed into a personality Me In Thirty Seconds to highlight your character traits.

*'While supervising the accounts payable department I worked with each member of the team, helping them in their professional development. I enjoyed teaching the new accountants how things were done in the office. I helped the older members of the department level out their workloads so no one felt overwhelmed. Many of us in the department enjoyed reading the same authors and we formed an informal group where we would share our books with each other. There always seemed to be a feeling that we were a family.'*

In the above example you will note that there were still some ties related to the work environment. Yet, it also goes on to state that they enjoyed teaching, helping others, and sharing their books. An interviewer could draw from this Me In Thirty Seconds speech that the individual had a close enough relationship with each member of the department that there was a sense of family cultivated.

## Chapter 9 - Thirty Second Sandwich

It also indicates that the individual is a reader while not at work. There was also concern shown that no one in the department was being overworked.

In the next set of examples we will see how you might answer the following inquiries about your personal life. The interviewer is not prying, only trying to get a sense if you will be a good fit into the company's culture. In the first example the question was, 'Tell me what you like to do to relax' (or what do you do on your time away from work). This again is to see if your personality will match that of the company's culture.

*'I really enjoy backpacking on the weekends. There are so many hiking trails in the local mountains that I have not yet hiked them all. It really gives me a chance to recharge myself. I enjoy my work during the week and the challenges it provides me for growth and development, however, I do like the sounds of nature to give me some balance in my life. I take photographs while on the trail and have even sold a few pictures of the wildlife I have encountered. I believe that nature and the physical challenges allow me to be more appreciative of what I do have, including my job.'*

In this example, while telling of what occupies their time, there is the realization that there is a purpose to how the weekends are enjoyed. Besides the backpacking, they are interested in photography. Through photography a willingness to share is also shown. Knowing how to relax is as important as knowing how to work hard. Keeping balance between the two facets of our lives is important.

In the next example, a question might be asked to tell of your dream vacation and when you would like to take it. If you say next year you are planning to go around the world sailing you might have just shot yourself in the foot. Not that it is a bad dream vacation, but it should be a long-range goal.

*'I have always wanted to see Alaska. I have been saving for the past several years a little something every payday for such a trip. I hope to save enough in the next couple of years so I will be able to afford a cruise through the Inside Passage so I could see the glaciers and cities like Skagway, Juneau, and Ketchikan. I enjoy checking out books from the library about Alaska and reading about the Native American tribes. I admire their artwork and totem pole carvings. They are really amazing. Perhaps I will be able to get there in about three more years of saving.'*

In this example you can see that the individual has a goal and is already working toward its accomplishment. There is no doubt about the individual's interest in this trip and the strong belief that they will get there in the near future. The individual has invested a great deal of time to the study of Alaska and has read enough about the cultural heritage of the state. The cruise would fit within a two-week vacation window easily.

In the following examples we will see how a sensitive question could be handled. For example, "What is one thing that you regret doing at your last job?" No one is perfect, and yet few will ever say or acknowledge that they have regrets about their past behavior or choices they have made. See how a negative can be easily turned into a more positive by the changing of our attitude.

*'I guess I would have to say it was not taking advantage of the company's 401K savings plan. I thought I could better manage my money than they could. Another worker who was hired on at the same time took full advantage of the program. When he left the company a year ago, I was shocked at how much he had saved. My Certificates of Deposit were not even close to what he had accumulated. I now know that I would be better off to participate in this type of program.'*

*'My one regret would be that I failed to take advantage of the educational assistance the company had available. I believe that since I didn't continue my education I was passed over for several promotions. Since leaving that company I have gone back to school on my own full-time to complete the degree I started six years ago. I now have my degree and feel that with my experience I can contribute more to any company that I will work for in the future.'*

*'This is a tough question. I was referred to the job by a friend who said it would be easy work. It wasn't and my friend was terminated shortly after I was hired. I did all I could to learn the business and the functions of my job. It seemed that I couldn't do enough to please my manager. It finally came to a point where we decided that this was not the job for me. I regret that I spent almost a year in a job that I had no idea of what I was getting into. So now I research the company and the position to make sure it is something that I can do and will enjoy.'*

You are not supposed to beat yourself up over some regret from a previous job. Do your best and all you can to improve the position you now have. Then you will be ready for the next level.

The next section will be the conclusion and review.

# Section 9

# Conclusion And Review

This section has been all about how you can write a proper Me In Thirty Seconds (Elevator) speech. The balance of who will be considered for hiring for any open position will go to the one individual who can confidently tell who they are and what they can do. This is why the Me In Thirty Seconds speech is so important. It must be written properly and delivered with confidence. There is no excuse for not having several well-prepared Me In Thirty Seconds speeches ready to respond to any inquiry.

The Me In Thirty Seconds speech is used while networking to find job opportunities for someone with your skills and talents. It is also used during the job interview process so the interviewer can learn more about you than what was submitted on your job application or resume. It is your chance to be actually heard. It will demonstrate your communication and organizational skills. Employers want articulate individuals who can express themselves.

Carefully consider every word you write. Choose the best word that can express and highlight your qualifications. There is a certain magic in being brief and to the point. Grab the interviewer's attention and keep it with a well-written Me In Thirty Seconds speech. Be prepared to answer correctly the inquiry that is being made. Don't think you can use the same Me In Thirty Seconds speech to answer or respond to every question. Give the impression that you have taken your job search activities seriously by being prepared.

Make lists of your qualifications, experience, and skills that will match up with the position requirements. Make lists that have your accomplishments and achievements. Don't forget about your education and any specialized training that you have completed. Finally, don't forget to list some of your more positive personality and character traits.

Be sure to highlight your qualifications and then give them support with quantitative results. Let them know that you were in a situation, took action and had some positive results that helped the organization. When telling about any awards, achievements, or honors you have received you can use qualifying statements of what you did to deserve the recognition.

Be prepared to write, proof, edit, and rewrite your Me In Thirty Seconds speech. You must perfect it in writing and then test the message, by practicing out loud. Listen carefully to how it sounds. Make sure that it flows smoothly and in your natural voice. If they wanted a robot they would not be conducting interviews.

Adapt your Me In Thirty Seconds speech so you can answer the question being asked. You might have to change it 'on-the-fly', so be prepared. How you present your message is just as important as to what you have written. Make sure that you engage your listeners so they will pay attention to what you are saying.

One of the best ways to really improve your Me In Thirty Seconds speech is to make it more conversational by correctly using dialogue to move your story forward. This will be a bit more work, but well worth the effort. Remember, everyone being interviewed is deemed to have enough qualifications for the position. Now they want to see how you sound, compose yourself, and your level of self-confidence.

Consider all the possible questions that you could be asked in a job interview and see if you can change your Me In Thirty Seconds speech to adapt the correct response. Ask others to listen to you give your Me In Thirty Seconds speechand ask for an honest opinion of how it sounded and what they thought about your delivery. Take no offense to what is said. They are only trying to help you improve your message and delivery so you can get the job.

Use the worksheet that can be found after this section. Make several copies. Write dozens of Me In Thirty Seconds speechesthat will cover all your work-related experiences, education, and skills. Then make some more that will highlight your personality traits. Most importantly make some that highlight your job qualifications and the results you achieved through the actions you personally took.

We hope that you enjoyed the **Thirty Second Sandwich** and will take the time to look at our other menu items at the **Job Seekers Café**.

*Thank you and come back soon!*

# Chapter 10

# Skill Builder Special Salad

# Chapter 10
# Skill Builder Special Salad

Satisfy any interviewer with the correct answers to interview questions. With lots of options to build a super salad of answers, you will be able to handle any question with confidence and skill. Over 100 sample interview questions provided.

## Section Table of Contents

| | |
|---|---|
| Introduction | 285 |
| Prepare For The Interview | 287 |
| First Impressions | 289 |
| Making A Good Opening | 291 |
| Interviewer's Point Of View | 293 |
| Address Your Strengths | 297 |
| Questions You Should Ask | 299 |
| Closing The Interview | 301 |
| Follow Up Items | 303 |
| Each Interview Is Experience | 305 |
| Interview Questions | 307 |
| Work History Interview Questions | 309 |
| About You Questions | 319 |
| Position And Organization Questions | 335 |
| Thoughts Of The Future Questions | 343 |
| Conclusion And Review | 347 |

# Section 1

# Introduction

Welcome to the **Job Seekers Café**. This menu item is entitled **Skill Builder Special Salad**. You will find this menu item very satisfying. A complete salad will be more than just some lettuce on a plate. It will have several additional items to make it more complete. Some of these items you may expect are some tasty croûtons, tomato, radishes, onions, olives, and a pleasing salad dressing for some extra flavor. You might desire to have some grilled chicken or other meats to top it off.

Just like a salad with various ingredients, a job interview will come with various questions. The questions will range from asking about your work history and previous job experiences, to questions about who you are, the position you are applying for, what you might want to know about the organization, and about your future plans.

You will notice that on the outer margins of this and most other pages there are Scholar Margins, where you can make notes or comments about what impressed you when reading the material. Perhaps you might have a question and you will put a question mark to remind you that you need to find clarification of the text and the concept presented.

Each interviewer and each organization will have their own set of questions specific to the position being offered. While there is an infinite number of questions that can be asked, some positions might have only a few that need to be answered. Other positions might require more detailed information about your qualifications so the organization can make the best selection to meet their needs.

Nearly all interview questions have been developed over the years with psychological overtones. This doesn't mean that the interviewer is trying to figure your mental condition. It is a reflection of how various individuals respond to certain questions that will reveal a bit more about the job candidates so the best qualified can be offered the position.

Most interviewers have done many interviews and realize that you might be a bit intimidated. They will try to make you feel welcome and comfortable. The better prepared you are the less stress you will experience during the interview. Relax and take the time to listen carefully to each question. Make sure you understand the question before you answer it. Take a deep breath and then answer the question with confidence.

In this eBook you will be introduced to some common customs that apply to job interviews. Some might seem a bit old-fashioned and others might seem silly to you. Over the years one thing has not changed, the interviewer is a human being and will make judgments about you based on how you look and how you respond to the interview questions.

Right after this introduction there will be a couple of sections that will give you information on how to dress, groom, and conduct yourself during the interview. Other sections will give you insight into what is going on that you might not be aware of as the interview progresses.

The best advice anyone can give you is that you need to be prepared—completely prepared. Don't go into an interview with the idea that you will dazzle the interviewer with your wit and charm, or try to give clever answers to the questions. The interviewer has seen hundreds, if not thousands of job candidates and has seen it all, or close to it. Be professional and respect the process. Your chance of being offered the position depends upon it.

The interview questions will be broken into the four areas that are generally what the interviewer is likely to ask. Each question will be next to what would be your best response.

Reference will be made throughout this eBook to concepts that can be found in some of the other **Job Seekers Café** menu items. While each eBook is a standalone publication about a given subject, the entire collection of menu items has been prepared to help a job seeker be totally prepared to reduce the time it takes to get a job.

# Section 2

# Prepare For The Interview

The better you prepare for the interview the better the results you can expect. Like everything else in life, things are much easier if you are prepared. By this point in your job seeking quest you should have several important tools at your command. You should have your Master Job Application Form filled out completely, as well as a resume written that will be read and will provide the results you desire. The words you choose to use will also be important. Power statements and your Me In Thirty Seconds should be practiced until they sound like your natural voice. You should have also spent some time researching the organization so you will be able to ask questions that demonstrate you have an interest in working there.

Normally you would have submitted an application for the position you are seeking. The application could have been prepared on-site or online. Many organizations will request your resume to be sent online or in the mail. Others will just ask that you bring it to the interview if you meet the qualifications they are looking for.

Since they have the advantage of having, in most cases, both the application and your resume, they have enough information about you to make a judgment about your qualifications for the position. Odds are there will be several other worthy candidates being considered also. Your task at hand is to create some differentiation between you and the other candidates. The interview is where you can demonstrate that you are the best candidate for the position.

One of the easiest and best ways to differentiate yourself from the others is how you present yourself for the interview. Dressing for success is not a myth. Many qualified candidates were summarily dismissed because of their choice of clothing and grooming. There are some standards of expectations for those who are seeking employment. Like them or not, society has its own 'rules' of acceptable clothing to wear to an interview, not to mention that the interviewer has in his or her mind just what they expect to see when a candidate enters the interview.

The confidence you demonstrate in your choice of words in answering the questions will make an impression. State your case with ownership words. You are selling yourself and no one knows you better than you do. Use "I am ...", "I have ...", and "I can ..." to show ownership of the statements you are making. It will also demonstrate that you take pride in who you 'are', what you 'have' done, and what you 'can' do. The best use of these ownership beginning lines is to show how you meet all the qualifications for the position being offered.

Write out several ownership statements and practice them until your natural voice smooths them out. The same should be done with the interview questions found in a later section in this eBook. Have a friend or someone you trust ask you the questions and then provide you the feedback you need to improve your delivery of the answers.

In the next section you will learn the importance of making that first impression.

# Section 3

# First Impressions

Good news! You got a call from an organization you had submitted an application and resume and they want to set up an interview. They are inviting you to come see them to meet and discuss the position you applied for. Now is the time for you to be flexible to their schedule to meet with them at their convenience, not yours.

Since you will be just one of a number of candidates to be interviewed you need to make preparations. If you are not sure of the exact location where the interview will be conducted, you might (should) do a test run so you will know approximately how long it will take to get there. If your appointment is at 10:00 am, do your test drive to see how the traffic is so you can arrive about fifteen minutes early for your appointment. It is much better for you to be waiting for them, than to have them waiting for you. If you arrive at 10:00 am you will be considered late for your appointment.

Your choice in what you wear is critical. Some schools of thought say that you should dress one step up from what you would wear working in the position being offered. The best advice is to wear clothing that is considered professional business attire. If everyone in the room waiting for their appointment is wearing a t-shirt and denim pants, you will make a more lasting first impression by wearing a business suit. Over the years there have been many stories about the interviewer who came out to get the first candidate and, seeing how everyone was dressed, dismissed all but those who were dressed professionally.

How you speak and comport yourself tells a lot about you. If you walk with confidence and hold yourself up with confidence you will be noticed in a positive way. Those who lack confidence can easily be picked out in a crowd. Remember, there are many reasons the interviewer has to make cuts to get to the right candidate. Your appearance and lack of self-confidence are causes that can eliminate you from consideration.

The next section deals with the best practices of making a good opening with the interviewer.

# Section 4

# Making A Good Opening

How you enter the interview room will be part of the interview process. Will you just walk in and wait to be told what to do, or show some initiative by demonstrating your confidence? Your role in the opening of the interview is to create a sense that you are the best candidate interviewing for the position.

Enter with a warm smile. This means it is a sincere smile and not a forced smile. Make eye contact when spoken to and when you speak. When shaking hands, make it a firm handshake, not a "dead fish" handshake. Have a tone of confidence in your voice when you speak. If you were referred by a common acquaintance, be sincere in acknowledging your appreciation for their assistance in helping you get the opportunity for the interview.

Above all else, be prepared. Know what is on the application that you submitted and what you stated on your resume. Don't look confused when asked about something you provided in advance to the organization. This will create a cloud of doubt about everything else you submitted to them.

Shortly after the greeting, the interviewer might ask you to tell them something about yourself. Here is where you will use your Me In Thirty Seconds. If the interview began with a discussion about the position, then use your job-related Me In Thirty Seconds and make sure that it is relevant to the position you have applied for. If the discussion prior to the question was about you as an individual, then give the Me In Thirty Seconds about you personally.

As questions are asked of you by the interviewer, answer the questions using power statements to show that your qualifications match the requirements for the position. If the position is a new one created without a complete idea of what will be expected, you would choose a power statement about your willingness to "go boldly" into the unknown because of your confidence in your ability to solve things.

In the next section you will learn about the interview from the interviewer's point of view. You might think you know what they are doing and you may be right, or you might gain insight as to where they are going with each question.

# Section 5

# Interviewer's Point Of View

The purpose of the interview is to determine which candidate is the best qualified for the position and will be the best fit into the organization's culture. Many times it is a weighted average between the two objectives of the best qualified and best cultural fit. This can be a delicate balance that will result in a consultation with management and supervisors that might require a second round of interviews to obtain a consensus of the best candidate.

There will be several "bars" or "hurdles" that will be used to make some of the initial cuts determining which candidates will be considered. Many organizations will use the education level as the initial bar to pass over. While many positions will not require a college degree, the organization would still like to have their employees demonstrate a proficiency in language and reading skills.

Over many years certain positions have gone from those who have a high school diploma to those who have a college degree. There are many jobs that will require a college degree due to some technical or specialty knowledge that will be required to properly handle the functions of the position. There are other positions which might require some certification or license in order to perform the functions of the job. These requirements might be a regulation imposed by local, state, or federal law.

It is the primary function of the interviewer and the hiring manager to do what is best for the organization. Because you need a job and really want the position they are offering will not be a valid reason for them to hire you. You must meet the requirements they post for the position to even be considered.

If the choice is between a candidate with experience or a candidate without experience, the organization usually will opt for the one with experience. This saves the time it takes to train a new hire. Besides that, the candidate might be able to bring some better ideas about work methods and have ideas about improving production.

Your appearance will also be taken into consideration. The type of clothing you wear to the interview is a reflection of your character. Everyone does judge a "book" by its cover. Your personal grooming will also be subject to scrutiny. Now is the time to be a little more conservative in your standards of dress and grooming. Don't let your ego cost you the opportunity to even be considered for the position. Once hired, if you are, you can see how the other employees dress and groom themselves. Then you can adjust your standard to that model. Don't go too radical in the beginning. If you are going to change make it gradual so you don't draw attention to the changes made.

Evaluating a candidate's ability to fit in with the organization's culture can be difficult. That is why there are several interview questions that will reveal details about your character and personality. The answers you give will help the interviewer gain a better understanding of you and how you might relate to the culture that currently exists within the organization.

Interviewers are not trying to "trap" you with the interview questions they ask. There will be several questions that are very similar that will be asked to see if your answers are consistent with each other. They will also be confirming the information you submitted on the application and what was stated in your resume. The interview is a relatively short period of time to gather a great deal of information about you and your qualifications. The interviewer isn't trying to trick you or catch you; there is no time to be wasted asking questions just to see if you can't keep your "story" together. Time is too important to be wasted in this manner.

If you have a negative item in your past that "haunts" you, be up front about it and be totally honest. Don't go into a blame game about the issues. Take responsibility for what happened and how you have worked hard to overcome the obstacle it presents. Some issues we bring with us through life will take a long time to get over. Others will pass quickly as we move on.

When you get a chance to discuss a negative point about yourself, try turning it in to a positive point. For example you might have spent too much time trying to make something perfect and it caused delays and overcharges in the past. This is where you will take that negative and make it positive by stating what you learned about the importance of asking for additional help to keep projects on time. This demonstrates how you learned that you know when you are in over your head and that you need to get the help required.

The following section will deal with how to address questions where you can show ownership by the way you begin your answers.

# Section 6

# Addressing Your Strengths

There are a few key words that will help you demonstrate ownership of your statements or answers. These are called ownership words. When you use them, speak them with 'positive' confidence. Do not use them where you have no knowledge or experience, at least the "I am" or "I have". If you want to answer a question where you lack knowledge or experience you could use the "I can" ownership opening. "I can learn to operate that equipment. I've had to learn how to operate several pieces of equipment in the past that I was unfamiliar with. I would enjoy having the opportunity to be taught how to use this equipment properly so I could meet both safety and production expectations."

With each of the ownership opening words there are certain words that are generally associated with each of them. Here are a few of those words:

- **I am** qualified
- **I am** willing
- **I am** a team player
- **I am** loyal
- **I am** trustworthy

The words you use after the "I am" opening will need to be supported by the rest of the words you speak. Taking the first one on the list, this would be an appropriate way to complete your statement:

"I am qualified for this position based on the requirements posted. My education and experience show how qualified I am."

Now we will look at the next ownership word set, the "I have" statement:

- **I have** experience
- **I have** education
- **I have** demonstrated
- **I have** license

Once again you will have to add words to support your claim. This time we will take the last item on the list:

"I have licenses to sell insurance for life, health, and property from the state of California which expire at the end of next year."

Finally, we will look at the last ownership word set, the "I can" statement:

- **I can** follow instructions
- **I can** learn quickly
- **I can** do the job
- **I can** operate

Here is an example of how you take ownership of the "I can" with words that will support your statement:

"I can operate a forklift. With a current safety certificate and over eight years of experience without a single accident, I have the qualifications you are looking for in hiring an operator with at least five years of experience."

You have many strengths and talents. Take ownership of them and use them to your advantage by putting them in a statement to answer a question from the interviewer. If you are not willing to take ownership for who you are, then don't expect anyone else to do it. They can't and won't. Only you can take ownership for who you are.

The next section will cover asking questions of the interviewer and when they are appropriate.

# Section 7

# Questions You Should Ask

I am sure that you have plenty of questions of your own. There is a right time to ask a question and a wrong time to ask a question, just as there are questions you should ask and those you should not ask. Many of your questions will be answered during the orientation phase of employment if you are offered the position.

During the course of the actual interview you should let the interviewer ask all the questions. However, if you do not understand a question being asked of you and you want it repeated or rephrased, then it is acceptable to ask that the question be repeated or rephrased so you might know what is being asked. If you don't have a clear understanding of what is being asked of you it is hard to truly answer it correctly. Better to be safe than to give the wrong answer to a question that you did not understand.

Generally near the end of the interview, the interviewer will ask if you have any questions. You should have a couple of questions thought out in advance of the interview. Certainly you do not want to seem to be trying to think of something just for the sake of asking a question.

Appropriate questions to ask might be about how soon you could expect to hear back from them. When will they make their final decision. And how soon would they want you to start after an offer has been made. Be careful not to ask a question that was answered about the subject during the interview. You will look like you were not paying attention or listening to the interviewer. Consider asking a question of when it would be appropriate for you to contact them about the position, or when will they be making their final decision.

Some good questions to ask of the interviewer once they have completed their questions would be if there is anything else they would like to know about you, if they had enough information from you to make a fair decision about your suitability for the position, and if there any other positions within the organization that they might feel you would be qualified to fill.

The closing of the interview will be presented in the next section.

# Section 8

# Closing The Interview

It is during the end of the interview that you will have your last chance to make a lasting impression. By this time you should have relaxed some and have found yourself in a comfort zone. You will also realize that you have come to the conclusion of the interview and you are still alive. This is good.

Ask the interviewer for their business card so you will have their name and contact information. You will need this information as you will discover in a later section of this eBook.

Keep making eye contact and with a warm smile, thank them by name for the opportunity to have the interview. You can show an interest in making a closing statement about how you look forward to working for the organization or being part of their winning team. Be sure to gather up everything you brought into the interview so you don't have to go back to retrieve anything.

Before you leave the interview make sure you have a good understanding of when you might expect a call from them, or when you should make a follow-up call to see if you got the position. Some organizations will wait and see what candidate is willing to keep in contact, demonstrating a sincere interest in the job.

Remember that as you came into the building you came in contact with a receptionist or another individual who was responsible for letting the interviewer know that you had arrived and were waiting for the interview. Be sure to acknowledge them by thanking them before leaving the building.

In the next section you will be shown the proper way to follow up with the organization.

# Section 9

# Follow Up Items

If the organization stated they will call you by the end of this or next week, give them some consideration by waiting for them to call. After that, a courtesy call could be made stating that you had not heard from them and asking if the position is still open. There are many reasons that the interviewer or the hiring manager may not be able to contact the candidates to let them know that the position has been filled. They could have had a family emergency, their manager might be waiting for approval from someone higher-up in the organization, or a candidate has not yet been selected for any number of reasons.

If they asked you to contact them on a certain date, make sure you call them in the morning on that date. Remind them they had requested you contact them about the position and you were just following up with them. Be pleasant and thank them for whatever information you receive from the call. They are looking out for the best interests of the organization and you must respect their final decision.

If by some chance you were not the successful candidate, you might ask if there are any other positions within the organization that you might be qualified to fill. This gives the impression that you have an interest in working for the organization. Someone in another department might quit, be terminated, or be promoted to another position. There will be an immediate need to fill the position. Knowing that you have an interest or would consider another position might get you that opportunity to be hired.

With the contact information you have on the interviewer's or hiring manager's business card, use the information to send a short thank you card or note expressing your gratitude for the opportunity and the time they gave you to be considered for the position. Even if you are not the successful candidate this will leave a good impression about you with that individual.

An interview is a learning experience and in the next section you will learn why and how to gain from each one.

# Section 10

# Each Interview Is Experience

After an interview you should be recording on your job search activities log the experience you had. This is the time you need to write down how you felt about the interview overall. You should also reflect on what you did well and where you might need to improve. By keeping a record you will be able to look back at it and build on those positive items and improve your weaker ones. At the end of this book there is an **Interview Evaluation Form** you can use to help you improve your interviewing skills. **(See Appendix - Interview Evaluation Form)** We all reflect back, thinking I should have said this, or why did I say that? This is normal behavior. We all second guess what we have done. Now is the time to record how you feel so you will be able to work on improving your interviewing skills. You might have felt nervous and uncomfortable. Ask yourself what you could do to overcome those feelings. You might ask a friend or someone you trust to help you find a way to build up your confidence level.

With each interview it should become easier for you to relax and enjoy the process. While it might be discouraging to have lots of interviews, without them you would not even be considered for hiring. You will just have to keep making appointments for interviews until you are hired. You might feel that your Me In Thirty Seconds or your power statements might not be as effective as they could be. Rewrite them and try the new ones. Don't get discouraged. Little adjustments to your delivery might be just the change you need to make.

There have been those who will seek an interview with a company with no intention of accepting any position. They just wanted to get the experience of an interview so they could become more comfortable with the process. A word of caution though, because you might be so prepared and have a very positive interview you may be offered a job. If you have been looking for a long period of time, you might consider accepting the position to help your current financial situation. This will take some pressure off of you so you can reconsider your options and perfect your job-seeking skills.

In the next section you will be introduced to some common and not-so- common questions that might be asked in an interview.

# Section 11

# Interview Questions

This section will cover the four areas of interview questions. The first area is about your work history and job experience as it might relate to the position being offered. The second area will be more about learning who you are as an individual. The third area is about the position being offered and about the organization in general. The fourth and final area is about your thoughts about the future.

Carefully read each question so you will understand what is actually being asked. Several questions might sound similar, yet each one will require a specific answer that might be slightly different. You might want to use some scratch paper and write out your answer so you can compare it to the sample answer provided. By doing this you will be able to take what you wrote down and improve it so it is closer to the suggested answer. This will help you bring in your natural voice to your answer.

Answer all interview questions with complete honesty. Don't try to shade your answers so it makes you sound better than you are. Most interviewers know when the bull is being tossed about. Some answers could be tough to get out because you might have some sensitivity about them being a bit too personal. If you are uncomfortable about answering a question, let the interviewer know. They don't want to make you uncomfortable and will move on to another question.

Your answers should be delivered as power statements that reveal you have the qualifications for the position. When possible use the ownership words when giving your answer. The "I am", "I have", and "I can" lead-ins to your answers let the interviewer know that you own your statement. No matter what, let your voice sound confident. Maintain good posture and enjoy the experience.

## Let the questions begin!

# Section 12

# Work History Interview Questions

| | |
|---|---|
| **What was your last position and title?**<br><br>• In my most recent position I was a manager in the accounting department with the title of Accounts Payable Manager where I managed two supervisors who each managed four accountants. I reported directly to the Chief Financial Officer.<br><br>• My most recent position was as a lead or head cashier in a retail store. My title was Head Cashier and I reported to the assistant store manager who was over the cashier department. I was responsible to help train the new cashiers on the registers and with customer service skills training. | *The interviewer is verifying what you had written down on your job application and resume.*<br><br>*Write your best response here:* |
| **What were your expectations from your last job and to what extent were they met?**<br><br>• I took the job with the expectation of learning how to read blueprints and then to be trained on how to draw them. After two months I was able to read the blueprints and understand them. Then after six months I was enrolled in a drafting class learning how to draw plans for single family homes.<br><br>• I expected to work into a supervisory position. After three months I was put into a supervisor skills training program. After my training I received a certificate for successfully completing the course and received a promotion as a supervisor. | *The interviewer wants to see if you felt your last job met your expectations and how you felt about the experience.*<br><br>*Write your best response here:* |
| **What were your responsibilities in your last job?**<br><br>• I supervised a department of twelve workers. I was responsible to schedule the workers to ensure sales floor coverage on the retail sales floor to match our customers' shopping patterns. I did the vacation schedule and kept management informed as to the department staffing requirements.<br><br>• I was responsible to handle the accounts payable department. I also assisted with the payroll preparation every other week. If there was an issue with an employee over the number of hours worked, I would verify all time records and make corrections if required. | *The interviewer wants to know if you knew your responsibilities on your last job and how you handled them.*<br><br>*Write your best response here:* |

# Section 12

# Work History Interview Questions

| | |
|---|---|
| **Were there any challenges you faced and how did you handle them?**<br><br>• We were facing a cash flow problem and I was able to negotiate a repayment program with several of our vendors. This helped to ease the situation and still satisfy our vendors.<br><br>• I managed a team of technicians who had fallen behind schedule installing new computers and software programs. I brought the technicians together and we identified several issues and agreed on how best to overcome the obstacles. We not only got back on schedule, we completed the project two weeks earlier than the original deadline. | *Here the interviewer wants to see how you handled a challenging situation.*<br>**Write your best response here:** |
| **What did you like about your last job?**<br><br>• I liked the people I worked with. It was a friendly atmosphere and we all put in our best efforts as a team to complete all our projects on time and by doing so we never had to delay or rework a project. I really enjoyed going to work every day.<br><br>• I would say I liked working with the customers. I liked to help them find the right product for their needs and at the same time give them the best value for their money. I liked the feeling of making the customer feel comfortable. | *The interviewer is trying to see if you liked your last job and why you liked it.*<br>**Write your best response here:** |
| **What didn't you like about your last job?**<br><br>• I felt that I could not advance in my department. I decided to further my education by finishing my degree so I could find a position with another company. Once I completed my degree the company did offer me an opportunity to be the supervisor of my department so I did not have to leave the company.<br><br>• When I started with the company I felt I knew my role in my position. I was discouraged that I was not being given enough responsibility. After expressing my concerns with my manager, he took the time to explain what I needed to know to reach higher levels of responsibility. His caring changed my attitude. | *The interviewer wants to see if you hold any grudges or negative feelings about your last job.*<br>**Write your best response here:** |

# Section 12

# Work History Interview Questions

| | |
|---|---|
| **What did you find most rewarding about your last job?**<br><br>• I found the most rewarding part of my last job was seeing the satisfaction on the customer's face at the conclusion of the sale. I am also a customer and I know that I have to be satisfied and I should not expect less for my customers.<br><br>• I would have to say it was when I was asked to help train the new hires. To help 'my co-workers' learn their position and to see their rapid development build into becoming productive team members. It was also rewarding to have management recognize my efforts and the success of the hires that contributed to better morale in the office. | *The interviewer is seeking to find what you value as a reward in doing your job.*<br><br>**Write your best response here:** |
| **What did you feel was least rewarding about your last job?**<br><br>• I had worked hard on a project to have it completed within the deadline. Once I finished it, the manager rejected it in favor of another employee's project. I was upset until I took a look at the other project and realized that it was better than mine. I learned that it was more important to have the best project go to the customer.<br><br>• Once I had an idea about a promotion that at the time seemed to be summarily dismissed by my supervisor. What I didn't know was that his manager had tried it a few years earlier and it was a complete failure. My supervisor spared me some embarrassment. | *The interviewer wants to see if you felt your efforts were not rewarded and how you dealt with it.*<br><br>**Write your best response here:** |
| **What was your biggest accomplishment you achieved on your last job?**<br><br>• I would have to say I was able to reduce the office supply expenses by consolidating what was ordered by taking advantage of eliminating some items and buying other items in bulk. Our costs were reduced by 15% in the first year!<br><br>• I would say it was when I was asked to supervise a department that lacked a 'team player' attitude. I talked with each member to see how they felt about the situation. A few asked to be moved to another department and some new members were added. I brought the team together by setting some common goals. | *Many won't tell an interviewer about any of their accomplishments because they don't see themselves as having achieved anything.*<br><br>**Write your best response here:** |

# Section 12

# Work History Interview Questions

| | |
|---|---|
| **What was your biggest failure in your last position?**<br><br>• I would have to say not reaching my goal of perfect attendance. I was involved in a serious accident that required me to take two months off to heal properly. Once I was able to get my doctor's release to return to work, I still kept up my perfect attendance efforts.<br><br>• I was put in charge of a project that was beyond my abilities. I discussed my feelings with my manager who put a more qualified individual in charge, but asked me to be his assistant so I would gain the experience and skills required for the next project. | *The interviewer is trying to understand how you deal with failure.*<br><br>**Write your best response here:** |
| **How did you get along with your last supervisor?**<br><br>• I feel I had a good working relationship with my supervisor. We would work together in solving issues before they got out of control. He would ask me what I would do, and then would confirm it or help me find a better solution by asking questions that would lead me where we needed to go.<br><br>• In the beginning it seemed we were not going to be a good fit. After a few weeks though we began to respect each other's role by focusing on the customer and what was best for the company. I learned that he was there to help me and I needed to let him. | *The interviewer is trying to see how you feel about your last supervisor. Did you respect the individual, the position, or both?*<br><br>**Write your best response here:** |
| **How did you get along with your co-workers?**<br><br>• I am proud of the fact that we as a department were supportive of each other. If someone made a mistake, the rest of us would help the individual correct it so they would know how to avoid making that mistake in the future.<br><br>• I have always tried to be professional with my co-workers. Although we came from different cultures, educational levels, and skill sets, we each went with our strengths with everyone making a contribution. We really enjoyed working together and learning more about each others' customs. | *The interviewer wants to see if you are a team player or a loner and how you felt about your co-workers.*<br><br>**Write your best response here:** |

# Section 12

# Work History Interview Questions

| | |
|---|---|
| **What was it like working for your last supervisor?**<br><br>• I appreciated his willingness to listen to me and to take the opportunity to turn it into a training moment. He always made sure that I fully understood what was expected of me and he made sure that I always had the tools, materials, and resources.<br><br>• I can honestly can say it was a pleasure to work for her. She was supportive of our training. She was also very generous with her praise for any improvement we attained. She always challenged us to improve ourselves at work and in our home life. | *The interviewer wants to see how you feel about your last supervisor and what you learned or gain while working for them.*<br><br>*Write your best response here:* |
| **What were some of your expectations of your last supervisor and were they met?**<br><br>• I appreciated being able to work in an environment that made personal connections with all employees. My supervisor made sure that everyone was treated fairly. Everyone was always given a part in every project. We were all satisfied with his leadership.<br><br>• My supervisor took the time to get to know my strengths and weaknesses. Then he took the time to help me discover how I could improve my weaknesses and at the same time add to my strengths so I could contribute more to the organization. | *The interviewer wants to see if you had some expectations of how your supervisor would interact with you and to what extent.*<br><br>*Write your best response here:* |
| **Can you describe your best boss and why?**<br><br>• I have had some great bosses over my career. Some would take an interest in me and I felt they were more of a mentor than a boss. One in particular was always challenging me to improve my self-confidence. This led me to be able to stand in front of a training class and teach others about my position.<br><br>• My best boss seemed to take an interest in giving me a variety of professional experiences that helped me improve my customer service skills. I still use these skills after having left that company over fifteen years ago. | *Here the interviewer is trying to see what you like in a boss. This is to see if you will fit into the organization's culture.*<br><br>*Write your best response here:* |

# Section 12

# Work History Interview Questions

| | |
|---|---|
| **Can you describe your worst boss and why you feel that way about them?**<br><br>• I have learned from each boss that I have worked for. From the good ones, I learned what to do. From the more challenging ones, what not to do.<br><br>• In a previous job I had a manager who challenged everything. We would agree to disagree on many issues. We kept things professional and did what was in the best interest of the customer and the company. | *The interviewer is trying to see how you worked with a difficult boss and how you handled it.*<br><br>**Write your best response here:** |
| **If we were to ask those who know you best why we should hire you for this position, what do you think they would say?**<br><br>• My friends would say you should hire me because I have ten years of experience in this position, and that I will bring to the position a sense of pride in always doing my best.<br><br>• My friends would say you should hire me because they know that I meet or exceed your requirements for the position. They will also tell you that I am hard working, professional, and a team player. | *The interviewer is trying to see how a third party might feel about your ability to fill the position from your perspective.*<br><br>**Write your best response here:** |
| **Can you give me some examples of teamwork?**<br><br>• In my last job our department encouraged open and frank discussion how best to divide up the work load. Each member did their share of the work, so the work was completed as a team.<br><br>• Years ago while participating on a softball team I had to work with others, yet I still had to develop my own skills and abilities to be a contributing member of the team. I believe each of us has a role, like a piece of the puzzle, that is an important part of making the team complete in purpose and in fulfilling of the requirements for a project. | *The interviewer wants to see if you can give examples of teamwork and know if you understand the what term "teamwork" means.*<br><br>**Write your best response here:** |

# Section 12

# Work History Interview Questions

| Question & Sample Answers | Interviewer's Intent |
|---|---|
| **Tell me about a difficult work situation and what you did to overcome it?**<br><br>• My supervisor gave us an unreasonable deadline for a project. I brought my team together to find a solution and presented it to our supervisor. He approved our suggestion and the project was completed on time.<br><br>• At my last job we had a situation that got out of control. Some members of my department felt we were given a project from another department who failed to complete it. It turned out that the project had been changed by the customer and that our department was better prepared to complete it for the customer. | *The interviewer is trying to see how you dealt with a difficult situation and how it was resolved.*<br><br>**Write your best response here:** |
| **Can you tell me about a time when you had a heavy workload and how you handled it?**<br><br>• In my last job several members of the department were out sick for some time. We were falling behind everywhere. I talked with my supervisor and we were able to get some qualified help from the other departments to get caught up.<br><br>• On a previous job we received a new manager who had never worked in our area. She seemed to be making promises that we could not keep to our customers. I asked if I could talk to her. She listened to how our department was set up and the policies we had to follow. Together we prioritized what was to be done. | *The interviewer is trying to see how proactive you were when you were given a heavy workload and how you dealt with it.*<br><br>**Write your best response here:** |
| **Can you give me an example of how you used strategic thinking in your last position?**<br><br>• I was a member of the strategic planning committee for the company. The committee assigned me the task of long range information technology support requirements. I successfully presented a solution that saved over $250,000.00 the first year.<br><br>• At my last job I was asked to use strategic thinking on how we could reverse the loss of fifteen percent of our customer base. I assembled a team and we discussed various options. Our strategic thinking ended up erasing the loss of our customer base and in gaining an additional ten percent increase in customers. | *The interviewer is trying to see if you are familiar with strategic thinking and how you have used it in the past.*<br><br>**Write your best response here:** |

# Section 12

# Work History Interview Questions

| | |
|---|---|
| **Will you tell me about a time you demonstrated initiative and being assertive to get something accomplished?**<br><br>• My past supervisor did not like confrontation and avoided dealing with two individuals who would not work together. When it began to affect the other co-workers I stepped up and challenged my supervisor to resolve the problem before it got out of hand. The two were moved to another department.<br><br>• There was an issue that didn't seem that important, however everyone was talking about it and morale was being destroyed. I went to my supervisor and presented my views on the issue. These were taken to management who immediately resolved it. | *The interviewer is trying to find out if you take initiative and then act assertively in solving an issue.*<br><br>**Write your best response here:** |
| **Can you describe to me how you solved a problem at work?**<br><br>• I noticed that we were using outdated production methods that were causing a forty percent rejection rate. I called in the engineers and we were able to put into place new methods that reduced the rejection rate to less than two percent.<br><br>• I found that we had several workers who were duplicating what others were doing. We brought in management to help write new procedures for each position. Together we established clear and detailed processing procedures that eliminated duplication and resulted in a sixty percent increase in work processed and a twenty-seven percent increase in customer satisfaction. | *Here the interviewer wants to see if you have solved problems at work and what your role was in making the change.*<br><br>**Write your best response here:** |
| **Can you tell me about a time when you had to adapt to changes at the last minute on a project you were working on?**<br><br>• On my last job last-minute changes were a routine part of the job. I found it best to step back and discuss the change and how to divide the time and costs of the project so an appropriate solution could be implemented.<br><br>• I was about to finish a complex project when the client decided to make some drastic changes. I spoke directly to the client so I could have a better understanding about the need to make the changes. By having a better understanding we were able to deal with the changes and still maintain on-time delivery to the client. | *The interviewer wants to know if you have had to deal with change and if so how did you handle it.*<br><br>**Write your best response here:** |

# Section 12

# Work History Interview Questions

| | |
|---|---|
| **Can you tell me about a time when you had an impossible deadline and how you handled it?**<br><br>• When I was told about a deadline that was unreasonable, I went to the sales department to discuss the deadline. I explained how it was not possible since we were waiting for the materials from various suppliers. The customer was contacted and the new deadline was only one week later.<br><br>• There was a project that was given a deadline before we even had all the specifications for the project. I took this up with my supervisor and the other department was called in to discuss the issue. The customer was contacted and we got the missing details. | *The interviewer wants to know how you dealt with this situation.*<br><br>**Write your best response here:** |
| **Tell me about an idea that you presented to your boss that was rejected. How did you handle the situation?**<br><br>• I had proposed that some of the older office equipment be replaced. My manager explained that replacement of office equipment was not in the current budget. It was put into the next year's budget and the new equipment arrived early in the year.<br><br>• I proposed an idea to extend the store hours to help increase the number of customers we served. My manager told me that the hours were reduced before I was hired since there was not enough customer traffic to justify the extra labor costs. He gave me a valid reason which I readily accepted. | *The interviewer is trying to find out how you react to rejection of your ideas.*<br><br>**Write your best response here:** |
| **Can you describe a recent situation you were confronted with under pressure and how you reacted?**<br><br>• I recently had two projects assigned to my department and when I reviewed them there was a conflict of the two deadlines. Both were valuable customers whose projects we had always finished on time. I talked to both customers and came to an agreeable solution about the delivery dates.<br><br>• I was asked to travel out of state during a time I was handling some staffing issues. I went to my supervisor and explained the situation. He agreed to postpone the out-of-state trip until I resolved my department's staffing issue. | *The interviewer wants to know how you deal with pressure and how you react to it.*<br><br>**Write your best response here:** |

# Section 12

# Work History Interview Questions

| | |
|---|---|
| **Why have you been out of work for so long?**<br><br>• I was going to school to finish my technical certification in welding. My previous job did not allow me enough time to go to school. I thought it best if I got my certificate and then find the job I was qualified for.<br><br>• My aging parents needed my help caring for them on a daily basis. I was the closest child to where they lived. It seemed only natural that I would be the one to take care of them. They have both recently passed away and I am ready to return to full-time employment. | *The interviewer wants to see if there was a valid reason that kept you out of work for a long time.*<br><br>**Write your best response here:** |
| **What did you think of your last employer (company)?**<br><br>• I felt that they were fair and they did offer some tuition help so I could finish my degree. They worked at making everyone feel like they were part of the family and for most of us we did feel that family connection.<br><br>• I thought it was great that they spent so much time and effort in making sure that everyone got adequate training in their position. I think they wanted us as individuals to be our best so it would reflect in our work. | *The interviewer wants to know what you thought of the last employer (company or organization) that you worked for.*<br><br>**Write your best response here:** |
| **Your job history shows that you have left most of your previous jobs in less than a year. Can you give me specific reasons for leaving them after a short period of time?**<br><br>• My job before my last one was downsizing and I had the chance to get a job in a different company. Soon after I was hired they merged with another company and I was soon let go.<br><br>• Most of these jobs were obtained through temporary agencies for specific projects. Once the project was completed I had to find another project to work on. I know I have the experience and knowledge required for the position you have posted. | *Here the interviewer is trying to learn why you have changed jobs so often after just a short period of time.*<br><br>**Write your best response here:** |

# Section 13

# About You Questions

| | |
|---|---|
| **Tell me something about yourself.**<br><br>(Here is where you will use your Me In Thirty Seconds, aka "Elevator Speech". If you have been discussing items as they relate to the position, use your vocational speech. If you have been discussing items about you personally, use your more personal speech. You can find more information about the Me In Thirty Seconds and how it is written in the **Guide For A Job Seeker**, our **free** eBook offering, or purchase the **Thirty Second Sandwich** eBook from the **Job Seekers Café Menu**. Both can be found on our web site at:<br><br>**www.oldoakmediapartnersllc.com** | *The interviewer is listening to both your message and your confidence in 'selling' yourself. This is perhaps the most important question to be asked.*<br><br>**Write your best response here:** |
| **Why are you leaving your current job?**<br><br>• I finished my technical training as an electrician. Now that I have a certificate I am looking for a job as an electrician's helper so I can better learn the trade.<br><br>• I realized that there was no room for advancement or any other opportunities at that company. I am seeking employment where I can use my education and experience to remain in my chosen field. I know that I am qualified for the position I have applied for. | *The interviewer wants to understand why you are leaving your current job and if the reason is a valid one.*<br><br>**Write your best response here:** |
| **What is your reason for leaving your last job?**<br><br>• The company I was working for began to downsize. I saw this as an opportunity to move to a new job where I would be able to use my business degree in the field I studied for.<br><br>• After a few months it was apparent to management and myself that this was not the right fit for what they wanted. We left on good terms and I wish them the best. With my experience and education I would like to find employment where my qualifications can be put to good use. | *The interviewer wants to know what your reasons are for leaving your last job.*<br><br>**Write your best response here:** |

# Section 13

# About You Questions

| | |
|---|---|
| **Why were you terminated from your last job?**<br><br>• I was part of a reduction in the workforce. Having been there only a year put me on the first list to be let go.<br><br>• I was desperate for work and took the wrong job. After six months it was evident I made a mistake and the company knew I was not the right person for the position. We left on good terms even though I should have never taken the job in the first place. | *The interviewer is looking for a reason why you were terminated from your last job.*<br><br>**Write your best response here:** |
| **What have you been doing since you left your last job?**<br><br>• My parents are not in good health so I took care of them. Now we have arranged to have a full-time caregiver helping them so I can return to the workforce.<br><br>• I have been freelancing while looking for a permanent job that fits my qualifications. I like to keep myself busy and by doing some freelance work I have been able to make some money while still looking for a suitable job. | *The interviewer wants to know what you have done with your time since leaving your last job.*<br><br>**Write your best response here:** |
| **Do you have reliable transportation available to get to work?**<br><br>• I have my own car that is regularly serviced to keep it in top running condition. I have also checked on the schedules for the local public transportation and I still could arrive in plenty of time for work here at your company.<br><br>• I use only public transportation since I do not yet have a car of my own. Before coming to this interview I tried several different bus schedules and found a few that will get me to work on time. The bus stop by my house is less than one hundred yards away and the bus stops on the corner across the street from your company. | *The interviewer wants to know if you will have any issues with getting to work or going home after work.*<br><br>**Write your best response here:** |

# Section 13

# About You Questions

| | |
|---|---|
| **What are some of your strengths and can you describe how you used them?**<br><br>• My best strength is that I am dependable. This is supported by my being on time to work every scheduled day for the past seven years. My next best strength would be that I am devoted to meeting the deadlines set by the customer.<br><br>• I am accurate in my record keeping. I have done both accounts receivable and payable. For over fifteen years I have never been cited for anything out of line during an audit for receivables or payables. | *The interviewer wants to hear in your own words what strengths you have and how you have used them.*<br><br>**Write your best response here:** |
| **What would you consider your greatest strength and how you have used it in the past?**<br><br>• I would have to say my greatest strength would be listening and coming to an understanding concerning an issue that required a fact-based solution and not an opinion-based solution.<br><br>• I think my greatest strength would be my ability to make people comfortable. I work hard to build trust by understanding the customer's unique needs before I recommend the right product at the right price. | *The interviewer wants to know what you consider to be your greatest strength and how you have used it in the past.*<br><br>**Write your best response here:** |
| **What would you consider your greatest weakness and how do you deal with it?**<br><br>• I would have to confess that my greatest weakness is that I tend to review my work too often. I have a habit of wanting to do my best. Over the years I have found that I have held myself to a higher standard and want to be able to take pride in my work.<br><br>• I have to say it is taking full responsibility for something that goes wrong on my team. I don't like to blame others if I didn't do my job right and as the team's supervisor I feel it is my job to make sure things don't go wrong. I work with my team on a proactive basis to spot potential issues to avoid making mistakes. | *The interviewer wants to know if you see yourself as having any weaknesses and how you have dealt with them.*<br><br>**Write your best response here:** |

# Section 13

# About You Questions

| | |
|---|---|
| **Describe your last major mistake and what you did about it?**<br><br>• I had made a new schedule and forgot that two employees were attending school on days that I had scheduled them. When it was brought to my attention I quickly adjusted the schedule.<br><br>• I once asked a co-worker to handle taking inventory. After he completed it I realized it was done incorrectly. He had not been trained on how to do an inventory. I explained that it was my fault for not having trained him. He and I re-did the inventory as I trained him how to do it correctly. Now he is one of the best workers to do the inventory. | *The interviewer wants to know about a time when you made a mistake and how you took care of it.*<br><br>**Write your best response here:** |
| **How would you describe your typical workweek?**<br><br>• I start the week by making a list of what needs to be done by the end of the week. Some items are daily, some might take a couple of days, and some might take the entire week. I prioritize the list and then hold myself accountable to get it all done on time.<br><br>• I have over eight years of experience as a salesperson in the field. I take pride in keeping all my scheduled appointments and will find the time to take care of any emergencies that might come up. If I have time between appointments I am calling prospective new customers trying to get an appointment. | *The interviewer wants to know how you plan your workweek.*<br><br>**Write your best response here:** |
| **Do you take your work home?**<br><br>• Only when I need to, no problem. I wouldn't want to miss a deadline because of an hour or two. Normally I try to get all my work done while at work where I have all the resources available I will need to get the job done.<br><br>• I fully understand meeting deadlines and getting work done on time is important. I know that there are those rare exceptions that show up when least expected and action needs to be taken to make sure the project is completed on time for the customer. | *The interviewer wants to know if you always take your work home or if you try to finish it while at work.*<br><br>**Write your best response here:** |

# Section 13

# About You Questions

| | |
|---|---|
| **How many hours do you normally work?**<br><br>• I work as many hours as necessary to get the job done correctly and on time. I take pride in getting my projects done within the normal working hours.<br><br>• I try to stay organized and I prioritize what I have to do so I can get all my work done within normal work hours. I make sure that I have all my resources available so I am not delayed in meeting a deadline. If a few extra hours are required to complete the project to meet the deadline, I am fine with spending them to satisfy the customer. | *The interviewer wants to know if you work too many hours or not enough for the amount of work you are capable of doing.*<br><br>**Write your best response here:** |
| **Can you describe the pace at which you work?**<br><br>• I try to pace my work to finish ahead of schedule so it can be reviewed and corrected if needed. I do not like missing deadlines and the best way I have found is to work to get the project done early enough to have time to double check it.<br><br>• I prefer to work at a quick pace that makes the time seem to go by faster. The end result is I tend to get more accomplished because I do not watch the clock. As soon as I finish one project and it is reviewed and turned in for the customer, I will begin the next project. | *The interviewer wants to see how you pace yourself and how you feel about your pace.*<br><br>**Write your best response here:** |
| **How do you handle stress?**<br><br>• I would have to say that I tend to react to the situation itself and not to the stress. Stress is something we put upon ourselves and does nothing to change the situation. Address the situation and the stress goes away.<br><br>• If I feel overwhelmed I will step back and get some help to see what I am not seeing as a solution. I think taking a proactive stance eliminates most of the stress by getting a different person's perspective and jointly solving the problem. | *The interviewer wants to see how you deal with stress and what you would do to remove it or eliminate it.*<br><br>**Write your best response here:** |

# Section 13

# About You Questions

**How do you handle pressure?**

- I see pressure as an outside influence whereas stress is more internal. I do work better under some pressure. It helps me use my resources better while keeping me focused on the task at hand.

- I try to avoid stress and pressure whenever I can. I realize that I do put some pressure on myself to meet deadlines and this is a healthy pressure. I don't like to wait until the last minute to finish a project or to put off doing what I should be doing thinking it will make things easier.

*The interviewer wants to know if you can distinguish between pressure and stress and how you handle either one.*

**Write your best response here:**

---

**What motivates you?**

- I would say a sense of pride in doing my best, finding acceptance for what I have done, and being made to feel like I am part of a dedicated team.

- I like to be a positive influence and help others reach their potential. I enjoy sharing my knowledge, skills, and talents with others and seeing them grow and develop in life. You could say it is just having that good feeling for doing something for someone else, for no other reason that just doing it.

*The interviewer wants to know what you feel is your motivation for doing what you do.*

**Write your best response here:**

---

**What decisions do you find hard to make?**

- I had to make several difficult decisions in my last job as a supervisor. There were two employees who were caught stealing from the company and they had to be terminated. They had been good workers, yet it was the right thing to let them go.

- The hardest decision I had to make was when I had to hire a new truck driver. There were five exceptionally qualified candidates for only one open position. I was responsible to fill the position and finally went with the one candidate who had the most experience in the particular truck we used at our company.

*The interviewer is trying to see if you can make difficult decisions if necessary.*

**Write your best response here:**

# Section 13

# About You Questions

| | |
|---|---|
| **When was the last time you were angry and what happened?**<br><br>• I see anger as a loss of control. I don't lose control. I step back and take a deep breath and thoughtfully think through the situation to find a solution. I did so one time when we missed a critical deadline. I made some changes in procedures to avoid it happening again.<br><br>• I was very upset at a co-worker who broke my chair. At first I was starting to get angry, but realized it had always shown signs of its age and could have easily been broken by anyone who sat in it. I was happy that no one was injured, and the chair was replaced with a stronger one. | *The interviewer wants to see if you have a short temper and how you deal with it.*<br>**Write your best response here:** |
| **Do you have any pet peeves?**<br><br>• I really don't have any pet peeves. If something bothers me, I step back and analyze 'why' and find a solution. I don't let little things get in my way of doing my work.<br><br>• I would have to say it is when I am asked to do something and do not receive the complete information I need. I handle it by asking questions until I fully get all the information I need to complete the project. | *The interviewer wants to know what bothers you and how you cope with it.*<br>**Write your best response here:** |
| **What would you say is the most criticized about you?**<br><br>• There is no ongoing criticism. I am open to any personal and professional growth and welcome the opportunity to improve. I know that I can always improve and hope that I am doing that.<br><br>• I would have to say it is the enthusiasm I display each morning. I really look forward to helping the customers and seeing that their needs are met. I guess I am just a happy person. | *The interviewer wants to know if you are aware of any criticism and how you deal with it.*<br>**Write your best response here:** |

# Section 13

# About You Questions

| | |
|---|---|
| **If we were to call your previous employer or co-workers, what would they say about you?**<br><br>• They would tell you that I am a team player. One who enjoys working with others to be the best I can be. They would also say that I am hard-working and dependable, not to mention I am honest.<br><br>• They would tell you I am honest, considerate, and hard-working. Other things they might say about me would be that I am always upbeat and that I tend to deal with reality and not opinions expressed by others. | *The interviewer wants to know what you think your employers and co-workers might say about you.*<br><br>**Write your best response here:** |
| **How would you describe your relationship with your co-workers?**<br><br>• I am willing to work with anyone. I try hard not to let personal feelings interfere with my work. I treat all my co-workers like friends or family and hope they feel the same toward me.<br><br>• I can get along with my co-workers. I try to learn from them as much as I can and share what I know or a skill that will help them. This has helped me to have a positive relationship with them. | *The interviewer wants to know what you think your relationship is with your co-workers.*<br><br>**Write your best response here:** |
| **Tell me why you are comfortable working in a team environment.**<br><br>• I enjoy working as part of a team when each member does their part or helps others to obtain successful completion of a project. I feel that I learn and do more when working with a team than I could do on my own.<br><br>• In my past several jobs where I was required to be part of a team I learned things much faster. I enjoyed the sense of pride of being part of a winning team. | *The interviewer wants to know why you would be comfortable working as a team member.*<br><br>**Write your best response here:** |

# Section 13

# About You Questions

| **How do you feel about working independently?** | *The interviewer wants to know if you prefer to work independently or on a team.* |
|---|---|
| • I am comfortable working on a team or on my own. Some projects require a team approach while others require an independent solution. I have worked on many teams and on many projects on my own in the past.<br><br>• I believe that even working on a team it is still up to me individually to bring my best to the table. Each member of a team has a role to play individually, yet collectively as a team is how the project gets completed. I have participated in many projects independently and many others as a member of a team. | **Write your best response here:** |
| **What type of work environment do you prefer to work in?** | *Here the interviewer wants to know if you have a preference in your work environment.* |
| • I am flexible when it comes to my work environment. How would you describe the work environment for the position I am applying for?<br><br>• I prefer to work in an environment that fosters team spirit, yet will still allow for individual input through open discussion. I like to have an openness in the work area and have a balance of natural and artificial lighting as I have seen here in your office areas. | **Write your best response here:** |
| **How do you define success?** | *The interviewer wants to know what you think the word success means in your own words.* |
| • I evaluate success in different ways. At work, it is meeting the goals that were set along with expectations of management. In my personal life it is being content and comfortable with what I have, being self-reliant, and helping others.<br><br>• I define success as reaching a point in life where one becomes self-sufficient and can meet all their needs and still have enough extra where they can help others. Success is being happy with what you have and with the friends you associate with. True success is enjoying the journey of life, not what you reach at the end. | **Write your best response here:** |

# Section 13

# About You Questions

| | |
|---|---|
| **How do you evaluate or measure success?**<br><br>• I evaluate success as a measure of what is accomplished in the direction of personal improvement, or in the case of a company, how productive and profitable they are. Success can be measured qualitatively or quantitatively, or even by both measures.<br><br>• Success is continually growing and moving forward in life. I ask myself, "Am I better off today than yesterday? Last week? Last year?" If I find that I am better off then I feel that I have a measure of success. I think that any organization can use this same way to evaluate or measure their success or lack of success. | *The interviewer wants to know if you have an idea of how to evaluate or measure success.*<br><br>**Write your best response here:** |
| **How would you handle a situation where you knew the boss was 100% wrong about something?**<br><br>• It would depend on the situation and the personality of the supervisor. I'd ask for more information and discuss my concerns hoping he would see the flaw so corrective action could be taken early on in the project.<br><br>• I would never tell my supervisor he is wrong. I would begin by asking him what are the results he is after. I would then do it correctly to get the information he wanted. I don't think he minds how I got the information, as long as he got what he had requested. | *Here the interviewer is wanting to know how you would handle a sensitive situation.*<br><br>**Write your best response here:** |
| **What would you say is your strongest talent or skill and why?**<br><br>• I would have to say it is my skill at being organized. I have found over the years the better I was organized the more I could accomplish. I constantly re-evaluate my priorities so I can get the most important things completed first.<br><br>• My strongest talent as a photographer is to see the 'creative shot' not just the 'snap shot'. Over the years my photographs have won many awards for being creative in both subject matter and in composition. | *The interviewer wants to know if you know your strongest talent or skill and why you think so.*<br><br>**Write your best response here:** |

# Section 13

# About You Questions

| | |
|---|---|
| **How do you balance your work and your life at home?**<br><br>• I balance the two by leaving my work at work and my home life at home. These are two important parts of my life and I do what I can to keep them from interfering with each other.<br><br>• I have always budgeted my time for work and for my home life. Both are important and I understand how they must be balanced or both will suffer. I take the time to schedule what I do at work and at home, yet still leaving enough flexibility for those unexpected "occurrences or intrusions" that must be dealt with. | *The interviewer wants to know how you deal with the balance of work and home.*<br>**Write your best response here:** |
| **What do you like to do when you are not at work?**<br><br>• I enjoy going to the beach or a park with my family. I know the importance of spending quality time together. Sometimes we like to visit family or friends and have a barbecue and just enjoy spending some time sharing old memories or catching up on what has been going on in our lives.<br><br>• I like to travel to various points of interest within about a four-hour drive. It is amazing just how many things there are to see and do when you stop and look at what is so close to home. There are many historical sites, museums, theaters, parks, and hiking trails to explore. | *The interviewer wants to know what you like to do when not at work.*<br>**Write your best response here:** |
| **What do you do when you are not at work?**<br><br>• What I do when not at work is mowing the lawn, painting the house, and doing landscaping work. I can be found in the garden or even playing with our children in the yard.<br><br>• I can be found doing the shopping for the family. It could be groceries, for clothing, or other items. Laundry and cleaning the house is also a major time-consuming occupation. When time permits I practice the piano and spend some time teaching our children how to play the piano. | *The interviewer wants to know what you actually spend your time on when not at work.*<br>**Write your best response here:** |

# Section 13

# About You Questions

| | |
|---|---|
| **What interests do you have outside of work?**<br><br>• I am involved with a youth sports program for the at-risk children in my community. It gives me a great deal of satisfaction to give back what others gave to me when I was a child. Besides the youth sports program I enjoy reading about world history and learning about different cultures and their contributions to society.<br><br>• I enjoy camping, hiking, and backpacking. I really enjoy the great outdoors and all the wonders that nature has to offer. I like to take photographs and record all the images I see so I can share them with others to inspire them to see them firsthand. | *The interviewer wants to learn about what outside interests you have.*<br><br>**Write your best response here:** |
| **Can you give me three words that will describe you and tell me why you chose those words?**<br><br>• I am 'qualified' for this position based on my experience. I am 'outgoing' because of my love for creating a happy work environment. Finally, I am 'trustworthy' because my word is my bond.<br><br>• 'Organized' would be the first word since I list and prioritize the demands on my time, both at work and at home. 'Team player' because I believe that working together produces better results. "Reliable" since you can count on me to be to work on time and I will be there when you need me the most. | *The interviewer wants to hear in your own words how you would describe yourself using just three words.*<br><br>**Write your best response here:** |
| **Describe your communication style and why you feel it is effective.**<br><br>• I am a great communicator and feel that my style of being open-minded and listening to all input allows others to feel more comfortable with me. I think listening is the most important part of communication.<br><br>• I am open and honest in my communication and feel that others trust me when I make a commitment. I have a reputation of being one who gives detailed and complete information the first time. I pride myself in keeping an open door if someone has a question or concern about what we discussed. | *The interviewer wants to learn what type of communicator you are.*<br><br>**Write your best response here:** |

# Section 13

# About You Questions

| | |
|---|---|
| **Tell me how you feel about deadlines.**<br><br>• I understand the need for having deadlines. Without them who knows when anything might be finished. I believe that any reasonable deadline for a customer should be met and if it can't be met on time, the customer needs to be kept informed and an agreed-upon solution be engaged.<br><br>• I prefer to know the deadline at the beginning of the project. That way I can organize and prioritize my time and resources to be proactive from the start to the finish. I do my best to complete the project a little earlier so I have time to review and make sure it was done as specified by the customer. | *The interviewer wants to know your personal feelings about deadlines and how you deal with them.*<br><br>*Write your best response here:* |
| **Are you comfortable with change and can you tell me how you deal with it?**<br><br>• Without change there can be no growth. I am comfortable with change or changes when properly presented so the reasons can be understood and then I can support the proposed changes.<br><br>• I learned a long time ago that change is a constant part of life. I am comfortable in my ability to change and adapt to new ideas and procedures. Change is often very good to bring about a new way of doing and seeing things. I think change also allows for new opportunities to learn things from another perspective. | *The interviewer wants a sense of your feelings about change and how you react to it.*<br><br>*Write your best response here:* |
| **Tell me about your organizational style.**<br><br>• I prefer to use an electronic organizer so I can make changes immediately as needed. The first thing in the morning I make a list of what needs to be accomplished and then I prioritize the list. I keep it flexible so I can handle any emergencies or issues as they come up.<br><br>• I would be considered 'old school' because I use a notebook to list what I need to do. I leave the notebook on my desk when I am not there. I make changes based on priority and if I am away from my desk, my supervisor can see exactly what I am working on and what I still have left to do. | *The interviewer wants to know if you have an organizational style.*<br><br>*Write your best response here:* |

# Section 13

# About You Questions

| | |
|---|---|
| **Tell me how you work with unorganized co-workers.**<br><br>• I can work with just about anyone. I keep myself organized and focused on what I need to do. I try to help those less organized by teaching them how to keep better records of what needs to be done and what has been accomplished.<br><br>• I enjoy the challenge of helping others see how easy it is to be organized. I keep myself organized and hope that it sets the example in the workspace. When I am over a project, I will give specific instructions on when things need to be done and will hold those under me accountable. They must show me what they are working on and what still needs to be completed. | *Here the interviewer wants to know how you deal with unorganized co-workers.*<br><br>**Write your best response here:** |
| **Can you tell me how you set your priorities?**<br><br>• I make it a habit to work on the most important and difficult project first. That way everything else flows much faster and smoother. I want to know up front what is expected and when so I can set my priorities properly.<br><br>• When working with several departments I try to get a consensus from each one as to a realistic due date that everyone can live with. Then I keep each department updated as to the status of their project in case any changes may be requested or required so nothing is done in a vacuum. | *The interviewer wants to see how you set your priorities and how you deal with others who are involved.*<br><br>**Write your best response here:** |
| **How do you manage your time?**<br><br>• I am a firm believer that one must budget their money and their time. Both are important. With time I try to prioritize what I have to do and the time it will take to complete each project. I try to finish everything on time by keeping myself organized.<br><br>• I keep a 'to do' list on my desk with approximate times to complete each task. I keep track of how I am doing on each task so I can manage completing my list by the end of the day. I keep busy so I have time at the end of the day so I can begin to plan out the next day's work. | *The interviewer wants to know how you spend your time.*<br><br>**Write your best response here:** |

# Section 13

# About You Questions

| | |
|---|---|
| **Can you give me an example when you were unable to deal with a problem?**<br><br>• My department was given a new manager who micro-managed everyone. He did not appreciate the fact that we had been working together as a team for over three years on a project that he was not familiar with. Upper management was aware of the issue but left him in charge. Many of the team requested to be transferred to other departments. I was one of them.<br><br>• I can't think of a time when having an open communication was not able to find satisfactory resolution to any issue on the job. | *The interviewer wants to know if you have been unable to deal with a problem.*<br><br>***Write your best response here:*** |
| **You have not listed any references on your job application or resume. Can you give a reason for this?**<br><br>• I like to wait until the interview so those references are contacted only when there is a possible job offer made. I don't see the need to have them unnecessarily contacted.<br><br>• I have the utmost respect for my references and know that they will be honest with you if and when the time comes for you to contact them. I believe my references are confidential and do not want them contacted unless it is a requirement for final consideration or I have an offer of pending employment. I do have that list and it will be made available at the proper time. | *The interviewer wants to know if you have a valid reason for not submitting a list of references.*<br><br>***Write your best response here:*** |
| **What have you done recently to develop a skill or talent that was missing in your life?**<br><br>• I completed several computer classes at the community library last month. This was to improve my skills in both word processing and creating spreadsheets.<br><br>• I am currently enrolled and attending a creative writing class. I hope someday to write stories for children and young adults about life's challenges and how they can survive them. | *The interviewer wants to know if you are constantly trying to improve yourself.*<br><br>***Write your best response here:*** |

# Section 13

# About You Questions

| | |
|---|---|
| **What has been your greatest disappointment in your life?**<br><br>• I would have to say it was waiting too long to complete my education. I realize now that it has cost me many opportunities in both my vocational pursuits and in my personal life. I have finished my education and I am enjoying new opportunities as they appear.<br><br>• I think my greatest disappointment is having lost my parents before I graduated college. I wanted them to see me be the first to attend and graduate from college in our family. I know it meant a great deal to them to see me accepted into a college, but I was disappointed that they did not see me graduate. | *The interviewer wants to see if there are any disappointments that have not been resolved in your life.*<br><br>**Write your best response here:** |
| **If you could re-live the last ten years of your life, what would you do differently?**<br><br>• I lost my mother to cancer. I wish I had known more about the disease to help me through that difficult time. I have since learned more about cancer and how to cope with those feelings I had at that time. I have reached a point of acceptance now and don't hold myself to blame for what I did not know at that time.<br><br>• I am sure all of us think about what we would do if we could go back and do over the past ten years of our life. I really don't think I would change much. I have learned so much about myself through the experiences I have had, both the good and the bad. | *The interviewer wants to know if you are still holding on to something in the past that might still affect your feelings now.*<br><br>**Write your best response here:** |
| **What would you do differently if you were to start your working life over?**<br><br>• I would have finished my education earlier so I could have been able to contribute more for a longer period of time. Now I do my best to keep up with current trends in my field so I can be at the top of my game.<br><br>• I would have found a mentor or a job coach who could have helped me grow faster in my career. I can see now how those who had a mentor moved up the corporate ladder faster than I did. There is a great value one can gain from someone else's experiences and knowledge. | *The interviewer wants to see how you feel about how your career has turned out so far.*<br><br>**Write your best response here:** |

# Section 14

# Position And Organization Questions

| | |
|---|---|
| **Why are you looking for employment here with our company?**<br><br>• I have known of this company for many years and it has a great reputation of treating their employees fairly and with respect. In my research I have found your company to be a leader in the industry and I would like to work for a winning team.<br><br>• This company has a history of growing market share through innovation and strategic marketing programs. It is known for its quality and competitive pricing on all of its products. I feel that this company has what I am looking for in not only the position being offered, but for my future personal growth and development. | *The interviewer wants to know why you have selected their company as a choice for employment.*<br><br>**Write your best response here:** |
| **Why would you want to work for our organization?**<br><br>• From my research I have found that you have an excellent training program for both leadership and management skills training. My own personal career goals are to gain the experience required to be a member of the management team. I feel with my qualifications and your training both of us will benefit.<br><br>• I have several friends who currently work here and they have told me how much pride all the workers have in doing the best job they can. That there is a special 'team spirit' that can be felt as everyone is contributing to a project. I know that I can be a valuable team member as this company expands into new markets. | *The interviewer wants to know why you would want to work for this company.*<br><br>**Write your best response here:** |
| **What do you know about our business and company?**<br><br>• My research into your company revealed that you are a leader in the local sporting goods retailing. I have personal experience shopping in your stores and appreciated the professional customer service I received every time I came into one of your stores. I know that this attitude comes from the top down.<br><br>• Your company is well known in the auto parts industry. Your stores use the latest technology for inventory control that keeps parts in stock when the customer needs them. If it is out of stock they will search the database and find another store that has it, then either have it transferred in or let the customer pick it up. | *The interviewer wants to see if you know anything about the company or its business.*<br><br>**Write your best response here:** |

# Section 14

# Position And Organization Questions

| **What do you find that interests you in this company or position?** | *Here the interviewer wants to see what interested you about applying for the position and with this company.* |
|---|---|
| • I am interested in this position because of what it has to offer for future advancement. This company is growing and expanding into new markets and I would like to be part of that future. I know that my qualifications and experience can help contribute to that future growth.<br><br>• I have enjoyed working in retail sales and working with the customers. I like to help the customers by satisfying their needs with the right product at a competitive price. Your company has a great reputation for having a wide selection of products to suit every taste and budget. | ***Write your best response here:*** |

| **Why do you want this job or position?** | *The interviewer wants to know why you would want this job or position.* |
|---|---|
| • I feel that this is an opportunity for me to help others. I can share my talents and skills to help others become more productive. At the same time it will allow me to develop more skills so I can be even more productive.<br><br>• I am looking for a career in this field and I see this position as an important part of a solid foundation. I look forward to learning not only this position but those around me so I can someday become a productive manager. Does this company offer leadership and management training as part of its succession plan? | ***Write your best response here:*** |

| **What makes you think you can do this job?** | *The interviewer wants to hear you state why you think you can do this job.* |
|---|---|
| • I have the education and over five years of experience working in this position in my last job. I started out as a clerk and after two years I was the department manager. I supervised on average twelve clerks and two supervisors. I reported directly to the operations manager.<br><br>• I am qualified for this position. Your job posting required a minimum of five years of truck driving experience and I have over eighteen years of experience. My commercial driver's license and medical records are currently up to date and will not expire until the end of the year. | ***Write your best response here:*** |

Chapter 10 - Skill Builder Special Salad

# Section 14

# Position And Organization Questions

| | |
|---|---|
| **What would you guess to be the most challenging part of this position?**<br><br>• From what I know and have experienced it would be becoming familiar with the local customers and vendors for this market. I have found that in each location I worked in there were always slight differences in the local cultures. I have always been quick to adapt to those local customs and cultures.<br><br>• I am up to most challenges and I will do my best to learn the expectations and policies as fast as I can. I am not afraid to ask questions or seek help when I find that I don't know something. I like to learn and to do my best in every position I have worked. | *The interviewer wants to know if you are aware of any challenges you might face in the position.*<br><br>**Write your best response here:** |
| **Why do you think you are the best qualified person for this job?**<br><br>• I have read your list of the qualifications you require for this position. I know that I meet and exceed them all. I have the education and the experience you are looking for. I have been in this field for over twelve years.<br><br>• I have the required licenses and certificates to sell your insurance products. I have nine years of experience selling insurance products and over twenty years of retail customer service experience. My licenses are current and I am proud to have an unblemished record with the state insurance commissioner's office. | *The interviewer wants to know why you think you are the best candidate for the job.*<br><br>**Write your best response here:** |
| **What do you feel you can contribute to this company?**<br><br>• I can contribute positive enthusiasm to your customer service. I enjoy working with customers to make sure they are satisfied with both the product they are purchasing and with the level of customer service they receive. A happy customer is a repeat customer.<br><br>• I have in the past twenty years built a strong reputation with the customers I have serviced of being available when they need me and not at my convenience. Many of these customers are loyal to me because they know I can be counted on to do the right thing and all of them will want me to be their sales representative. | *The interviewer wants to know what you feel you can contribute to the company.*<br><br>**Write your best response here:** |

# Section 14

# Position And Organization Questions

| | |
|---|---|
| **What experience do you have for this position?**<br><br>• I have seven years of experience operating this particular piece of equipment. I received my training from the factory on how to operate and maintain this equipment. This has reduced the costs of outside repair and maintenance fees by over $18,000 per year.<br><br>• I have over seven years of experience as a receptionist. I have a proven track record of multi-tasking while setting appointments and tracking sales. I have been responsible for generating reports for management that included sales, returns, and inventory. | *The interviewer wants to know what experiences you have had in the past.*<br>**Write your best response here:** |
| **Do you feel you have the qualifications for the position?**<br><br>• Yes I do. I have the education and experience listed on the job posting. I am able to handle the supervision of the medical billing department. I began my career as a medical billing clerk and later became the department supervisor. With over six years of experience as a supervisor I know I can handle this position.<br><br>• I have over eleven years of long haul trucking experience. I have a current commercial driver's license with the required endorsements for the position posted. I also have a current copy of my driving record if you would like to see it. | *Here the interviewer wants you to tell them if you feel qualified for the position.*<br>**Write your best response here:** |
| **Do you feel you are over-qualified for this job?**<br><br>• I am perfectly qualified for this position based on my work history and training. Is there really such a thing as being over-qualified for any position? You do want the best you can find don't you?<br><br>• I wouldn't say I was over-qualified. I feel that my experience gives me an advantage. I am able to help others learn more about the position and help them be more productive in their work. You are interested in increasing production aren't you? | *The interviewer wants to know if you feel over-qualified for the position.*<br>**Write your best response here:** |

# Section 14

# Position And Organization Questions

| | |
|---|---|
| **Are there any days you would prefer not to work if you had a choice and why?**<br><br>• I would prefer not to work on Sundays. I take my family to church and it is important that we all go together. I am willing to work on Saturday in order to have Sunday off if possible.<br><br>• I currently attend all-day classes on Tuesdays and Thursdays to finish my Associate of Arts degree. I should be finished by the end of the year and would be able to work any day that would be required. | *The interviewer is trying to see if you wanted days off that would justify adjusting your schedule and still meet required staffing.*<br><br>**Write your best response here:** |
| **Are you willing to work any shift you are scheduled?**<br><br>• I know almost everyone wants to work the day shift and I believe that it should be earned based individually on one's performance. I am willing to take any work shift in order to prove myself and my ability to be productive.<br><br>• I would be open to any shift, however I care for my mother in the evenings. I would be able to work the day shift or the overnight shift so I can tend to my mother in the evening hours. | *The interviewer wants to know your willingness to work any shift.*<br><br>**Write your best response here:** |
| **Are you willing to work any schedule you are assigned?**<br><br>• I am willing to work the assigned schedule. If it is flexible I prefer not to work on Sundays if possible. If I work on Sunday I would prefer the evening shift so I could attend church with my family on Sunday mornings.<br><br>• I would be willing to work any schedule that I am assigned. Is there a possibility of a change of schedule in the future? Are the schedules fixed or do they rotate? How are requests for days off for medical or dental appointments handled? | *The interviewer wants to know if you are flexible in working any schedule.*<br><br>**Write your best response here:** |

# Section 14

# Position And Organization Questions

| **What can you bring to this job that you experienced in the past?** | *The interviewer wants to know what you can bring to the job that you did in the past.* |
|---|---|
| • I have ten years of customer service experience where I have learned to meet the customer's expectations or exceed them. I know that I can bring this skill to this job.<br><br>• I am knowledgeable about the products and their applications so I can easily match the customer to the best product to meet their needs. As sales manager I have helped the members of my department increase sales by over eighteen percent in my first year. I know how to set goals and achieve them and hope to be doing that here for your company. | *Write your best response here:* |

| **Tell me what makes you unique to fill this position.** | *The interviewer wants to know if there is a reason you are uniquely qualified for the job.* |
|---|---|
| • I am qualified for this position based on my education and experience in the field. I have had seven of my studies and reports published in trade magazines. I have been the keynote speaker at three trade shows for this industry. Therefore I feel that I am uniquely qualified to fill this position.<br><br>• I have the unique ability to help others not only see, but to realize their potential by helping them write their personal goals to achieve what they want in life. I have authored fourteen books to help individuals get what they want out of life. I have also presented eight seminars on the subject of setting goals. | *Write your best response here:* |

| **Are you willing to relocate?** | *Here the interviewer wants to know if you would be willing to relocate to another location if that is where the job is located.* |
|---|---|
| • I am recently married and my wife and I are still attending college locally in the evenings to complete our degrees. I would possibly consider relocating in the future once we have both completed our degrees.<br><br>• I had never given much thought about relocating. It might be something I would consider after I discussed it with my husband. He is self-employed and can work almost anywhere there is an Internet connection available. Where might some of the other locations be? | *Write your best response here:* |

# Section 14

# Position And Organization Questions

| | |
|---|---|
| **Are you willing to travel?**<br><br>• I would possibly consider traveling if I knew how much time I would be away from home. How much travel is required for this position?<br><br>• I do have some family commitments that might interfere with extensive travel. If it is under five days per month we might be able to find an agreeable travel schedule. What amount of travel is now required for this position and are there any plans to add more travel days in the future? | *The position might require some travel and the interviewer needs to know if you will travel if it is part of the job.*<br><br>**Write your best response here:** |
| **There are several applicants for this position that have been interviewed with more experience than you have. Can you give me a reason why you think we should hire you?**<br><br>• I have the qualifications and experience you are seeking to fill this position. I am ready to step into the position and give it my best from day one.<br><br>• I don't know the other candidates. To have reached this point we each should be equal as to the requirements for the position. The difference you must consider is the individual personality each of us has. I bring to the table an enthusiastic management style that encourages teamwork to complete every project. | *The interviewer wants to hear your reason why you feel you should be hired over several other more qualified applicants.*<br><br>**Write your best response here:** |
| **What do you require as compensation or salary?**<br><br>• What is the current salary for someone in this position with my qualifications and experience?<br><br>• I would expect to be paid fairly for my qualifications and experience. What is your pay range for this position? | *The interviewer wants to know if you know what you expect to get paid. Safest answer is to ask a question and not put out a figure.*<br><br>**Write your best response here:** |

# Section 15

# Thoughts Of The Future Questions

| | |
|---|---|
| **What are you looking for in your next job?**<br><br>• I am looking for the opportunity to learn new skills and talents to help me improve my performance and productivity. I believe that each of us can improve and have a responsibility to improve ourselves.<br><br>• I am hoping to expand my knowledge of the industry and how I can help improve my role with the company. I would like to receive training for a supervisory position and then later on a management position. | *The correct answer should be related to the position you are seeking at this company, not the one after this job.*<br>**Write your best response here:** |
| **What is important to you in your next job?**<br><br>• I feel it important to know that there is opportunity for advancement within the organization. That there is also educational assistance available and the company appreciates my efforts and has a willingness to help me grow and develop.<br><br>• I would like to be able to use both my education and experience in helping the company reach their production and financial goals and objectives. In some past jobs I felt that I was not used to my full potential. I feel that this position will allow me to use all my resources. | *The interviewer wants to know what you feel is important to you in your next job.*<br>**Write your best response here:** |
| **What can you tell me about your career goals?**<br><br>• I want to know more about this industry so I can become a salesperson and eventually a sales manager. I know I already have the customer service skills required and need the sales experience and management training to get to my goal.<br><br>• I see myself working through the ranks to gain the experience and knowledge required to be an influential leader in this organization. I hope to make a career in this industry and with your company. | *The interviewer wants to hear you speak about where you see your career going.*<br>**Write your best response here:** |

# Section 15

# Thoughts Of The Future Questions

| | |
|---|---|
| **Do you plan to pursue any additional education?**<br><br>• I would like to. Does this company help with tuition expenses for education related to my position?<br><br>• I have a bachelor's degree in business and have a goal to get my master's in business administration. Is there a program here in this company that will help me with those expenses? | *The interviewer is interested in finding out if you have any plans to continue your education.*<br>―――――――――<br>***Write your best response here:*** |
| **What will you do if you do not get this position?**<br><br>• If you find a more qualified candidate I can't blame you for hiring them. I will still continue my job search activities to find that perfect match for my talents and abilities.<br><br>• I will reflect back on this interview and my answers to your questions to see where I must improve in my interview skills. I will also look into what abilities and talents that I am lacking now and see if I can improve myself to eventually become the perfect candidate for this position. | *The interviewer is seeking to know how you would handle not getting this position. Are you too sensitive about rejection?*<br>―――――――――<br>***Write your best response here:*** |
| **What do you hope to be doing five years from now?**<br><br>• I hope to be working here with your company as your office manager.<br><br>• After you hire me to fill this inside sales position I hope to be promoted to outside sales. By the time I will have been here five years I hope to be your sales manager. | *The interviewer is trying to see if you feel you will still be working here if you are hired.*<br>―――――――――<br>***Write your best response here:*** |

# Section 15

# Thoughts Of The Future Questions

| | |
|---|---|
| **What are some of your goals for the next ten years?**<br><br>• I would like to get a graduate degree so I will be able to contribute more skills to my company and more money to my favorite charities. I would like to visit Hawaii by then also.<br><br>• One of my goals is to establish an investment portfolio that will be more than adequate to support my family when I retire. This will give me a more secure feeling that retirement will be taken care of so I can concentrate on the other facets of my life. | *Here the interviewer is wanting to know if you have any long-term goals.*<br><br>**Write your best response here:** |
| **How do you plan to achieve your goals in the next ten years?**<br><br>• I am a firm believer in the power of setting goals and then planning each step to accomplish those goals. I have some long-term goals, medium-term goals, and some short-term goals that I am working on. I have weekly goals that I accomplish so I am always moving toward my goals.<br><br>• I have found a mentor and a job coach to help me achieve my vocational goals. With my wife, we have set goals for our family and track them weekly to make sure we are always moving toward our goals. | *The interviewer wants to know if you have a plan to achieve your goals.*<br><br>**Write your best response here:** |
| **What do you consider to be your life's goal?**<br><br>• My life goal is to be the best I can be in all that I try and do. I know that I won't be the best in the world, but I can be my best. I think it is important to develop and maintain good character and have people respect you for who and what you are.<br><br>• My life goal is to live my life as an example to my children and grandchildren. I hope that I can instill in them the qualities of honesty, integrity, and trustworthiness. I hope they will also learn to respect nature and be of service to those less fortunate in this world. | *The interviewer wants to see what you think your life's goal or purpose is in your own words.*<br><br>**Write your best response here:** |

# Section 16

# Conclusion And Review

Not all of these questions will be asked in an interview. But many of them will be. Some positions will have detailed questions related to special skills or talents that will be required. We hope that you will see that there is a pattern to how to answer the interview questions.

Most interview questions will be open-ended, meaning you will have to 'explain yourself' in sentences. Even the closed-ended question should be answered in one or two sentences. Your answer to both types of questions should contain part of the question you were asked. This indicates to the interviewer that you listened to the 'whole' question.

Where you can try to answer the question with your qualifications, do so. It is important to make your answers sound like you own them, that you stand by your answer, and that you have confidence in what you say. Avoid a one-word answer that will not allow you to demonstrate your confidence in yourself. Practice these questions with a family member or friend until you are comfortable with how you present yourself. You may even videotape yourself during these practice sessions so you can see how you look.

During an interview you should sit up, leaning in a bit like you are listening to every word. Pause for a second or two before answering to make sure you understood the question. Don't try to guess the next question before you answer the one just asked. Some interviewers will mix up the questions from the different areas so you don't get too comfortable in one area.

Remember to prepare for the interview. There are many things that you must do before you are ready for the interview. You should have a master job application filled out, a well-written resume, and some good Me In Thirty Second speeches to showcase your qualifications. You should have plenty of power statements that will demonstrate that you own those statements.

The way you appear will have a great bearing in how you will be perceived. Dress for success, not for comfort. You must make a great initial impression with the way you hold yourself. Stand tall and show confidence in your mannerisms and voice. Review page 6 of this eBook about making a good opening. This will set the tone for the rest of the interview.

Try to understand the interviewer's point of view. The organization has a position to fill and the interviewer will be part of that selection process. The questions the interviewer will be asking will help them decide if you possess the right qualifications and experience they are looking for. The questions will also reveal your personality and how you deal with issues that come up.

Address your strengths. You are now in a sales position, selling yourself. Know who you are, what you have done, and what you can do. Before you go to an interview try writing a list of the talents and skills you have that can be associated with the position being offered. That way when you answer a question you can tie into your qualifications.

You should not be afraid to ask questions of your own. There are only a few places during the interview process where they will be appropriate to ask. Respect the process and ask questions only when asked or if you need help in understanding a question that has been asked.

How you close the interview is also important since it will be the last impression you will make with the interviewer. After the interview you should follow up with the interviewer with a thank you card. If you have agreed to contact them at a later date make sure you do so. Remember they have interviewed many applicants so don't feel bad if the interviewer doesn't remember you when you call them.

Remember, each interview is an experience. If you are unsuccessful in getting this position reflect back upon the interview and figure what you could have done better. Make the necessary changes in your interview presentation so you can improve your chances of being hired on the next interview.

Review and practice the interview questions, answering them for the position you will be applying for. The sample answers provided are just that, samples. Write your best response to the questions and practice speaking them out loud until they come in your natural voice. You will sound more natural and relaxed which will show how confident you are.

We hope that you enjoyed the **Skill Builder Special Salad** and will take the time to look at our other menu items at the **Job Seekers Café**.

## *Thank you and come back soon!*

# Appendix

# Forms

# Appendix
# Forms

# Form Table of Contents

Action Step Form ............................... 355

Goal Setting Form ............................. 356

Interview Evaluation Form ................. 357

Job Search Activity Log ...................... 358

Job Search Checklist .......................... 359

Master Job Application Form ............. 360

Me In Thirty Seconds Worksheet ........ 362

Mentoring Plan ................................. 366

Network And Resouce List ................. 367

Objective Form .................................. 368

Power Statement Worksheet ............... 369

Resume Worksheet ............................. 375

Scripting Form .................................. 379

Simple Budget Form .......................... 381

**Action Step No.** _____ For My Goal:

Facet

| Start Date | Target Date |

My Objective

My Plan

My Resources

My Results

| **My Goal** |
| --- |
| |
| |

| Facet |
| --- |
| |

| Start Date | Target Date |
| --- | --- |
| | |

| My Objective |
| --- |
| |
| |
| |

| My Plan |
| --- |
| |
| |
| |
| |

| My Resources |
| --- |
| |
| |
| |
| |

| My Results |
| --- |
| |
| |
| |
| |

# Interview Evaluation Form

| Company/Organization | Interviewed With | Date of Interview |
|---|---|---|
| | | |

| | | | Comments |
|---|---|---|---|
| I was totally prepared … | ☐ Yes | ☐ No | |
| I accomplished what I wanted … | ☐ Yes | ☐ No | Comments |
| I presented myself well … | ☐ Yes | ☐ No | Comments |

### Items Discussed
1.
2.
3.

### What Went Well

### What I Need To Improve

### Items To Follow Up On

| | Complete By Date: |
|---|---|
| 1. | |
| 2. | Complete By Date: |
| 3. | Complete By Date: |

### Referrals To Add To Network List

| 1. Name | Telephone | Fax |
|---|---|---|
| Email | Address | |
| 2. Name | Telephone | Fax |
| Email | Address | |

Appendix

Page 357

# Job Search Activities Log

| Company/Organization Name | Contact Individual | Date of Initial Contact |
|---|---|---|
| Address | Referred By | Application Submitted |
| City, State, Zip | E-mail Address | Resume Submitted |
| Phone Number | Company Website Address | Interview Scheduled |
| Fax Number | Other Contact Information | Thank You Note Sent |

| | | |
|---|---|---|
| First Contact | Items Discussed | Follow Up Items |
| Second Contact | Items Discussed | Follow Up Items |
| Third Contact | Items Discussed | Follow Up Items |
| Fourth Contact | Items Discussed | Follow Up Items |

| Company/Organization Name | Contact Individual | Date of Initial Contact |
|---|---|---|
| Address | Referred By | Application Submitted |
| City, State, Zip | E-mail Address | Resume Submitted |
| Phone Number | Company Website Address | Interview Scheduled |
| Fax Number | Other Contact Information | Thank You Note Sent |

| | | |
|---|---|---|
| First Contact | Items Discussed | Follow Up Items |
| Second Contact | Items Discussed | Follow Up Items |
| Third Contact | Items Discussed | Follow Up Items |
| Fourth Contact | Items Discussed | Follow Up Items |

# Job Search Checklist

| Complete | Item | 1st Draft | 2nd Draft | 3rd Draft | 4th Draft |
|---|---|---|---|---|---|
| | Master Job Application Form | | | | |
| | Resume | | | | |
| | Me In Thirty Seconds (1) | | | | |
| | Me In Thirty Seconds (2) | | | | |
| | Me In Thirty Seconds (3) | | | | |
| | Me In Thirty Seconds (4) | | | | |
| | Me In Thirty Seconds (5) | | | | |
| | Power Statement (1) | | | | |
| | Power Statement (2) | | | | |
| | Power Statement (3) | | | | |
| | Power Statement (4) | | | | |
| | Power Statement (5) | | | | |
| | Career Goals | | | | |
| | Network & Resource List | | | | |
| | Introductions & Greetings | | | | |
| | Interview Questions & Answers | | | | |
| | Mock Interview | | | | |
| | Video Interview & Review | | | | |
| | Dress & Grooming Standards | | | | |

# MASTER JOB APPLICATION FORM

This generic Master Job Application Form complies with federal and state laws against discrimination; however, the user must exercise caution by checking local laws that might have additional restrictions. This form when filled out will contain personal information that you might wish to keep confidential.

## GENERAL INFORMATION

| Name (Last) | (First) | (Middle Initial) | Home Telephone ( ) - |
|---|---|---|---|
| Address (Mailing Address) | (City) | (State) | (Zip Code) | Other Telephone ( ) - |

| E-Mail Address | Are you legally entitled to work in the U.S.? ☐ Yes ☐ No |
|---|---|

## Position

| Position or Type of Employment Desired | **Will Accept:** ☐ Part-Time ☐ Full-Time ☐ Temporary | **Shift:** ☐ Day ☐ Swing ☐ Graveyard ☐ Rotating |
|---|---|---|
| Are you able to perform the essential functions of the job you are applying for, with or without reasonable accommodation? ☐ Yes ☐ No | | |
| Salary Desired | Date Available | |

## Education and Training

High School Graduate or General Education (GED) Test Passed? ☐ Yes ☐ No
If no, list the highest grade completed:

### College, Business School, Military (Most recent first)

| Name and Location | Dates Attended Month/Year | Credits Earned Quarterly or Semester Hours | Credits Earned Other (Specify) | Graduate? | Degree And Year | Major or Subject |
|---|---|---|---|---|---|---|
| | From | | | ☐ Yes | | |
| | To | | | ☐ No | | |
| | From | | | ☐ Yes | | |
| | To | | | ☐ No | | |
| | From | | | ☐ Yes | | |
| | To | | | ☐ No | | |
| | From | | | ☐ Yes | | |
| | To | | | ☐ No | | |

| Occupational License, Certificate or Registration | Number | Where Issued | Expiration Date |
|---|---|---|---|
| Occupational License, Certificate or Registration | Number | Where Issued | Expiration Date |
| Occupational License, Certificate or Registration | Number | Where Issued | Expiration Date |

Languages Read, Written or Spoken Fluently Other Than English

## VETERAN INFORMATION (Most recent)

| Branch of Service | Date of Entry | Date of Discharge |
|---|---|---|

## SPECIAL SKILLS (List all pertinent skills and equipment that you can operate)

# Appendix

## WORK EXPERIENCE (Most Recent First)   (Include voluntary work and military experience)

| Employer | Telephone Number (   )   - | From (Month/Year) |
|---|---|---|
| Address | | To (Month/Year) |
| Job Title | Number Employees Supervised | Hours Per Week |
| Specific Duties | | Last Salary |
| | | Supervisor |
| Reason For Leaving | May We Contact This Employer?  ☐ Yes  ☐ No | |

| Employer | Telephone Number (   )   - | From (Month/Year) |
|---|---|---|
| Address | | To (Month/Year) |
| Job Title | Number Employees Supervised | Hours Per Week |
| Specific Duties | | Last Salary |
| | | Supervisor |
| Reason For Leaving | May We Contact This Employer?  ☐ Yes  ☐ No | |

| Employer | Telephone Number (   )   - | From (Month/Year) |
|---|---|---|
| Address | | To (Month/Year) |
| Job Title | Number Employees Supervised | Hours Per Week |
| Specific Duties | | Last Salary |
| | | Supervisor |
| Reason For Leaving | May We Contact This Employer?  ☐ Yes  ☐ No | |

| Employer | Telephone Number (   )   - | From (Month/Year) |
|---|---|---|
| Address | | To (Month/Year) |
| Job Title | Number Employees Supervised | Hours Per Week |
| Specific Duties | | Last Salary |
| | | Supervisor |
| Reason For Leaving | May We Contact This Employer?  ☐ Yes  ☐ No | |

## Check List

- ☐ Correct contact information and phone number
- ☐ All addresses are correct
- ☐ All dates have been verified
- ☐ All education is correctly listed
- ☐ Resume complete
- ☐ Me In Thirty Seconds complete
- ☐ Power Statements complete
- ☐ Job Search Activity Log entries made as contacted

# ME IN THIRTY SECONDS WORKSHEET

Use this worksheet as a guide to help you craft a well-written Me In Thirty Seconds speech. You should have made several lists of your qualifications, accomplishments, education, experiences, and personality traits. Begin with why you think you are qualified for the position by writing a Me In Thirty Seconds speech that aligns your qualifications to the requirements of the job posting. Keep your message as close to thirty seconds as you can. Time it as you speak it out loud. You may have to edit the words to make it fit within thirty seconds.

Make sure that you are quantifying any results by using numbers, dollars, or percentages. If you are qualifying an achievement, award, or recognition be sure to state some facts that can be used to support your statement. Use action verbs and keywords to grab attention and keep the listener engaged. Make your Me In Thirty Seconds speech conversational to involve the interviewer.

Now write a Me In Thirty Seconds speech that will highlight some of your qualifications for the position and then one stating some accomplishments you achieved in your past employment.

**Qualification**

**Accomplishment**

# Appendix

Write a Me In Thirty Seconds speech that states how your education relates to the position. Then continue on writing one about your experience and any awards you may have received.

**Education**

**Experience**

**Awards**

Write a Me In Thirty Seconds speech stating what honors you have received. Then continue on writing one about your personality and one stating your leadership skills or abilities.

**Honors**

**Personality**

**Leadership**

# Appendix

Write a Me In Thirty Seconds speech stating how you employ the concept of teamwork. Pick one you have written and take it to the next level. Then pick one and polish the dialogue.

**Teamwork**

**Taking It To The Next Level**

**Polishing Dialogue**

# Mentoring Plan

| Mentored (Mentee) | Contact Information |
| --- | --- |
| Mentor | Contact Information |

| Start Date | Target Date |
| --- | --- |

**My Plan**

**My Resources**

**My Results**

# Network And Resource List

| No. | Name Of Resource | Contact Information (phone number, address, email) | Priority |
|---|---|---|---|
| 1. | | | |
| 2. | | | |
| 3. | | | |
| 4. | | | |
| 5. | | | |
| 6. | | | |
| 7. | | | |
| 8. | | | |
| 9. | | | |
| 10. | | | |
| 11. | | | |
| 12. | | | |
| 13. | | | |
| 14. | | | |
| 15. | | | |
| 16. | | | |
| 17. | | | |
| 18. | | | |
| 19. | | | |
| 20. | | | |

## Objective Form

| Mentored (Mentee) | Contact Information |
|---|---|
| Mentor | Contact Information |

| Start Date | Target Date |
|---|---|

**My Objective**

**My Resources**

**My Results**

# POWER STATEMENT WORKSHEET

Use these Power Statement Worksheets to create your unique and individualized power statements that will best describe who you are. Keep to the facts and support your claims with qualitative or quantitative results. Power statements are most powerful when you begin them by taking ownership by stating that *"I am ..."*, *"I have ..."*, or *"I can ..."*. You can also start them off by stating what you did, such as *"I managed ..."*, *"I taught ..."*, or *"I developed ..."*. Just remember, whatever it is you are claiming or stating you must: 1) Give the situation; 2) What action you took; and 3) What were the results obtained. Power statements can be categorized as being about your accomplishments (ownership), your qualifications (education or experience), your personality (character traits), or used as a branding statement (concise description of what you can offer).

### List nine things you can take ownership of:

| | | |
|---|---|---|
| 1. | 4. | 7. |
| 2. | 5. | 8. |
| 3. | 6. | 9. |

### List nine power words to describe what you are taking ownership of:

| | | |
|---|---|---|
| 1. | 4. | 7. |
| 2. | 5. | 8. |
| 3. | 6. | 9. |

### List the nine situations:

| | | |
|---|---|---|
| 1. | 4. | 7. |
| 2. | 5. | 8. |
| 3. | 6. | 9. |

### List the nine actions you took:

| | | |
|---|---|---|
| 1. | 4. | 7. |
| 2. | 5. | 8. |
| 3. | 6. | 9. |

### List the nine results you achieved (quantify or qualify):

| | | |
|---|---|---|
| 1. | 4. | 7. |
| 2. | 5. | 8. |
| 3. | 6. | 9. |

Using the information you have written above, begin writing nine ownership power statements in the following boxes.

# POWER STATEMENT WORKSHEET

Write nine ownership power statements:

| 1. |
|---|
| 2. |
| 3. |
| 4. |
| 5. |
| 6. |
| 7. |
| 8. |
| 9. |

List nine qualifications you have for the position:

| 1. | 4. | 7. |
|---|---|---|
| 2. | 5. | 8. |
| 3. | 6. | 9. |

List nine power words to describe your qualifications:

| 1. | 4. | 7. |
|---|---|---|
| 2. | 5. | 8. |
| 3. | 6. | 9. |

# POWER STATEMENT WORKSHEET

**List nine situations where your qualifications were used:**

| 1. | 4. | 7. |
|---|---|---|
| 2. | 5. | 8. |
| 3. | 6. | 9. |

**List nine actions you took because of your qualifications:**

| 1. | 4. | 7. |
|---|---|---|
| 2. | 5. | 8. |
| 3. | 6. | 9. |

**List nine results achieved because of your qualifications:**

| 1. | 4. | 7. |
|---|---|---|
| 2. | 5. | 8. |
| 3. | 6. | 9. |

Using the information you have written above, begin writing nine qualification power statements in the following boxes.

| 1. |
|---|
| 2. |
| 3. |
| 4. |
| 5. |
| 6. |
| 7. |

# POWER STATEMENT WORKSHEET

| 8. |
|---|
| 9. |

List nine positive personality traits you have:

| 1. | 4. | 7. |
|---|---|---|
| 2. | 5. | 8. |
| 3. | 6. | 9. |

List nine power words to describe your personality traits:

| 1. | 4. | 7. |
|---|---|---|
| 2. | 5. | 8. |
| 3. | 6. | 9. |

List nine situations where you used your personality:

| 1. | 4. | 7. |
|---|---|---|
| 2. | 5. | 8. |
| 3. | 6. | 9. |

List nine actions you took using your personality:

| 1. | 4. | 7. |
|---|---|---|
| 2. | 5. | 8. |
| 3. | 6. | 9. |

List nine results you achieved from using your personality (quantify or qualify):

| 1. | 4. | 7. |
|---|---|---|
| 2. | 5. | 8. |
| 3. | 6. | 9. |

Using the information you have written above, begin writing nine personality power statements in the following boxes.

**Appendix**

# POWER STATEMENT WORKSHEET

| 1. |
|---|
| 2. |
| 3. |
| 4. |
| 5. |
| 6. |
| 7. |
| 8. |
| 9. |

    Once you have completed the above you are ready to begin building your branding statements. Start by finding the key or power words that best describe what you can do, have done, or can offer to a prospective employer. List all the words first and then build powerful branding statements to use on your resume or cover letters.

**List as many key or power words as you can from your ownership, qualification, and personality power statements. Then write out your branding statements in sentence or list form.**

| 1. | 7. | 13. |
|---|---|---|
| 2. | 8. | 14. |
| 3. | 9. | 15. |
| 4. | 10. | 16. |
| 5. | 11. | 17. |
| 6. | 12. | 18. |

# POWER STATEMENT WORKSHEET

1.
2.
3.
4.
5.
6.
7.
8.
9.
10.
11.
12.
13.
14.
15.
16.
17.
18.

Your are off to a great start. There is no such thing as having too many power statements. Make as many as you can. Read them, practice them, and state them with confidence. The more prepared you are the better your chances of getting the job you are seeking.

# RESUME WORKSHEET - Chronological Type

**CONTACT HEADING** *Required*

*Name, Address, City, State, Zip Code, Telephone Number, Cell Phone Number, Email Address*

**BRANDING STATEMENT** *Optional*

*Enter your personal Branding Statement here*

## RESUME OF WORKING EXPERIENCE

**DATES AND JOB DATA - JOB DESCRIPTION** *Required*

*Dates of Employment or Experience - **Most Recent First***

| Starting Date (month/year) | Ending Date (month/year) or if currently working: Present |
|---|---|

*Job Data - Last Position, Last Title, Name of Company, Company's City and State*

| Last Position and Title | Name of Company | Company's City and State |
|---|---|---|

*Job Highlights of Accomplishments with Supporting Statements*

Appendix

Page 375

# RESUME WORKSHEET - Chronological Type

**CONTACT HEADING** (Required)

*Name, Address, City, State, Zip Code, Telephone Number, Cell Phone Number, Email Address*

**BRANDING STATEMENT** (Optional)

*Enter your personal Branding Statement here*

## RESUME OF WORKING EXPERIENCE

**DATES AND JOB DATA - JOB DESCRIPTION** (Required)

*Dates of Employment or Experience - **Most Recent First***

| Starting Date (month/year) | Ending Date (month/year) or if currently working: Present |
|---|---|

*Job Data - Last Position, Last Title, Name of Company, Company's City and State*

| Last Position and Title | Name of Company | Company's City and State |
|---|---|---|

*Job Highlights of Accomplishments with Supporting Statements*

Appendix

# RESUME WORKSHEET - Chronological Type

**DATES AND JOB DATA - JOB DESCRIPTION** (Required)

*Dates of Employment or Experience - The One Just Before the One Listed Above*

| Starting Date (month/year) | Ending Date (month/year) |
|---|---|
| | |

*Job Data - Last Position, Last Title, Name of Company, Company's City and State*

| Last Position and Title | Name of Company | Company's City and State |
|---|---|---|
| | | |

*Job Highlights of Accomplishments with Supporting Statements*

|   |
|---|
|   |
|   |
|   |
|   |
|   |
|   |

---

**DATES AND JOB DATA - JOB DESCRIPTION** (Required)

*Dates of Employment or Experience - The One Just Before the One Listed Above*

| Starting Date (month/year) | Ending Date (month/year) |
|---|---|
| | |

*Job Data - Last Position, Last Title, Name of Company, Company's City and State*

| Last Position and Title | Name of Company | Company's City and State |
|---|---|---|
| | | |

*Job Highlights of Accomplishments with Supporting Statements*

|   |
|---|
|   |
|   |
|   |
|   |
|   |
|   |

---

## EDUCATION

**EDUCATION** (Required)

*Name of Most Recent Educational Institution, Location - City and State, Year Degree - Diploma - Certificate or Units Earned*

| | | |
|---|---|---|
| | | |
| | | |
| | | |
| | | |
| | | |

# RESUME WORKSHEET - Chronological Type

## MILITARY SERVICE
**MILITARY SERVICE — Required**

*List your branch of service and dates, your highest rank achieved, any special skills or abilities acquired while serving, and awards.*

## SKILLS
**SKILLS — Required**

*List skills you have such as: Computer programs, equipment you can operate, technical trained abilities, etc.*

## REFERENCES
**References — Optional**

*You should only state on your Resume: **Available On Request**. You should have them available should they ask for them. You should have a minimum of three references and no more than six references who can talk about your personality and your qualifications for the position you are applying for.*
*Be sure to provide current contact information for each name provided, this includes their street address, city, state, zip code, telephone number, cell phone number, and email address.*

# Scripting Form

Before you call someone you should know exactly why you are calling them, what you will be discussing, and what questions you will be asking. The best way to keep your call organized is to use a script.

There are six parts to your script. 1. A greeting. 2. A question - "Is this a good time to talk?" 3. Explain why you are calling. 4. Deliver a brief Me In Thirty Seconds. 5. Ask the three networking questions. 6. A close that includes a thank you for their time and any names they may have provided.

There are three types of scripting calls. 1. Someone you know. 2. Someone you were referred to call. 3. Someone you don't know.

This Scripting Form contains outlines for each of the three types of scripts. These are presented for the purpose of helping you write your own scripts. Your scripts should sound like your natural voice. Practice reading your scripts until you no longer have to read them during your networking calls. You can use this form to check off each part of the script to make sure you cover them all.

Your purpose in calling is to get answers to the three networking questions. Make sure these are part of every networking call you make.

1. Do you know of any job openings in your company that might fit my qualifications?

2. Can you recommend anyone who hires or manages people who do what I do?

3. Do you know two people who work in my field of experience who might be able to help me?

**NOTE:** Use a blank piece of paper to write out your own script in your own words.

## Calling Someone You Know

### 1. Greeting

"Hello*, _____ (name of contact) this is _____ (your name).

### 2. Question if now is a good time to talk.

*"Is this a good time for you to talk to me for a minute or two?"*

### 3. Explanation for your call.

*"I am currently in the job market and looking for a job."* (This could be followed with: *'in my current field'*, or *'making a career change that is more in line with my education and training'* as appropriate.)

### 4. Insert a brief Me In Thirty Seconds or a couple of power statements.

_____
_____
_____
_____
_____
_____
_____

### 5. Ask the three networking questions.

(Get two names to add to your network and resource list with their phone contact information.)

### 6. Closing and thank you.

*"Thank you for your time and the names you have given me. I really appreciate you helping me."*
_____

* You could use the following instead of *"Hello"*: *"Good morning"*, *"Good afternoon"*, or *"Good evening"* depending upon the time of day you are calling.

# Scripting Form

## Calling Someone Referred To You

**1. Greeting**

"Hello*, _____(name of contact) my name is _____ and _____ (name of person who referred you), suggested that I call you."

**2. Question if now is a good time to talk.**

"Is this a good time for you to talk to me for a minute or two?

**3. Explanation for your call.**

"I am currently in the job market and looking for a job." (This could be followed with: 'in my current field', or 'making a career change that is more in line with my education and training' as appropriate.)

**4. Insert a brief Me In Thirty Seconds or a couple of power statements.**

**5. Ask the three networking questions.**

If you get a "Yes" to your first networking question and you are speaking to a manager or the hiring manager ask for an appointment for an interview. If the answer is "No" then continue with the other two networking questions. (Get two names to add to your network and resource list with their phone and contact information, if possible.)

**6. Closing and thank you.**

"Thank you for your time and for the names you have given me. I really appreciate you helping me."

_____

* You could use the following instead of "Hello": "Good morning", "Good afternoon", or "Good evening" depending upon the time of day you are calling.

## Calling Someone You Don't Know

**1. Greeting**

When the receptionist answers the phone you will ask who is the owner, manager, or hiring manager. Write down the name and title.

Say, "Thank you. May I please speak to _____ (name of owner, manager, or hiring manager). Once connected say, "Hello*, _____ (name of contact) this is _____ (your name).

**2. Question if now is a good time to talk.**

"Is this a good time for you to talk to me for a minute or two?

**3. Explanation for your call.**

"I am currently in the job market and looking for a job." (This could be followed with: 'in my current field', or 'making a career change that is more in line with my education and training' as appropriate.)

**4. Insert a brief Me In Thirty Seconds or a couple of power statements.**

**5. Ask the three networking questions.**

If you get a "Yes" to your first networking question and you are speaking to a manager or the hiring manager ask for an appointment for an interview. If the answer is "No" then continue with the other two networking questions. (Get two names to add to your network and resource list with their phone contact information.)

**6. Closing and thank you.**

"Thank you for your time and for the names you have given me. I really appreciate you helping me."

_____

* You could use the following instead of "Hello": "Good morning", "Good afternoon", or "Good evening" depending upon the time of day you are calling.

| SIMPLE BUDGET | | |
|---|---|---|
| Month | Year | |
| **Income** | **Projected** | **Actual** |
| Salary/Wages | | |
| Passive Income | | |
| Other Income | | |
| **Totals** | | |
| **Expenses** | **Projected** | **Actual** |
| Rent/Mortgage/Housing | | |
| Food | | |
| Transportation/Auto | | |
| Insurance | | |
| Clothing | | |
| Utilities | | |
| Phone/Internet | | |
| Medical | | |
| Savings | | |
| Investments | | |
| Rainy Day Fund | | |
| Charitable Contributions | | |
| Education | | |
| Loans | | |
| Other | | |
| Other | | |
| Other | | |
| **Totals** | | |
| **Income** | | |
| **- Expenses** | | |
| **Over/(Short)** | | |

www.ingramcontent.com/pod-product-compliance
Lightning Source LLC
Chambersburg PA
CBHW081829170426
43199CB00017B/2684